GW00493875

Palgrave Studies in the History of Subcultures and Popular Music

Series Editors
Keith Gildart
University of Wolverhampton, Wolverhampton, UK

Anna Gough-Yates
University of West London, London, UK

Sian Lincoln
Liverpool John Moores University, Liverpool, UK

Bill Osgerby
London Metropolitan University, London, UK

Lucy Robinson
University of Sussex, Brighton, UK

John Street
Vancouver, British Columbia
Canada

Peter Webb
University of the West of England
Cambridge, UK

Matthew Worley
University of Reading, UK

From 1940s zoot-suiters and hepcats through 1950s rock 'n' rollers, beatniks and Teddy boys; 1960s surfers, rude boys, mods, hippies and bikers; 1970s skinheads, soul boys, rastas, glam rockers, funksters and punks; on to the heavy metal, hip-hop, casual, goth, rave and clubber styles of the 1980s, 1990s, noughties and beyond, distinctive blends of fashion and music have become a defining feature of the cultural land-scape. The Subcultures Network series is international in scope and designed to explore the social and political implications of subcultural forms. Youth and subcultures will be located in their historical, socio-economic and cultural context; the motivations and meanings applied to the aesthetics, actions and manifestations of youth and subculture will be assessed. The objective is to facilitate a genuinely cross-disciplinary and transnational outlet for a burgeoning area of academic study.

More information about this series at
http://www.springer.com/series/14579

Kirsty Lohman

The Connected Lives of Dutch Punks

Contesting Subcultural Boundaries

palgrave
macmillan

Kirsty Lohman
University of Surrey
Guildford, UK

Palgrave Studies in the History of Subcultures and Popular Music
ISBN 978-3-319-51078-1   ISBN 978-3-319-51079-8   (eBook)
DOI 10.1007/978-3-319-51079-8

Library of Congress Control Number: 2017947730

Cover illustration: Claire Carrion/Stockimo/Alamy Stock Photo

Printed on acid-free paper

This Palgrave Macmillan imprint is published by Springer Nature
The registered company is Springer International Publishing AG
The registered company address is: Gewerbestrasse 11, 6330 Cham, Switzerland

ACKNOWLEDGEMENTS

The process of writing a book is long and arduous but ultimately a greatly rewarding experience. This project was conceived back in 2008, and I have benefitted greatly over the last eight years from insightful supervision by Hilary Pilkington. Without Hilary's intellectual guidance, her critical eye, her unwavering support and her friendship this project would not have been possible. Working alongside her has been an honour and an experience to be cherished, and the lessons I learned from her will be drawn on throughout the rest of my academic life. Anton Popov provided valuable advice, good humour and assistance, reading and commenting on many drafts in the latter stages of this project, for which I am eternally grateful.

My thanks go to the AHRC for funding the doctoral studentship that enabled this research, to the excellent editorial staff at Palgrave Macmillan for guidance throughout the publishing process, to my anonymous peer reviewer for their comments and suggestions, and to everyone who has read draft chapters at all stages of this project.

I have benefited from stimulating conversations with so many colleagues over the years, in my department as well as at conferences. I can't begin to name all individuals who have inspired me academically and apologise to any that I inevitably leave out from this list. Particular thanks go to Matt Worley and Cath Lambert for their recommendations. Thanks also to the rest of the 'Punk Project'; Ivan Gololobov, Ivana Mijić, Yngvar Steinholt, Ben Perasović and Aimar Ventsel, the Subcultures Network, and the Punk Scholars Network. Mick Carpenter,

Alice Mah, Maria Do Mar Pereira, Keith Popple, Martin Price, Mae Shaw and Deborah Lynn Steinberg have provided further support over the years. Helen Anderson, Rowenna Baldwin, Mark Carrigan, Joanna Cuttell, Louise Ellis, Izzy Gutteridge, Michelle Kempson, Milena Kremakova, Harriet Palfreyman, Joelin Quigley-Berg all helped enormously and made the writing experience far more fun.

In doing this research I was inspired to finally pick up a guitar and make some punk noise myself. Cookie, Jim Donaghey, Marcus Green, Sham Jaffer, Freja Sohn Frøkjær-Jensen, Dan Kerr, Jo Oldham and Snowy Snowdon all indulged me in fulfilling this dream—it has been an honour to share stages with them all. Jenny Holden, Jess Kitchen, Ruth MacDonald, Rowena Scarbrough and Lara Staal all offered their continued and valued friendship despite my habit of disappearing into my books for months at a time. My family, Margaret, Joost and Ishbel Lohman have all been endlessly patient and supportive of me. My partner, Ruth has been a true inspiration to me, academically, personally, and creatively, and has encouraged me at every turn.

Finally, a huge thank you to all those who participated in this research, for sharing your stories and experiences with me, and for inspiring this book, I hope that you feel it does justice to your lives.

CONTENTS

LIST OF FIGURES

LIST OF TABLES

CHAPTER 1

The Connected Lives of Dutch Punks: Contesting Subcultural Boundaries

I arrived (by bicycle, of course) to an ex-squat, gig venue and practice space nestled underneath the motorway that divided the older part of Groningen from newer suburbs. As I cycled around to find somewhere to leave my bicycle, I saw lots of neat little modern family homes, a stone's throw from where the punk bands were unloading their equipment. It was a temperate evening in early April and no one was in a hurry to set up for the gig that night, instead the focus was on catching up with old friends.

The event was to be a tribute to recently deceased Phil Vane, co-vocalist of UK legends Extreme Noise Terror (ENT). Originally, ENT themselves had been due to play as part of a small Dutch tour the preceding night in Amsterdam, and on April 2, 2011, in Groningen. Upon the news of Phil's death in February, the members of the disbanded Groningen-based Extreme Noise Error (ENE) decided to reform to play a tribute set. Whilst ENE had been named as a nod to ENT, they had never strictly been a tribute band; they had their own songs and had even performed on the same bill as ENT in the 1980s. For this gig, however, they rehearsed ENT covers to play in honour of Phil. Hearing of this, ENT other's vocalist, Dean Jones, decided to join ENE for the two Dutch gigs. Also on the lineup were NFFU from the USA, Suicide State from Brabant in the southern Netherlands, and the Groningen-based band, Noodweer.

I had arrived at The Viadukt early to interview Bram who was playing later that night. We grabbed a beer from the bar and sat on the

© The Author(s) 2017
K. Lohman, *The Connected Lives of Dutch Punks,*
Palgrave Studies in the History of Subcultures and Popular Music,
DOI 10.1007/978-3-319-51079-8_1

stoop over the road. Bram's bandmate Wim joined us for the chat too, although we barely got going before both were pulled away to help with the soundcheck.

On our way back inside, Bram gave me a quick tour of the venue. There was a small bar to one side with room for a few tables and then the venue itself, with room for a couple of hundred punks. Off a few corridors were the many practice rooms and the lockup cupboards bands could rent to store their equipment. Bram let me dump my rucksack in his band's lockup; I needed only my voice recorder, camera, notebook, pen and some money for beer.

Whilst the bands had their soundcheck, I joined Ruben on the door. He had organised the show and was happy to be interviewed whilst taking admission fees, as long as I was happy to help out and to be interrupted. It was great way to meet people; every few minutes I was introduced to more and more of 'the crowd'. Many were interested— if a little bemused—by my presence; amazed that it was possible to study Dutch punk and pleased that I had left the beaten track around Amsterdam to see what they were up to in Groningen.

I spent the next hour on the door chatting with Ruben, hearing his motivation for putting on the event, the planning of it, and his past involvement with Groningen's punk scene. He had originally been an 'outsider'—a metalhead hailing from Hoogeveen—but on visiting Groningen a few times and falling for the cultural life of the city, moved to one of Groningen's many squats and got more involved with the punks, their music, politics and way of life.

Tonight was a somewhat nostalgic night for Ruben, not just due to the context of the gig but also because he had been less involved in punk and metal scenes of late. He and his wife had become parents a few years before. They consequently decided to move from living in squats into a rented accommodation; Ruben, therefore, needed to take a formal job to pay the bills. All these new demands meant he had less time for punk. He and his wife would usually take turns to go out to gigs, but as tonight was a special night, grandparents had been enlisted as babysitters and they both were out. It was two friends' birthdays that night, and 'everyone' from the old crowd would be turning out to pay tribute to Phil Vane.

But this was not your standard nostalgia punk night. Whilst there was a fair number of middle-aged men in their 30-year-old punk regalia reliving their youth, it was a fairly mixed crowd. In Groningen, the contemporary punk scene was made up of punks of all ages and genders. Some had been involved for decades, others were new to punk. This was highlighted by the local support band Noodweer, which had members ranging from their twenties to forties with men and women playing instruments. This was relatively common in Groningen, but less so in the rest of the country.

Sitting on the door I met punks who had travelled to be there that night—from Leeuwarden, from Alkmaar and even further afield—many of them who had previously been part of the Groningen punk scene. Others lived in Groningen now, like Ruben they had moved there *for* the punk scene from elsewhere in the Netherlands, or even from around Europe: Scotland, Ireland, and France.

Unfortunately, despite my excitement, I did not actually get to see many of the bands play that night. I was still on the door with Ruben as the first band played. After they finished Bram grabbed me, indicating that then would be the best time to talk. As we made our way to one of the empty practice rooms, he introduced me to a couple more people I should speak to that night. Bram and I then sat down for his history of punk in and beyond Groningen. His own story was intertwined with that of the city's squats and venues; places he had lived and practiced in and his escapades battling authorities who wanted to evict the squatters. He told me of all the countries he had toured over the years and the friends he had made worldwide through punk. He was an eloquent storyteller and easily switched between English and Dutch, common in this multinational, multilingual punk scene. But I did not want to take up too much of this important evening and so let him go after 35 minutes. He immediately sent me back into the practice room with Jolanda, followed by Suzanne and then Tom. So instead of seeing the next two bands I heard a variety of experiences of punk in the north of the Netherlands, and the ways in which it was different—or the same—as punk the world over. It was my last night in Groningen, so I was overjoyed to hang out and hear all these great stories. But none of us wanted to miss the headline act, so when they were due on stage, I called a halt to the interviews and went back into the main hall to dance the rest of the night away, first to ENT, then at the after-party with DJs, and finally at the after-after-party at the Crowbar, a small pub in the city centre where all the alternative people of Groningen hang out.

PUNK IN THE NETHERLANDS

Punk exploded to widespread attention in the Netherlands in 1977. Shows by established international bands such as the Sex Pistols and the Ramones drew massive crowds; waves of new bands formed in their wake ready to join in with this sensational new style. Punk clothes, music, zine culture and the do-it-yourself (DIY) approach swept the nation, finding a home in the infamous Dutch squats.

In the Netherlands there was a natural symbiosis between the oppositional politics of early punk and the anarchist squat scene. A strongly political Dutch punk scene flourished, producing bands such as Rondos, The Ex, Lärm, and later Balthasar Gerards Kommando (BGK). Notably, Dutch punks who reflected on their influences name bands such as Crass, The Clash and the Dead Kennedys, whose politics fitted well with the Dutch left-wing anarchist punk scene.

Even as punk 'died' in the UK it was going from strength to strength in the Netherlands. Buoyed by political ferment, along with the punk staples of critiquing societal sexism, racism and the threat of nuclear war, angry Dutch punks still had plenty to shout about. The 1980s in the Netherlands saw state repression of the squats in which the punks lived, practiced, and played, and an economic crisis resulting in unprecedentedly high levels of youth unemployment.

When commercial pop punk arrived in the 1990s this new form took off in the Netherlands; the Dutch band Heideroosjes toured with the Misfits and joined bands such as Bad Religion and The Offspring on Epitaph Records. During this decade Epitaph took the decision to open their European office in Amsterdam. Meanwhile, the DIY hardcore scene continued to produce popular bands such as Fleas and Lice, Vitamin X and Antillectual throughout the 1990s and the 2000s.

Despite the number of bands who have become known internationally, and the importance of Dutch venues on the European touring network, Dutch punk does not have a particularly high profile. This is reflected in the absence, until now, of academic work that has taken the Netherlands as a focus.

There has long been a preference within the academic world to focus on the countries in which punk originated: the UK and US. This stems in part from unhelpful notions of authenticity in punk; Hebdige famously sites this in "a distinction between originals and hangers-on" (1979: 122). Whilst this sharp differentiation has been critiqued

(Hodkinson 2002; Moore 2004; Williams 2011), the academic world has been slow to redress the imbalance. However, this is starting to change, with more research in recent years looking beyond the UK and US to 'non-originator' scenes. A myriad of studies have focused on how punk operates in other countries, ranging from Indonesia (Wallach 2008) to Russia (Gololobov et al. 2014) to Mexico (O'Connor 2003) and to Croatia (Perasović 2012), with Dunn (2016) taking a more comparative global approach. The study of the Dutch punk scene undertaken for this book extends this internationalisation of the field of punk studies and addresses new theoretical questions that emerge from consideration of punk in an as yet unstudied national context.

The Netherlands is both geographically and culturally close to the UK. Exceptionally high levels of English (as well as German and French) language capability mean that cultural trends from elsewhere can be easily picked up by the Dutch. Indeed, early punk came to the Netherlands on British and German television channels, broadcast on the Dutch cable network. However, the emergence of Dutch punk does not equate to simple cultural mimesis; each time punk emerges in a new context, it takes on new forms and meanings, shaped by locality.

Dutch punk is characterised both by its outward-looking position and by its specific historical context. On the one hand, it is influenced by and has close connections with punk across Europe and beyond. On the other hand, it is situated specifically within a strong national squatting movement. The Dutch squatting model influenced many across Europe in the late twentieth century; punk and squatting ties across Europe have thus come to resemble those in the Netherlands. Whilst not unique in being close to squatting movements, Dutch punk is highly entwined with squat culture. This particular facet of Dutch punk has intensified the political activism of individuals in the scene. Punks, globally, have a long history of engagement across the political spectrum, from far right to far left. In the Netherlands this is particularly acute, a fact attributable to the manner in which it has co-existed with and cross-pollinated other political activities.

Dutch punk is not notable for anything particularly 'Dutch' in the music or the art it has produced. Only a few bands sing in Dutch; English-language and American-style hardcore dominates the scene. But the Netherlands is where a very particular mix of UK, US, European and global punk influences come together, are fermented in the squat scene, and distilled to produce distinctive and multifaceted punk lives.

The especially close ties between the squat and punk scenes in the form of the 'cultural squat' model has proved particularly influential across Europe and the US, shaping the mobility and connectivity of global punk. Moreover, the embeddedness of Dutch punk within the squats places it at the forefront of a wider politicised subculture.

THE PROJECT

This research project was initially conceived as an ethnography of *Amsterdam*'s scene, tracing its historical development and analysing the contemporary situation. I arrived in Amsterdam in July 2010 with the intention of spending time with and interviewing people who either were or had been involved with punk. I wanted to understand the specifics of the local punk scene and was particularly interested in its engagement with wider political activism. I particularly hoped to see the impact of Amsterdam's squatting history on the scene. However, it soon became apparent that this aim was based on a conceptualisation of borders that was not applicable in the Netherlands. The size of the country and the small number of punks meant that it made more sense to investigate the way in which boundaries extended *beyond* the city, crossing regional and national borders. As such, the project's remit was broadened; it became an ethnography of the Netherlands' scene, with participants spread across the country.

What was particularly striking was the age of those who were (still) involved with Dutch punk. Whilst the academic literature on punk talks about a *youth* subculture, my own experiences in the Netherlands suggested that this was not an accurate reflection of the contemporary situation. For those who had been involved with punk for many years, this was no 'phase' but a significant portion of their lives. In attempting to understand the historical development of the scene, I also uncovered narratives of ageing *within* punk and the search for a homological fit between punk and other aspects of life.

The account I present here is therefore very different from what I envisioned when starting the research project. My original aim of "tracing the different forms of political activism of Amsterdam's punks (historically and contemporaneously)" has given way to an inductively driven project that situates punk within a far 'messier' social and cultural context.

This book aims to map the Dutch punk scene historically and geographically. The broadening of the remit of the project necessitates understanding how a nationally 'bounded' subculture operates and how this has developed. I chart the historical emergence of the Dutch punk scene and its trajectory to now, and I examine the way in which geographical location has shaped the scene and the ways in which participants engage with the scene.

This aim is borne out of the distinct lack of written information on the punk scene in the Netherlands. With little of an—academic—reference point, it is important to provide context before further analytical work can take place.

I further aim to contribute to understandings of 'punk', drawing especially on insights from a scene that has been under-researched. 'Punk' is notoriously difficult to pin down. This book does not attempt to offer a fixed definition; indeed, it argues that no such definition can be given. However, it does seek to contribute to knowledge of the myriad of ways in which 'punk' has meaning for its participants.

This aim speaks directly to the theoretical debates that will be outlined in Chap. 2. 'Punk' is a contentious term and has been conceptualised in various ways, from Hebdige's (1979) style-based practice to Thompson's (2004) DIY resistance of economic structures. However, my own involvement with punk suggested that these conceptualisations are often lacking. Punk has incorporated many forms of culture other than music and has encompassed a variety of ideological standpoints. Punk has been an identity and a lifestyle. Every new form of punk has brought with it a new way to understand what it means. But most importantly in a subculture that invests so much in its participants' creativity, "its followers were as much its creators as created by it" (Sabin 1999: 5). Meaning is generated by its participants as they constantly reshape what punk is. This project therefore seeks to develop definitions of punk that focus on participants' understandings.

This book also contributes to the debate over 'subculture', calling for a need to reground theory. The academic debate over 'subculture' has raged over the last few decades, and—as will be outlined in Chap. 2—it is clear that 'subculture' versus 'post-subculture' has reached an impasse. This book argues that to productively engage with this concept, we must reground the debate by focusing on the everyday *whole* lives of participants, recognising their connectedness to wider society.

I further aim to develop definitions of 'politics' by investigating the activities of politically active punks. This book takes the position that existing definitions of politics are inadequate and actively erase the political activities of many groups. It suggests a conceptualisation of politics that includes everyday resistant activities and individualised practices, as well as more traditional activisms. This aim carries with it the theoretical assumption that some of the practices and activities of punks can be read as 'political'. I conceptualise all forms of resistance, protest and activism as political (see Chap. 6). My initial experiences of punk highlighted its interactions with various forms of political engagement (for example, the 2004 Rock Against Bush campaign, vegetarianism and anarchism). An early formulation of my research questions focused on this as I asked, 'what is the relationship between punk and politics?' However, it became clear—again, in the early stages of the fieldwork—that my contribution would be broader than this. Participants understood a variety of their actions as *being* political, and thus I needed to address 'politics' as a concept.

Based on these aims, the book will answer four research questions:

- What is punk for its Dutch participants?
- How has this changed over time?
- What forms of politics are Dutch punks engaged with?
- How does participants' 'punkness' interact with and influence other aspects of their lives?

Research questions that interrogate the meanings and everyday implications of punk necessitate a methodological approach that focuses on punks themselves. In particular, I seek to uncover how individual punks understand their practices and where they find meaning in what they do. I take a constructivist, interpretivist approach to the social world, understanding that it is these punks themselves who create meaning with their practices and that, therefore, as researchers we have an obligation to centre these meanings in our analyses. As such, I utilised ethnographic methods, focused particularly on participant interviews and oral history techniques. These allowed punk participants' voices to direct the research. Whilst valuable research can be done (and has been done) by taking the cultural products of punk (for example, the music, style, art or writing) as a data source, these are beyond the scope of this project, which instead focuses on everyday punk *lives*.

A Note on Methodology

An ethnographic approach can entail a range of research methods, including (participant) observation and interviewing, as well as the collection of documents and other artefacts; most often, ethnographers combine a number of these techniques (Bryman [2001] 2008; Hammersley and Atkinson [1983] 1995). This approach enables a 'thick description of events' (Geertz 1973: 6), allowing the multiplicity, complexity and connectivity of the social world to emerge.

However, ethnographic projects have a chequered past, with exploitative practices that must be avoided (Punch 1986; Spivak 1988; Stacey 1988). I therefore take a feminist approach to my ethnographic and interviewing practices, recognising, claiming responsibility for, and working to minimise as far as possible, the power inequalities that exist between researcher and participant (Haraway 1991; Skeggs 2001). I did not pressure anybody into taking part in my research, only interviewing those who showed an active interest in participating, and I sought informed consent for all interviews. I further returned transcripts to interviewees in as many instances as possible for their further comment (or a later opportunity to withdraw) and to allow them to retain as much control over their words as possible (Duneier 1999; Oakley 1981).[1]

This project also utilises participant observation in which I recorded notes in a field diary. My field notes recorded the events that took place, demographic estimations, stylistic elements, the practices in which I and others participated in, my own emotional reactions to events as well as what I perceived others might be feeling. I also made notes from memory on any pertinent conversations held.

Key to my interviewing technique, especially amongst older punk participants, was an emphasis on uncovering *their* sense of the histories of Dutch punk. Interviews had an 'oral history' dimension in which participants were asked for their perspectives on how Dutch punk had developed and how their interactions with it had shifted over time. While this project only drew on oral history techniques and did not aim to produce full biographical life histories of all participants, the dimension through which 'a' history of Dutch punk (Chap. 3) is produced is an important element of the project's methodology.

The choice to focus the historical element of this project on oral history is in keeping with the overall theoretical framework in which participant voices and understandings are privileged. This is a particularly important element of oral history as it works to empower those whose voices are erased and are absent from more traditional forms of history (Thompson [1963] 1980) and allows us to focus on *people* rather than 'big structures and grand processes' (Klandermans and Mayer 2005: xvi).

The use of oral history techniques refocuses our minds on how histories (like any form of social research) are not produced in contextual vacuums—neither by academics, nor by participants. "In oral history, in fact, we do not simply reconstruct the history of an event but also the history of its memory, the ways in which it grows, changes, and operates in the time between then and now" (Portelli 2009: 24). In sociological studies, oral history is most often utilised in the form of narrativised life histories, or 'life stories', shifting the focus from events with which participants bore witness to, to their experiences. As Bertaux (1981) argues, "life stories are some of the best tools with which to elicit the expression of what people already know about social life" (39). These stories illuminate as much of the present context and "anticipated future realities" (Rosenthal 1997: 63), as they tell us of participants' understandings of their past.

Oral history relies on memory, which is notorious for shifting over time and place and reflects the contemporary situation as much as it does the past. As suggested by Portelli (2009), oral and life histories are greatly affected by the production of memory, which "is an experience of the present" rather than of the past (Mah 2010: 401). Oral history makes clear the tension between 'private' memories and 'official' memories, and privileges the former over the latter (Portelli 2009). Mah (2010) suggests with her concept 'living memory,' that: "local memories exist within the present as dynamic and changing processes and that they do not necessarily function as part of the social construction of official or unofficial collective memory" (403). 'Living memory' thereby captures the malleability of the nature of the stories told by participants in oral history interviews.

Given this, it is important to be aware of the wider context that might affect the stories told. Most notably for this research project (and as discussed in the introduction to Chap. 3) was the change to the legal status of squatting in the Netherlands at the time of my research. In light of shifting public opinions, participants may have sought to emphasise the importance of squats as part of a wider project of defending squatting. Their living memories, in this context, became a political tool in the battle for squatters' rights.

It was notable throughout my interviews that participants were most animated and keen to discuss their earliest experiences as part of the punk movement, I relate this to memory practices in which the most vivid memories are formed by 'new' experiences, rather than those that had become more commonplace after 5, 10, or even 20 years of experience as a punk. This ultimately impacts upon the manner in which oral histories are created.

INSIDER RESEARCH

An important element of any ethnographic study is the ability of a researcher to gain the acceptance of those whom they are researching. A number of ethnographers have discovered that 'insider' status has greatly aided them in this.

Insider status can be attained through a number of means. Within subcultural research, a distinction can be drawn between researchers such as Gololobov (2014) and Gordon (2005), who are 'insiders' to their *scene*, thereby having greater knowledge of the specifics of subculture in that particular location, and those such as Dunn (2016), Hodkinson (2002) and Leblanc (1999), who are insiders to their *subculture* but whose research takes them beyond their local scene where they are known. Therefore, whilst they might not always know the local bands or hangouts, they certainly trade in the same subcultural knowledge of style and practices and share this understanding with their participants.

'Insider' is of course a simplification, suggesting that all subcultural members share in one particular identity and set of practices, thereby erasing differences between individuals in a group (Carby 1982; Hodkinson 2005). Song and Parker (1995) elaborate that a researchers' position could simultaneously highlight commonality *and* difference with participants and therefore suggest a more nuanced approach to understanding researcher positionality based on "partial and unfixed modalities of identification" (254). Popov (2009) elaborates on this, saying that "identities of both the researched and the researcher are [constantly] (re)constructed throughout fieldwork interactions" (94).

It is important to note that just as identifications of 'insider' are partial and unfixed, they are also subject to spatial differences. Kempson (2015) writes about how participants themselves experience varying degrees of insider status as they move through subcultural spaces (in this case zinefests) in different locations. In some spaces, participants may identify as an insider, but should they travel to a zinefest elsewhere they might know fewer people and therefore feel less like an 'insider'. By understanding the spatial implications of differential insider/outsider status, we understand why Leblanc (1999) and Hodkinson (2002) found it useful to 'display' their subcultural affiliations to those who didn't know them.

Discussions of 'insider' status in ethnographic research tend to reify the position of the 'insider' researcher with little regard of the complexity with which such an identity operates. Hodkinson (2002) suggests that this reification is dangerous, noting that successful and nuanced ethnographies are produced by researchers who position themselves as 'outsiders' (such as Duneier 1999). A better approach would recognise the multiplicity of identity and intersubjectivity of selfhood, both in regards to research participants and researchers. By drawing on theorisations that place individuals in a series of communication interlocks (Fine and Kleinman 1979; see also Chap. 2) and by recognising that identities are produced in communication with (and with regards to) others, we recognise that researcher positionality is far more complex than a finite 'insider' or 'outsider' status. Acknowledging this 'connectedness' of individuals and the "implications of relational constructs of self" (Joseph 1996: 119), leads us to an even greater imperative to consider one's position when conducting fieldwork.

My Path into Punk and My Position in the Dutch Scene

I first started to get interested in punk music around the age of 14 with popular bands such as Green Day and The Distillers attracting my attention. Through friends, a devotion to BBC Radio 1's *John Peel Evening Sessions* and *The Punk Show*, and research into other bands on the Internet, I gained a wider interest in and knowledge of less mainstream punk and the ideas surrounding it.[2] I went to my first punk gig at 16 and fell in love with the energy at shows. At university I started to put shows on in the local town and went to gigs more regularly.

Whilst I had first bought a guitar when I was 15, it mostly sat gathering dust for several years. It wasn't until after my fieldwork—during which I had received much encouragement from research participants—that I formed (or joined) my first (and second and third) band(s).[3] The success of these bands and my continued dabbling in gig promotion meant that I regularly 'left' my desk-bound 'day job' of writing about punk to 'be' punk in the evenings.[4]

When I embarked on my fieldwork, my knowledge of punk was largely shaped by my location in the UK, and my local, Midlands scene; I didn't know much of the Dutch punk scene beyond its biggest bands. However, the cultural context of the Netherlands was not new to me, having lived there as a young child and periodically visited family members throughout my childhood.

In some senses, then, I had some shared 'insider' knowledge, social and cultural reference points, and was able, contextually to perform subcultural affiliation in the manner of writers such as Haenfler (2004), Hodkinson (2002), and Leblanc (1999). Moreover, being of a similar age to many participants and having accessed punk first through commercial pop punk provided a shared trajectory with many (see Chap. 3). This provided me with insight into the contentious 'commercialisation debate' in punk.

However, my *Dutch* punk knowledge was initially lacking, and during interviews I didn't always have knowledge of every band or artist that participants mentioned.[5] In some cases participants saw this as an opportunity to share their knowledge of Dutch punk, playing me excerpts of favourite bands, sharing their collections, and so on. However, others used this lack of knowledge to challenge my subcultural capital, to question who *I* was to be studying Dutch punk. I was occasionally questioned in what felt like a rather 'confrontational' manner as to whether I really did *like* punk and if so, what bands *did* I know.[6] The role of researcher and participant taking turns to 'display' subcultural capital (Thornton 1995) within interviews was a (naïvely) unexpected element that affected the way in which interviews were produced.

Events such as gigs left me feeling—certainly initially—more obviously an outsider. Whilst the hallmarks of the events were familiar—crowded and sweaty rooms, loud bands, queues at the bar, moshing (or sometimes static) crowds, leaflets and posters being handed out for the next event—it didn't *feel* like 'my' scene. The faces were unfamiliar, the bands not always to my taste, and my own anxiety about how quickly I should reveal my 'researcher' status underpinned many early interactions with others.

However, the longer I was in the field, the less unfamiliar my position felt and the more comfortable I became. Whereas at first I had wondered if others at the gigs found my presence there odd, soon I realised that these were not closed spaces in which only 'the usual crowd' were present. Given the mobility of the Dutch punk scene (see Chap. 4) and the turnover of people in the scene (particularly in the tourist hotspot of Amsterdam), 'new' faces were common and as such never marked me out as particularly noteworthy.[7] As I got to know more participants I more often went to shows where there were friendly faces. Whilst I therefore never shook the feeling of being an 'outsider' by dint of my role as a researcher (Hodkinson 2005), I certainly felt more comfortable in the scene as my fieldwork progressed.

The longer I spent in the field, the more I realised how the mobility of the Dutch punk scene might affect other gig attendees' positionality. When I got on a train and travelled for an hour to go to a gig, I was taking part in their practices; when I turned up in a different city and felt I didn't necessarily know many people, there were others in the same position. Mobility, as suggested by Kempson (2015), complicated the insider/outsider dichotomy as much for participants as for me.

Who Are the Punks?

Before embarking on my fieldwork it was necessary to define *who* I was interested in interviewing. Should I have sought out people who *identified* themselves as 'a punk', I would have greatly narrowed the pool of potential participants. As noted by Pilkington (2012), and by some of my participants (see Chap. 5), it is, after all, 'not very punk' to call oneself 'a punk'. This creates a dilemma for the ethnographer of a subculture in which 'genre evasion' is so pervasive (Steinholt 2012). As I was interested in uncovering the multiplicity of understandings of punk, seeking out only those who were invested in it in terms of an identity would preclude my findings. I therefore settled on seeking out those who were (or had been) involved in (or with) punk, either contemporaneously or historically. This may have been inelegant, but it ensured as wide a pool of potential understandings of punk as possible, therefore allowing me a richer understanding of Dutch punk.

Moreover, it was necessary to define *what* I was interested in; as highlighted in Chaps. 2 and 5, 'punk' even as a musical category is amorphous. Again, my approach was to take as broad a view as possible and to gather as much data as possible from which to draw conclusions. Whilst some participants might have identified more closely with 'hardcore' or 'punk rock' (as more general umbrella terms for different styles of punk rather than the many hundreds of punk subgenres), there was an understanding between myself and my participants that in talking about 'punk' we were also talking about hardcore and punk rock. Participants often used these terms interchangeably, although occasionally they reflected more on the specifics of what *punk* meant as opposed to hardcore or punk rock.

The majority of the fieldwork was conducted at gigs, many of which were in Amsterdam where I was based, but also in Groningen, Nijmegen and Leiden. Gigs are the prime location for punks to socialise. Gigs are not only where bands are on 'show' but also where merchandise, art, zines, and other (often political) literature are distributed. Especially in a fragmented punk scene, such as that of Amsterdam (see Chaps. 3 and 4), gigs were often the main location where punks would meet up beyond band practices and gatherings for close friendship groups. As gigs are open to the public, they therefore formed a prime research 'gateway' to the scene. In addition to this I also undertook participant observation in a variety of other locations, at more 'every day' subcultural venues such as record shops, squats, Amsterdam's anarchist bookshop, 'punk' bars, and at one band's practice session and another's recording session, as well as at more 'occasional' events including a participant's birthday party, a squatters' demonstration and a gig after-party. Two participants were kind enough to give me 'guided' tours to the 'best' punk places in other cities I visited; in Nijmegen and in Groningen. At one point in my research I also volunteered at a 'VoKu'[8] at a squat in Amsterdam-East, which entailed helping out with food preparation, cooking and serving, and then relaxing and eating with others later.

LAYOUT OF THIS BOOK

This book begins by setting out the theoretical framework that guided this research project. Chapter 2, 'Theories of Punk and Subculture', traces the emergence of the fields of subcultural studies and related academic understandings of punk. It places these within wider sociological developments before arguing for a need to 'reground' theory.

Chapter 3, 'Punk Lives On: Generations of Punk and Squatting in the Netherlands', takes the format of a historical overview of the trajectory of the Dutch punk scene, seen through the eyes of the participants in this project. It focuses particularly on the close ties between the punk scene and the squatters' movement, drawing out the influences each has had on the other. It argues against narratives that punk is 'dead', proposing instead that Dutch punk goes through 'highs' and 'lows'. New generations provide an upswing of activity and excitement, although from time to time activity dips. The chapter further unpicks narratives of the impact of different generations moving through punk and includes a discussion of individuals' positions as ageing punks. It finally examines the role of these ageing punks within the contemporary scene.

Chapter 4, 'Mobility and Connections: In and Beyond the Dutch Punk Scene', situates the geographical position of the Dutch scene. It discusses structural aspects of the Netherlands and its position within Europe to explain how participants are able to attain high levels of mobility. It details how personal relationships and connections bolster this mobility and how these networks are passed on to new generations of punks. It questions conceptualisations of locally bounded scenes when subcultural participants are hypermobile and hyperconnected, nationally and internationally. It also presents instances in which locally bounded scenes *are* present and explores how these 'senses of place' (Shields 1991) emerge. The chapter draws conclusions on the 'flow' of culture arguing for a conceptualisation based on punk as a 'rhizome' structure (Deleuze and Guattari [1987] 2003).

Chapter 5, 'Punk Is…', unpicks the complexities faced by both academics and participants in attempting to define punk. It destabilises fixed definitions of punk by drawing upon multiple, sometimes conflicting, definitions of punk discussed by research participants. Punk is discussed variously as an artistic form, an ideology, an identity and as a set of practices that could be social or individual. The chapter argues that there is space for all of these definitions to coexist and that recognising this is crucial to developing an academic understanding of 'punk'. Punk is necessarily a contested label.

Chapter 6, 'Punks' Wider Lives: Punks and Their Politics', further develops the theme of contextualising punk as *part* of individuals' lives as first explored in the context of ageing in Chap. 3. It focuses on punks' further political engagement beyond standard subcultural punk practices. It argues that the influences of punk ideology can be felt through the *activities* of punks themselves, beyond punk music, events and subcultural practices. It proposes a broad conceptualisation of political activism: beyond traditional notions of, for example, trade union agitation or party political activity, to the political importance of 'educative practices'. Punks who write zines, who educate themselves and who set up anarchist reading groups or distros are placed within historical practices of education as a means of spreading influence and potential mobilisation.

The conclusion to this book draws out the overarching themes of the book, contextualising the discussions of each chapter within broader arguments that we need to understand punk as *part* of individuals' lives, and as part of a connected cultural world. There are no clear boundaries to subcultural life. Whether or not an individual considers punk as part of their identity, the ideas, politics, and philosophies expounded by punk influence other aspects of their life. When individuals travel to gigs or other events, to band practices, or to visit friends elsewhere, the porous boundaries of a 'local' scene are made apparent, and in the contemporary Dutch punk scene these 'boundaries' have become so porous that it is difficult to delineate their existence. Punk itself is a shifting category: different generations, different scenes, different styles, different politics all claim to be or to do 'punk'. In trying to understand what this means for an academic conceptualisation, the possibility that punk necessarily has to be open to encompassing all these various ideas. This book aims to place punk within the messiness of people's individual lives and social practices and the globally connected nature of this subculture.

NOTES

1. Informed consent was obtained from all research participants prior to conducting the interviews. Pseudonyms have been used for all quotes from these interviews. However, in agreeing to be interviewed for this research, some participants quite explicitly hoped that their work, be that artistic or musical, might gain further attention in the UK. When (prior to interview) I explained that pseudonyms would be used, I was challenged by those who felt this to be a disappointment, sometimes repeatedly so. More often, however (both prior to and in subsequent communication with participants), the practice of anonymisation was met with bemusement; a number of participants suggested that they didn't mind or care if I used their 'real' names as they had 'nothing to hide'. However there were also participants who *did* welcome the use of pseudonyms in light of concerns about trouble with authorities or non-punk peers. As such, and in order to be consistent, I felt it appropriate to use pseudonyms across the board. In recognition that participants act both publicly and privately in providing interviews, band names and participant locations are retained (in keeping with Pilkington's [2014] practices). Such details provide a necessary richness to the book. Whilst this therefore risks reducing the anonymity of some participants, I have endeavoured to only provide details that participants were happy to share, and moreover in certain portions of the

book where anonymity was of greater concern, I have avoided disclosure by using neither a name nor pseudonyms. In quoted extracts that represent discussion between participant and interviewer I have retained my own name to highlight my presence within the field of research and in co-producing the data. Interviews were conducted in Dutch and/or English according to participant preference. Where interviews were conducted in English quotations provided have been largely unaltered except to remove hesitation. Grammatical errors and slightly unusual formulations in sentence structures have therefore been left as in the original transcriptions.

2. Most memorably at the time was the Rock Against Bush campaign in 2004, through which punk bands, led by Fat Mike of NOFX, campaigned for young people to register to vote. Later, through a local vegan hardcore group I came into contact with wider anarchist punk politics.

3. Not Right, Fear & Slothing, and Die Wrecked, respectively.

4. Indeed, my fieldwork further impacted my own subcultural practices; I set up the Revolt Feminist Library and Distro shortly after writing Chap. 6 in which I discuss similar practices amongst participants.

5. Although this improved the longer I was in the field.

6. These challenging moments were dissipated quickly enough with answers outlining a number of well-known and well-respected favourite bands, as well as a punk cliché of displaying subcultural capital with reference to obscure bands: my own opportunity to share some small local UK bands with participants.

7. As a white woman speaking Dutch I seemed no different to other travelling Dutch punks. Whilst the punk scene has more men than women, women were always present. The internationalism of the Netherlands, particularly in Amsterdam, meant that the presence of people of colour and those who spoke in other languages was not unheard of, but this would certainly have been a clearer marker of 'outsider' status.

8. A German acronym for 'Volks Küche' (transl. People's Kitchen), which is used widely in the Netherlands. VoKus provide cheap or free meals.

References

Bertaux, D. 1981. From the Life-History Approach to the Transformation of Sociological Practice. In *Biography and Society: The Life History Approach in the Social Sciences*, ed. D. Bertaux, 29–46. Beverley Hills, CA: Sage.

Bryman, A. [2001] 2008. *Social Research Methods, Third Edition*. Oxford: Oxford University Press.

Carby, H. 1982. White Women Listen!: Black Feminism and the Boundaries of Sisterhood. In *The Empire Strikes Back: Race and Racism in Seventies Britain*, ed. Centre for Contemporary Cultural Studies, University of Birmingham, 212–235. London: Routledge.

Deleuze, G., and F. Guattari. [1987] 2003. *A Thousand Plateaus: Capitalism and Schizophrenia*. London: Continuum.

Duneier, M. 1999. *Sidewalk*. New York: Farrar, Straus and Giroux.

Dunn, K.C. 2016. *Global Punk: Resistance and Rebellion in Everyday Life*. New York: Bloomsbury.

Fine, G.A., and S. Kleinman. 1979. Rethinking Subculture: An Interactionist Analysis. *American Journal of Sociology* 85 (1): 1–20.

Geertz, C. 1973. *The Interpretation of Cultures: Selected Essays*. New York: Basic Books.

Gololobov, I. 2014. On Being a Punk and a Scholar: A Reflexive Account of Researching a Punk Scene in Russia. *Sociological Research Online* 19 (4). Available from http://www.socresonline.org.uk/19/4/14.html. [13/05/2015].

Gololobov, I., H. Pilkington, and Y.B. Steinholt. 2014. *Punk in Russia: Cultural mutation from the 'Useless' to the 'Moronic'*. London: Routledge.

Gordon, A.R. 2005. *The Authentic Punk: An Ethnography of DIY Music Ethics*, PhD Thesis, Loughborough University: Loughborough.

Haenfler, R. 2004. Rethinking Subcultural Resistance: Core Values of the Straight Edge Movement. *Journal of Contemporary Ethnography* 33 (4): 406–436.

Hammersley, M., and P. Atkinson. [1983] 1995. *Ethnography: Principles in Practice, Second Edition*. London: Routledge.

Haraway, D. 1991. Situated Knowledges: The Science Question in Feminism and the Privilege of Partial Perspective. In *Simians, Cyborgs, and Women: The Reinvention of Nature*, ed. D. Haraway, 183–202. New York: Routledge.

Hebdige, D. 1979. *Subculture: The Meaning of Style*. London: Routledge.

Hodkinson, P. 2002. *Goth: Identity, Style and Subculture*. Oxford: Berg.

Hodkinson, P. 2005. "Insider Research" in the Study of Youth Cultures. *Journal of Youth Studies* 8 (2): 131–149.

Joseph, S. 1996. Relationality and Ethnographic Subjectivity: Key Informants and the Construction of Personhood in Fieldwork. In *Feminist Dilemmas in Fieldwork*, ed. D.L. Wolf, 107–121. Oxford: Westview Press.

Kempson, M. 2015. I Sometimes Wonder Whether I'm an Outsider: Negotiating Belonging in Zine Subculture. *Sociology* 49 (6): 1081–1095.

Klandermans, B., and N. Mayer. 2005. *Extreme Right Activists in Europe: Through the Magnifying Glass*. New York, NY: Routledge.

Leblanc, L. 1999. *Pretty in Punk: Girls' Gender Resistance in a Boys' Subculture*. New Brunswick: Rutgers University Press.

Mah, A. 2010. Memory, Uncertainty and Industrial Ruination: Walker Riverside, Newcastle upon Tyne. *International Journal of Urban and Regional Research* 43 (2): 398–413.

Moore, R. 2004. Postmodernism and Punk Subculture: Cultures of Authenticity and Deconstruction. *The Communication Review* 7 (3): 305–327.

O'Connor, A. 2003. Punk Subculture in Mexico and the Anti-globalization Movement: A Report from the Front. *New Political Science* 25 (1): 43–53.

Oakley, A. 1981. Interviewing Women: A Contradiction in Terms. In *Doing Feminist Research*, ed. H. Roberts, 30–61. London: Routledge.

Perasović, B. 2012. Pogo on the Terraces: Perspectives from Croatia. *Punk & Post-Punk* 1 (3): 285–303.

Pilkington, H. 2012. Punk—But Not As We Know It: Punk in Post-Socialist Space. *Punk & Post-Punk* 1 (3): 253–266.

Pilkington, H. 2014. Punk, But Not As We Know It: Rethinking Punk from a Post-socialist Perspective. In *Punk in Russia: Cultural mutation from the 'Useless' to the 'Moronic'*, ed. I. Gololobov, H. Pilkington, and Y.B. Steinholt, 1–21. London: Routledge.

Popov, A. 2009. Ethics, Identities and Economics of Fieldwork: Reflection on Ethnography in Southern Russia. *Ethnologia Actualis Slovaca: The Journal of Ethnographical Research* 9: 86–96.

Portelli, A. 2009. What Makes Oral History Different. In *Oral History, Oral Culture, and Italian Americans*, ed. L. Del Giudice. Basingstoke: Palgrave Macmillan. [E-book version].

Punch, M. 1986. *The Politics and Ethics of Fieldwork*. Beverley Hills, CA: Sage.

Rosenthal, G. 1997. Reconstruction of Life Stories: Principles of Selection in Generating Stories for Narrative Biographical Interviews. In *The Narrative Study of Lives*, ed. A. Lieblich and R. Josselson, 59–91. London: Sage.

Sabin, R. 1999. Introduction. In *Punk Rock: So What?: The Cultural Legacy of Punk*, ed. R. Sabin, 1–13. London: Routledge.

Shields, R. 1991. *Places on the Margin: Alternative Geographies of Modernity*. London: Routledge.

Skeggs, B. 2001. Feminist Ethnography. In *Handbook of Ethnography*, ed. P. Atkinson, A. Coffey, S. Delamont, J. Lofland, and L. Lofland, 426–442. London: Sage.

Song, M., and D. Parker. 1995. Commonality, Difference and the Dynamics of Disclosure in In-Depth Interviewing. *Sociology* 29 (2): 241–256.

Spivak, G. 1988. Can the Subaltern Speak? In *Marxism and the Interpretation of Culture*, ed. C. Nelson and L. Grossberg, 271–313. Basingstoke: Macmillan.

Stacey, J. 1988. Can There Be a Feminist Ethnography? *Women's Studies International Forum* 11 (1): 21–27.

Steinholt, Y.B. 2012. Punk is Punk but By No Means Punk: Definition, Genre Evasion and the Quest for an Authentic Voice in Contemporary Russia. *Punk & Post-Punk* 1 (3): 267–284.

Thompson, E.P. [1963] 1980. *The Making of the English Working Class*. London: Gollancz.

Thompson, S. 2004. *Punk Productions: Unfinished Business*. Albany: State University of New York Press.

Thornton, S. 1995. *Club Cultures: Music, Media and Subcultural Capital.* Cambridge: Polity Press.

Wallach, J. 2008. Living the Punk Lifestyle in Jakarta. *Ethnomusicology* 52 (1): 98–116.

Williams, J.P. 2011. *Subcultural Theory: Traditions and Concepts.* Cambridge: Polity Press.

CHAPTER 2

Theories of Punk and Subculture

In academic discussions of punk there are two (near) certainties: that the Sex Pistols and Malcolm McLaren will be namechecked, and that the work of Hebdige will be discussed. Hebdige's (1979) book *Subculture: The Meaning of Style* was foundational in theories of punk. More than this, however, the book proved to be central to the development of a theory of 'subculture'. The academic history of punk has, ever since, been intertwined with developments in the conceptualisation of subculture.

Over the decades much has been written about subculture. The original literature spawned a range of new conceptualisations: 'post-sub-culture', 'scenes' and 'neo-tribes', alongside retentions of—or returns to—'subculture'. This chapter will provide a brief review of the history of 'the subculture debate' before turning to more concrete discussions of how theorists might proceed in such a contentious discussion. More specifically, the development of a body of academic work on punk will also be examined throughout this chapter.

The first two sections of the chapter provide the 'pre-history' of the subculture debate, introducing first, the concept's origin in the work of the Chicago School before moving on to consider the work of the University of Birmingham's Centre for Contemporary Cultural Studies (CCCS). I then go on to discuss the evolution and debate that has occurred around 'subculture' and 'punk' and contextualise these within the wider theoretical developments of late modernity, individualisation and globalisation.

© The Author(s) 2017
K. Lohman, *The Connected Lives of Dutch Punks*,
Palgrave Studies in the History of Subcultures and Popular Music,
DOI 10.1007/978-3-319-51079-8_2

Although important theoretical work has been done by both subcultural and post-subcultural theorists, I argue that in order to proceed with an academic analysis of a subculture the concept needs to be regrounded (Bennett 2011; Pilkington and Omel'chenko 2013). To do this, the academic lens should be refocused in order to place subcultural participants within their wider historical, social and geographical contexts. I advocate for a view of the connectedness (Smart 2007) of all these facets, arguing that a holistic approach will ultimately result in a greater understanding of the significance of subculture.

SUBCULTURE AND THE CHICAGO SCHOOL

The use of subculture as an analytical framework first came to prominence with the work of sociologists at the Chicago School. Their work focuses on a variety of aspects of urban culture, most notably gang culture and deviancy (Cohen 1955; Whyte [1943] 1955).

The work of the Chicago School took place at a time (the early twentieth century) when there was great preoccupation, and consternation, with delinquency amongst the young. Whyte's descriptions of gang culture in *Street Corner Society* ([1943] 1955) set the foundation for a focus on delinquency within the school's work on subculture. This would shift with subsequent theoretical development; however, the setting up of subcultures as either against or separate from normative cultures remains a distinct element of the concept.

Whilst the Chicago School's conceptualisation did not foreground a requirement of 'youth' for membership of subcultures, the groups they focused on certainly were young. The 'rise' of the teenager during the 1950s led to more acute concerns amongst wider society regarding the delinquency of these 'youth subcultures' (Goodman 1960). Subculture, therefore, became inherently linked with youthful practices. This discourse remains, rather erroneously, today, even as more recent research has noted that subcultural practices persist into and through adulthood (Bennett 2006; Bennett and Hodkinson 2012).

In A.K. Cohen's (1955) theorisation, subcultures arise in a 'problem' solving capacity. Where individuals lack status in wider society, they will group together, forming new norms that imbue them with alternate modes of claiming status. In this we see the kernels of later developments of 'subculture' that focus on resistance to wider society (Clarke et al. [1975] 2006; Williams 2011), or the claiming of subcultural capital (Thornton 1995).

SUBCULTURE AND THE CCCS

The concept of 'subculture' found a new home in the UK during the 1960s and 1970s. A move towards a Gramscian emphasis on the role of cultural hegemony in Marxist class struggle led to the emergence of the field of cultural studies, first at the CCCS. Subcultural work at the CCCS focuses on the cultural expression of disaffected working-class youth in the UK, most notably groups such as the Teds, Mods, Skins, Punks, and Rastas (Hall and Jefferson [1975] 2006).

Two particular strands emerged from studies produced at the CCCS. The first draws more explicitly on the Chicago School and conceptualises the practices of *resistance* amongst these youth groups. The second formulation of subculture, encapsulated most famously by Hebdige (1979), focuses on the *stylistic* practices of young people.

Subcultural Resistance and Class

The CCCS conceptualisation of subculture proposes that such groups consist of predominantly working-class young people; subcultures were positioned as subgroups of working-class culture. Subculture is viewed as a response to class oppression and the hegemonic cultural domination of the middle class. However, as a subgroup of the working classes, these young people's resistance was deemed to be against their 'parent(s')' culture' rather than middle-class hegemony. Thus their resistance is understood as symbolic, rather than as a direct political challenge (Clarke et al. [1975] 2006).

In contrast, middle-class youth are viewed as members of 'counter cultures' rather than subcultures. Counter cultures, whose resistance was against their parent(s') middle-class culture, were considered to have more political potential. "Even when the working-class subcultures are aggressively class-conscious, this dimension tends to be repressed by the control culture, which treats them as 'typical delinquents'. Even when the middle-class counter-cultures are explicitly anti-political, their objective tendency is treated as, potentially, political" (Hall and Jefferson [1975] 2006: 48). By dint of their supposed different class positions, subcultures' and counter cultures' political potential was viewed differently.

There has therefore been much debate over the political potential of these working-class youth subcultures. As their resistance was largely determined to be symbolic, without posing any material challenge to the status quo, subcultures were viewed as inadvertently *reinforcing* social structures (Clarke et al. [1975] 2006; Cohen [1972] 1997; Willis 1977).

Debate over the structural determinism of the CCCS understanding of 'subculture' has raged, forming one facet on which 'post-subculture' came to be based (see later in this chapter). Although the CCCS did not negate the influence of other structural factors (for example race, see Critcher [1975] 2006; Hebdige 1979), it is argued that they laid the emphasis on class as the most important factor determining the social nature and political relevance of the subcultures (Muggleton 2000).

Later defences of 'subculture' suggest that critiques of the CCCS's structural determinism were based on a misinterpretation on the part of the post-subculturalists (Shildrick and MacDonald 2006; this is discussed in more detail later in this chapter).

Subcultural Style

One of the most outwardly notable aspects of these 'new' subcultures were their stylistic practices. These formed the basis of Hebdige's (1979) work. Hebdige conducted a semiotic analysis of the clothing and behaviours of Teddy Boys, mods, punks, rastas and skins. In mundane everyday objects, he argues, members of subcultures seek to create their own identity; by appropriating and recontextualising artefacts through practices of *bricolage*, they seek to challenge the rest of society.

In placing so much emphasis on the outward style, particularly the clothing, Hebdige's readings of subcultures position practices of consumption as central to subcultural identity and resistance. Although widely critiqued, this influence is felt throughout later theorisation on subculture, and more specifically on punk.

Internal Critiques in the CCCS

Whilst many later theorists have critiqued the work of the CCCS as a whole, it is important to remember that the CCCS was a collective: a number of academics working in a similar field but with often distinct positions. As such, some of the criticisms of the CCCS's body of work as a whole come from *within* the CCCS itself. McRobbie and Garber ([1975] 2006) lamented the gender bias in the work of their colleagues and how this affected 'subculture' as an analytical framework. The majority of the CCCS's output had focused, rather uncritically, on male-dominated subcultures. McRobbie and Garber worked to redress this balance through their focus on feminine 'bedroom' subculture.

A methodological critique came from within the CCCS, from G. Clarke ([1982] 2007) who said; "attention should be focussed on what youth actually *do*, [...] rather than 'reading' the stylistic nuances of a chosen sub-culture. Where styles are considered, the analysis should fully take into account their importance for working-class youth *after* what has been taken to be a moment of incorporation" (249). G. Clarke therefore recognised that subculture has wider influences on young people's *practices* as well as on their style.

Willis (1972) proposed that the CCCS as a whole needed to spend more time locating subculture within wider culture, arguing that: "[t]here has not been a vigorous analysis of the status of the culture a sub-culture is supposed to be 'sub' to. The notion implies a relative positioning which seems to give an altogether misleading sense of [the] absoluteness and dominance of the main culture" (Willis 1972: xlv–xlvi, quoted in Blackman 2005: 6). Subcultural theorists should, therefore, consider the relationship(s) between subcultures and wider cultures.

PUNK AS STYLE, PUNK AS ART

Punk Style

The foundations for the academic understanding of punk were laid by Hebdige (1979) in *Subculture: The Meaning of Style*. His focus on the 'spectacular' style of punk pertains within and beyond academia.

Hebdige, in line with the rest of the CCCS, focused particularly on the homological 'fit' between punk style and punks' (supposed) working-class position. "Punk claimed to speak for the neglected constituency of white lumpen youth [...] 'rendering' working classness metaphorically in chains and hollow cheeks, 'dirty' clothing [...] and rough and ready diction"(Hebdige 1979: 63). "The safety pins and bin liners signified a relative material poverty which was either directly experienced and exaggerated or sympathetically assumed, and which in turn was made to stand for the spiritual paucity of everyday life" (Hebdige 1979: 115). The stylistic practices of working-class young people formed a large part of his focus and analysis of subculture.

However, through punk's 'signifying practices', Hebdige argues that punks occupy a rather different position in regards to class resistance than the other working-class subcultures studied by the CCCS. Through absurdity and their 'otherness', punks, rather than being positioned inside the working classes and resisting their parent culture, are positioned *outside*. "The punk ensembles [...] did not so much magically resolve experienced contradictions as *represent* the experience of contradiction itself" (Hebdige 1979: 121). Punk was therefore set apart from other subcultures in terms of its resistant potential.

Problematic, for punks and for theorists, was Hebdige's construction of punk authenticity and his emphasis on practices of consumption. He (justifiably) bemoaned consumer culture's tendency to appropriate subculture, "irrespective of the startling content of the style: punk clothing and insignia could be bought mail-order by the summer of 1977" (96). With this Hebdige set up a hierarchy that recognised only those punks who shopped in London's Kings Road as 'original' punks. "As soon as the original innovations which signify 'subculture' are translated into commodities and made generally available, they become 'frozen'" (96). Punks who had not witnessed its inception could not claim to understand it. "The style no doubt made sense for the first wave of self-conscious innovators at a level which remained inaccessible to those who became punks after the subculture had surfaced and been publicized. Punk is not unique in this: the distinction between originals and hangers-on" (122). This discourse thereby erases as authentic the experiences of punks from anywhere other than London and from a very specific time frame (Cobley 1999). It also removes agency from anyone who interacts with mass culture, positioning them as passive consumers of whatever the media is currently pushing (Hodkinson 2002).

The most glaring errors in Hebdige's work stem from his methodology. He understands himself to be an objective outsider, schooled in reading the underlying meanings attached to punk's symbols, able to gain a better understanding of punk than the punks themselves; "it is highly unlikely, for instance, that the members of any of the subcultures described in this book would recognize themselves reflected here" (Hebdige 1979: 139). This attitude would see generations of later academics, with personal experience of punk, criticise his appropriation: "[I] was left feeling that it had absolutely nothing to say about my life as I had once experienced it" (Muggleton 2000: 2). In Chap. 5, some of the participants in this research project discuss their own ideas of punk and subculture.

Laing's (1985) *One Chord Wonders* followed Hebdige in adopting a semiotic approach. Laing rehearsed Hebdige's analysis of the clothes and behaviours of punks, but widened the scope. Laing investigated the *artefacts* of punk (recorded music, zines and clothing), the *events* of punk (key performances of punk both live or on television, also including instances of censorship) and the *institutions* of punk (shops and record labels, record companies and the press) (vii).

Studying punk in the context of post-punk developments, Laing was able to take a broader and less deterministic view of the implications of punk. Laing made it clear that punk was not only a working-class subculture, and further critiqued the emphasis on purchased punk clothing: "true punks made their own outfits, the 'posers' merely bought theirs" (1985: 124). He interrogated the political economy of punk record labels and distribution networks, a theme that would continue to dominate academic studies of punk (see later in this chapter). His understanding of punk recognised that it is complex, perhaps only coalescing around an 'alternative', but 'recognizable' 'identity' (131).

Punk Art

The next major trend within punk studies was the interpretation of punk as an artistic movement. A number of studies emerged that argued the central position of the Sex Pistols and, in particular, Malcolm McLaren's role in early UK punk (Marcus 1989; Nehring 1993; Savage 1991). These three works all drew out the links between punk and art school graduates (or drop-outs), placing punk in a lineage of avant-garde, Dada, and Situationist art.

The power of Hebdige's emphasis of the importance of 'original' punks over 'hangers on' was compounded by the importance that these three texts placed on the Sex Pistols and Malcolm McLaren. This pervasive discourse has led to this band continuing to dominate punk theory (see Crossley 2008) and cultural representations of punk in television documentaries and museum retrospectives. This led to Sabin's (1999) complaint; "how many more times must we hear the Sex Pistols story?" (2). The discourse that punk 'died' with the end of the Sex Pistols is, therefore, a powerful one. This is especially true amongst UK-based scholars, as post-1979 the dominant cultural 'leftover' was post-punk, positioned self-consciously as different to punk. Around the rest of the world, however, punk mutated into other forms; punk therefore lives on (Gololobov et al. 2014; O'Connor 2004; O'Hara 1999; Thompson 2004; Wallach 2008).

LATE MODERNITY: INDIVIDUALISATION AND GLOBALISATION

Later developments in subcultural theory, namely the shift from sub-culture to post-subculture(s), took place under the influences of wider shifts in sociological thinking. Subcultural theory had drawn heavily on postmodern semiotic methods. However, in the late twentieth century postmodernism came under fire from a group of theorists who believed that there had been insufficient social change to justify the concept of *post*modernism, instead proposing that *late* modernity was more appropriate. Late modernity, as a concept, placed emphasis on the individual, a conceptual development that proved key to post-subcultural debates. There was also a rise in debates on issues of globalisation that proved influential to later theoretical developments that aimed to move beyond the CCCS's ideas of locally bounded subcultures.

The importance of theories of late modernity, individualisation and globalisation go beyond their impact on later developments in the 'subculture debate'. They also contribute to discussions later in this book regarding how punk itself is conceptualised. I later show that punk came to be defined (academically) largely by its social practices, however Chap. 5 will argue that there is also value in understanding the individual's role within the subculture.

Late Modernity

Late modernity, also known as liquid modernity (Bauman 2000), was proposed as an alternative theory to postmodernity. It is argued that in late modern society, the key tenets of the shift from pre-modernity (or traditional society) to modernity continue to have effect. The governance of the nation state as well as the dominance of scientific and technological developments remain important in late modernity and continue to drive social change (Giddens 1994, 2000). This continuity places society within a longer period of modernity, rather than in a new—post—modernity.

Bauman (2000) argues that liquid modernity can, however, be marked out as distinct from modernity due to two factors: firstly, the loss of the narrative that society, technology and science could 'progress' us towards a utopia; secondly, a rise in the levels of deregulation and privatisation of economies. These have accompanied a shift in our roles in society from citizen to individual.

A change in our relationship with space and time, Bauman (2000) and Giddens (1991) argue, is a key factor shaping pre-modern, modern, and late modern periods. Globalisation, hyperconnectivity and hypermobility form the distinct late modern element of our understanding of time and space.

Individualisation

It is suggested that the 'detraditionalisation' (Heelas 1996) of modern society has given rise to greater individual agency: 'individualisation' (Beck 1994; Beck and Beck-Gernsheim 2002). Individuals have many more choices available and far greater opportunities to shape their own lives. For example, whereas 'traditionally' a son would follow his father's career, "work is now rarely approached as fate" (Giddens 1994: 91). Moreover with marriage no longer as closely tied to property rights, there has been an erosion of societal demands to make a 'good match' (Beck and Beck-Gernsheim 2002). The availability of education to all arguably gave rise to far greater social mobility and control over the choices that one might make in life than in earlier traditional societies. In these areas, and many more, these theorists propose that individuals are faced with a plethora of choice in which the challenge is "to stage manage [...] one's own biography" (Beck and Beck-Gernsheim 2002: 4). Choice is therefore crucial in the creation of identity in theories of individualisation.

With the emphasis in late modern times on 'living one's own life' (Beck and Beck-Gernsheim 2002), far greater importance was placed on every choice made. If we accept this individualisation thesis, it is no logical leap to understand how the management of one's (sub)cultural life can be seen to be driven by choice. Indeed, the possibility and fluidity of the process of individualised biography construction is a central aspect to the post-subculturalists' critiques of 'subculture'.

However, both Giddens' and Beck's understandings of these phenomena as twentieth century developments are problematic. Smart (2007) rightly criticises this as ahistorical (see later in this chapter), with high levels of individual agency present throughout history. Smart suggests that despite this problematic aspect, theories of individualisation should not be disregarded but that their foregrounding of individual agency should be tempered. She reminds us that individual agency is "embedded in culture and history, with these qualities manifesting themselves through forms of everyday behaviour which are not radically different to action in the past" (Smart 2007: 26). Smart puts forward a theory of society based around 'connectedness' rather than 'individualisation'.

> The point about the idea [of connectedness], however, is that it sets the sociological imagination off on a different intellectual trajectory to the one initiated by the individualization thesis. With the latter, one is directed towards gathering information and evidence about fragmentation, differentiation, separation and autonomy. And it also becomes a mindset or inferential framework through which information is interpreted. This tendency needs to be counter-balanced by an awareness of connection, relationship, reciprocal emotion, entwinement, memory, history and so on. (Smart 2007: 189)

This theory of 'connectedness' will prove key to the arguments presented in this book. I will endeavour to gain a closer understanding of Dutch punk by 'embedding' (Pilkington and Omel'chenko 2013) individuals' lives in their connected social world; be that historically, spatially, or socially.

Globalisation

With the rise of individualisation and detraditionalisation in late modernity came the dominance (certainly in Western understandings) of globalisation (Beck and Beck-Gernsheim 2002). The twentieth century saw an exponential growth in connectivity between disparate areas of the globe, heightened mobility for many, and greater transnational economic structures. This posed great problems for social theorists more used to discussing locally bounded society and cultures. Work on globalisation theories had previously encompassed models of discrete local or national societies communicating and interacting with each other, often unevenly. Dominant conceptualisations focused on the relationship between cultural 'centres' and 'peripheries' (Shils 1975; Wallerstein 1974).

For those working on processes of individualisation in late modernity, globalisation offered yet more evidence of the erosion of traditional communities in which people lived their lives. Now, "people spread their lives out across separate worlds. Globalization of biography means place polygamy; people are wedded to several places at once" (Beck and Beck-Gernsheim 2002: 25). Globalisation therefore has implications for individualised identity construction in late modernity.

The cultural implications of heightened global connections were huge. For Appadurai (1996), increases in cultural flows contributed primarily to the way in which people understand their place in the world: for global, connected cultural communities to be possible, if often largely *imagined* (for 'imagined communities' see Anderson [1983] 2006). Appadurai (1996) recognised that, for the majority of the twentieth century, the United States had formed a cultural centre to which much of the rest of the world was peripheral. However, he argued that the late twentieth century rise of mass media and increased migration resulted in a change to the modern experience of culture. Mass media "tend to interrogate, subvert, and transform other contextual literacies" (3). The immediacy of these new media possibilities, taken together with the mass migration of people "create diasporic public spheres" (4). He argued that cultural flow was exceedingly complex, and "the United States is no longer the pup-peteer of a world system of images but is only one node of a complex transnational construction of imaginary landscapes" (31). Globalisation has resulted in cultural flow operating in multiple directions.

However, a lot of sociological work on theories of globalisation have taken a more nuanced view of the limited opportunities of globalisation. Discussions encompassed issues of continued locality, of changing perceptions of spatiality with the 'shrinkage' of the world, and of historically contingent uneven interactions between economic/cultural centres of the west and the rest of the world.

One concept that emerged, and which was picked up in post-subcultural theory (see later in this chapter) was 'glocal'. Robertson (1995) first applied 'glocal' to sociological discourses of globalisation, borrowing the term from the business world in which it is used to describe "the tailoring and advertising of goods and services on a global or near-global basis to increasingly differentiated local and particular markets" (28). He argues that discussions about the globalisation or Westernisation of the world had lost sight of the role of the 'local'. Historically, the construction of 'local' identities (such as nations) occurred in parallel with the development in understandings of the 'global'. Therefore we see that, conceptually, glocal and local have always been dependent on each other. Robertson states that adopting the term 'glocalization' would reassert the place of the local in these debates, allowing a refocusing on the ways in which global and local concerns may intersect.

A number of theorists critique the emphasis on a rather flat model of globalisation in which everyone had access to its benefits, and few experienced its disadvantages. Pries (2005) reminds us that whilst "[t]hese increases in flows and movement have created new dimensions of lived experiences and perceptions, and have broadened mental maps and spatial imaginaries" (168), the application of these flows have been "distributed very unequally over the globe" (167). Hannerz (1992) agrees, arguing therefore for a retention of the 'centre/periphery' conceptualisation in the context of a global flow of culture in recognition of these inequalities. Hannerz suggests that any sphere of culture has its own centre, or potentially multiple centres, of influence with culture flowing in multiple directions between them. This multiplicity enables a deeper understanding of cultural 'flow' whilst maintaining a theoretical framework that allows this 'flow' to be unequal.

> People from both center and periphery, and from different centers and different peripheries, engage in the ongoing management of meaning within them to a greater extent as both producers and consumers, in a joint construction of meaning and cultural form. Although a relatively even distribution of knowhow among them provides the basis for some degree of symmetry in the management of meaning, however, elements in the organization of these cultures still draw them into the center/periphery framework. (Hannerz 1992: 249)

Massey (1993) argues for a deep understanding of the multifaceted levels at which people's access to globalised mobility takes place. Massey highlights how this shapes culture in uneven ways depending on who has access to higher levels of mobility. Massey further reminds us of the importance of considering mobility and cultural flow in the context of social relations that are both borne out of and also affect mobility and cultural flow. "Different social groups have distinct relationships to this anyway-differentiated mobility: some are more in charge of it than others; some initiate flows and movement, others don't; some are more on the receiving end of it than others; some are effectively imprisoned by it" (61). Globalisation has therefore not been a force for universal good.

Discussions of individualisation and the position of individuals and subcultures in a global world have shaped many of the subcultural debates that followed and will be discussed in the rest of this chapter. Moreover, Chap. 4 of this book will return to these debates, focusing particularly on Massey's (1993) mobility as a facet of cultural flow to situate the Dutch punk scene in a global punk context.

POST-SUBCULTURE

In the wake of the rise of the concept of individualisation, theories pertaining to subculture experienced similar shifts. With academic focus now on individuals and their agency, the CCCS's conceptualisations of subcultural groups came to be viewed as overly rigid and fixed around structurally determined group identities. Muggleton and Weinzierl (2003), amongst others (Bennett and Kahn-Harris 2004), developed an argument that contemporaneous youth groupings were *post*-subcultural.

Muggleton's (2000) work focuses on style. He argues against the CCCS position that style has meaning for a semiotician to read, proposing instead that style is "a symptom of postmodern hyperindividualism" (6). Subcultures, therefore, are "manifestations of self-expression, individual autonomy and cultural diversity" (167). Style and the postmodern fluidity of style became the most important subcultural indicator in many strands of post-subcultural theory.

The rise of post-subcultural theory led to a questioning of the very usefulness of the term subculture. Redhead (1990) charged that "subcultures were produced by subcultural theorists, not the other way around" (25), whilst Bennett (1999) stated that subculture "has arguably become little more than a convenient 'catch-all' term" (599). This opened up the floodgates for waves of theorists to coin new terms they felt best fitted the groups on which their own studies were based. Bennett (1999) and Malbon (1999) describe dance cultures as *neo-tribes*, Straw (1991, 2001) and Stahl (2004) prefer *scenes*, whilst Hodkinson (2002) argues for a modification of 'subculture' for goths.

Neo-Tribes

'Neo-tribe' is a concept postulated by both Bennett (1999) and Malbon (1999), utilising Maffesoli's (1996) concept of *tribus*. "[T]he wandering mass-tribes [...] [which are] less a question of belonging to a gang, a family or a community than of switching from one group to another [...] characterized by fluidity, occasional gatherings and dispersal" (Maffesoli 1996: 76). Theorists' emphasis has shifted away from conceptions of the fixed group identities of subcultures to highlighting individuals' temporal identities, arguing that just as these identities are fluid, so are the 'groups' around which they coalesce. The fluidity of these neo-tribes forms a stark contrast to the cohesive groups that formed the core of the CCCS's subcultural studies.

Within a particular neo-tribe there is no strong adherence to rigid styles or tastes. This freedom, Bennett (1999) explains, stems from late modern consumer society. This retains the CCCS's emphasis on consumption as contributing to the formation of identity but views consumption as a site of *pleasure* rather than symbolic resistance. Blackman (2005) and Hesmondhalgh (2005) view the concept of the 'neo-tribes' as focused rather uncritically on practices of consumerism above other social practices with which young people might be involved. However, Bennett (2005) counters that his understanding of consumption is far broader and 'includes dancing, listening to the radio, watching television, reading magazines, and so on' (256).

Malbon (1999) suggests a theory of 'experiential consumption': the storing of experience as memory that contributes to identity. Malbon is especially interested in the way in which 'the crowd' is experienced and how this experience is consumed and reproduced, thereby acting as part of *sociality*. Malbon does not view post-modern society as structure-less; he uses Maffesoli's (1996) concept of 'sociality' as his structural framework. "Sociality may be defined as the common sense or human nature that underlies the more formal aspects of social life. [...] Sometimes seemingly invisible, at times secretive, and often elusive, sociality has been described as the dark underbelly of society and society's norms, mores and civilising processes" (Malbon 1999: 24). The crowd therefore remains important, this 'being togetherness' as a form of *empathetic sociality*, which Malbon translated into a collective form of 'experiential consumption' (Malbon 1999). Similar themes would later emerge, drawing on Fine and Kleinman (1979), to argue for the importance of understanding affective social bonds (Pilkington et al. 2014).

Scenes

The concept of 'scene', as proposed by Shank (1994) and Straw (1991, 2001), puts more emphasis on geographical location and musical heritage than either 'subculture' or 'neo-tribe'. The concept 'scene' has been used to describe groups that draw upon international music culture (Straw 2001). However, it has also been used to describe specifically local groups that rely on face-to-face contact (Shank 1994). These differing conceptualisations have proven confusing. "In many cases, the term seems to be used to invoke a notion of the musical (and music-associated) practices occurring within a particular geographical space.

[...] Meanwhile, other writers are using the term to denote a cultural space that transcends locality" (Hesmondhalgh 2005: 29).

For Harris (2000), however, this multiplicity was part of the attractiveness of 'scene' as a concept as it reflected the complexity of the geographical space in which musical practices operate. "The implication is that scenes include everything, from tight-knit local music communities to isolated musicians and occasional fans, since all contribute to and feed off a larger space(s) of musical practice" (25).

Despite this confusion, 'scene' proves useful in retaining a focus on the geographical and the historical. The concept allows for both spatial and temporal differences within a worldwide movement such as punk—useful, as the term 'punk' has been understood in very different ways in its many incarnations all over the world. The emphasis on geographical locations, when looking at each specifically local cultural heritage can help in explaining this diversity. 'Scene' also retains an emphasis on music, an important aspect that is all too often lost in favour of analysis of style, consumption and ritual.

However, beyond the musical, historical and geographical, 'scene' largely lacks much further sociological rigour; it does not address other aspects of the social such as identity, ideology, structure, style, consumption or politics.

'Scene' is further complicated by being in common vernacular usage, especially by punks. "When punks use the term 'scene' they mean the active creation of infrastructure to support punk bands and other forms of creative activity. This means finding places to play, building a supportive audience, developing strategies for living cheaply, shared punk houses, and such like" (O'Connor 2002: 226). Scenes can also be non-local: "The 'scene' is the Punk community and the word they use to describe it. There are local scenes, national scenes, and worldwide scenes. The subsections of the Punk movement also use the term to describe themselves, e.g., the Straight Edge scene" (O'Hara 1999: 16). Similar to O'Hara and O'Connor, when 'scene' is used in this book it is used in terms of the punk *vernacular* rather than pertaining to any of the differing *concepts* of 'scene'.

Moving Beyond Post-subculture, Defending Subculture

Not all theorists agreed that the terms 'subculture' should be dismissed (Hodkinson 2002, 2004; Shildrick and MacDonald 2006). Some felt that there was enough merit in the CCCS concept that, with a little updating, it was still workable.

Shildrick and MacDonald (2006) charge that the post-subculturalists misread the work of the CCCS when critiquing its overemphasis on structure. Particular importance was therefore placed on the interaction between structure and agency in the 'subculture debate'. Shildrick and MacDonald (2006) criticise the post-subculturalists for taking the assertion of individuals' agency too far, arguing that "social divisions still shape youth cultural identities" (126). They suggest reviewing the way in which the CCCS approached the matter, pointing towards their more nuanced "intertwin[ing]" (137) of social structure and individual biography than are present in the concepts offered by post-subculturalists. They also draw attention to the CCCS's emphasis of subculture as shaped by *three* factors: culture and biography, in addition to structure (Clarke et al. [1975] 2006).

Some, such as Hodkinson (2002, 2004), therefore choose to retain the nomenclature of 'subculture'. He called for an emphasis to be placed on determining subculture through four indicative criteria of *identity, commitment, consistent distinctiveness* and *autonomy* (2002: 29). In doing so he hopes to move beyond (working) class resistance to focus on the diverse cultural practices and identifications of those involved whilst retaining some degree of cohesiveness. It is on the basis of these four indicators that he concludes that the UK goths of the late 1990s could be understood as a subculture.

> It remains important to recognize that even the most substantive of subcultures will retain elements of diversity, that some individuals will adopt elements of their values without any particular commitment, and that even the most committed participants are not somehow isolated from other interests or priorities. At the same time as emphasizing these elements of fluidity, though, this book seeks – by focusing in relative terms on levels of identity, commitment, coherence and autonomy – to infer that subcultures are more notable for their substance than for their ephemerality. (Hodkinson 2002: 33)

Crucially, in setting out four determinants for 'subculture', Hodkinson (2002) suggests that the concept should not be applied uncritically to a group. Instead the practices should be evaluated to test whether or not 'subculture' is more appropriate than one of the other, more fluid, post-subcultural terms such as neo-tribe.

REGROUNDING THEORY

More recently there has been a move away from this 'subculture debate' towards a regrounding of theories of youth cultural practice (Pilkington and Omel'chenko 2013). Bennett himself noted that much of the work of the post-subculturalists had lacked an "in-depth analysis of the dynamic interplay between structural experience and cultural consumption in the formation of local instances of youth cultural practice" (Bennett 2011: 502). Such interplay is crucial to regrounding subcultural theory.

This theoretical work draws on the best of subcultural and post-subcultural theory, to produce "a more effective mapping of a contemporary youth cultural terrain in which youth identities forge an increasingly complex mix of global and local cultural influences" (Bennett 2011: 502). Pilkington and Omel'chenko (2013) aim to prioritise "neither 'structure' nor 'culture'" and instead study "the social structures that include/exclude young people; individuals' negotiations of them; and the youth cultural trajectories that ensue" (209). Some theorists retain the terminology of 'subculture', whereas others do not.

Williams (2011) places his work within the paradigm of 'subculture'. His conceptualisation is developed through a symbolic interactionist framework. He strikes a balance between the fluidity and fixedness of groups of people, focusing on the way that subcultural norms develop through interactions between (and beyond) members. "Subcultures refer to culturally bounded, but not closed, networks of people who come to share the meaning of specific ideas, material objects, and practices through interaction" (39). In this reconceptualisation of subculture, Williams treads carefully between elements of structure and agency, fixity and fluidity. Moreover, by understanding that subcultural practices are affected by interactions with those *beyond* the subculture itself, he embeds participants in their wider social and cultural contexts.

A key component to these developments is Fine and Kleinman's (1979) concept of 'communication interlocks', drawn on by both Williams (2011) and Pilkington et al. (2014). Fine and Kleinman suggest that cultural communication takes place through a variety of connections. "Small groups are connected with many other groups through a large number of interlocks, or social connections" (Fine and Kleinman 1979: 8). These may consist of individuals who have membership in multiple groups, intergroup communication, multigroup communication or communication between groups and non-members (8). Subcultures are hereby understood not as fixed worlds, separate from the rest of society but embedded within wider social and cultural practices. Subcultures are "affected by outside cultures just as it affects them" (Williams 2011: 42).

In these conceptual developments, therefore, the subcultures themselves are embedded within wider culture. In starting from this position it is possible to understand how subcultures spread and operate. Williams (2011) argues that subcultural practices, artefacts, and ideas may spread via these 'communication interlocks': "subcultures are not restricted to particular groups or areas, but can spread through whatever channels of social interaction exist" (Williams 2011: 40). Moreover, the embeddedness of subcultures within wider culture allows us to view cultural practices as constrained by social structures, whilst allowing individuals the possibility to (re)negotiate these.

I argue that the grounding of subcultural theory in understandings of connectivity can be further extended. A model of intersubjectivity (Crossley 1996) can help us understand the process by which meaning is shared and created within the relationships in multiple intersecting communication interlocks. 'Intersubjectivity' explains how verbal and non-verbal means of communication operate through shared systems of meanings, which are based on assumptions that both/all parties are privy to (Crossley 1996). It also explains how cultural meanings are created and shared "*between* individuals" (Wan 2012: 109). Intersubjectivity does not require meaning to remain fixed: rather, cultural meanings, processes and understandings are able to evolve (Crossley 1996; Wan 2012). Crossley explains 'intersubjectivity' in terms of community cohesion:

> Much is acquired [...] in education of both a formal and an informal form. We grow up and live in communities and those communities both structure our learning experiences and teach us about life and how to live it. This ensures that assumptions are shared and thus that the symbolic cement of the lifeworld is reproduced through both time and space. Having said this, common-sense assumptions are not static. They change as the structure of communal life changes. (Crossley 1996: 92)

The applicability of intersubjectivity to subcultural research can be seen in the way that understandings of the foundations of subculture, for example, its systems of thought and common practices, are created intersubjectively. This occurs not only within communication between participants but also with those in other communication interlocks; subcultural (or punk) meanings are created as much by shared assumptions within the group as with shared assumptions beyond it. Intersubjectivity is therefore crucial to understanding the creation of a "sense of [subcultural] self" (Crossley 1996: 71) and recognition of these identities (Gillespie and Cornish 2010; Honneth 1995).

Substance and Everyday Practices

Having established the importance of viewing subcultures as embedded in wider cultural life, it is not a large leap to recognise the importance of embedding subcultural practice in everyday practice. In failing to pay enough attention to this, earlier subculture and post-subculture theorisations often achieved only a partial understanding of the subject positions that members inhabit.

> One of the major problems with subcultural theory was its emphasis on a 'subcultural identity' which while arising out of structural positions also seemed to transcend all other identities that members of subcultures could inhabit. As Angela McRobbie puts it, 'Few writers seemed interested in what happened when a mod went home after a weekend on speed.' Members of musical scenes are not simply 'teds,' 'mods,' 'punks' or 'northern soulies,' but also mothers, sons, husbands, and workers. Furthermore, they may also, for example, be fans of 'Coronation Street' or the Stoke City football club. (Hollows and Milestone 1998: 96; with reference to McRobbie 1990: 68–69)

Discussions of 'everyday life' should therefore be brought to bear on understandings of 'subcultural life' (Pilkington 2014a: 14). Understanding intersubjectivity in 'communication interlocks' (Fine and Kleinman 1979) allow us to see how "common cultural reference points and practices are diffused both across (sometimes apparently hostile) 'subcultural' groups and between 'mainstream' and 'subcultural' groupings" (Pilkington 2014a: 13).

To this end, Pilkington suggests concerning ourselves with the substantive *cultural practices* in which individuals take part, without attempting to separate out those practices that may be 'alternative' from the 'mainstream'. This is important because "'subcultural' lives are not separate from but embedded in and constrained by 'whole lives'" (13). Whilst the mundanity of many everyday cultural practices has left them marginalised in subcultural debates, Pilkington argues for the "inclusion in the field of vision of a range of everyday communicative, musical, sporting, educational, informal economy and territorial practices, not just 'spectacular', style-based, cultural practices" (13).

The investigation of individuals' everyday cultural practices allows us to understand their whole lives, both the elements over which they retain agency and the structures that constrain them. We see how they participate in their chosen subculture and how their practices affect others, and this helps inform us as to what subcultural practices consist of. Moreover, we can better locate the subculture itself within wider social practices and structures. Taking this into account, Chap. 6 will draw on participants' wider political activities in order to understand the political significance of punk.

Beyond Youth

Refocusing the lens from the spectacular to the whole lives of participants further enables us to view how interactions might shift as people age. 'Subculture' as an analytical framework has historically centred on the cultural practices of groups of *young people* through the early work of the Chicago School. This was consolidated by the CCCS and much of the post-subcultural literature. However, any empirical evidence of contemporary subcultural gatherings will confirm that a wide variety of age groups are, and have been, involved. By retaining a focus on young people we negate the opportunity to both fully represent the subculture, and see how, for example, "punk as an identity [...] must be managed and negotiated in the context of other everyday circumstances" (Bennett 2006: 226).

However, there is a growing trend to critique the ties between youth and subcultural engagement. Recent work (Bennett 2006; Bennett and Hodkinson 2012; Davis 2006; Hodkinson 2011; Pilkington 2014b) has sought to pay more attention to the ways in which ageing and the presence of different age groups affects subcultures.

A key facet of this work has been the way in which subcultural members must negotiate 'adult' responsibilities as they age. Hodkinson (2011, 2012) has particularly focused on older goth couples negotiating childcare and raising (goth) children. Pilkington (2014b) and Fogarty

(2012) discuss the ways in which subcultures come to resemble families as older members 'mentor' and 'advise' younger individuals. Bennett (2012) situates subcultural life alongside everyday work commitments, and Hodkinson (2011, 2012) and Haenfler (2006, 2012) discuss how everyday commitments as well as aspects of the ageing body coalesce to result in different approaches to stylistic practices.

A number of these themes, particularly the solidarities and tensions (Pilkington 2014b) between different generations are examined in terms of the trajectory of the Dutch punk scene in Chap. 3.

Resistance

'Resistance' and its role in the conceptualisation of subculture remains contentious. Subculture's origins in studies of delinquency mean that youth cultures have historically been positioned in opposition to middle-class or mainstream hegemonies. Whereas Hodkinson's (2002) reconceptualisation of subculture sought to explicitly sever "its automatic link with resistance [and] class conflict" (29); for Williams (2011) 'resistance' remains central, as subcultures exist for and because of marginalised, non-normative young people searching for an "antidote to everyday life" (10).

Leblanc (1999) and Haenfler (2006) also contend that resistance remains an important facet of subculture: in Haenfler's case, for straight edge, and for female punks in Leblanc's study. Both argue that these forms of resistance do carry political potential, unlike the model of resistance espoused by earlier understandings in which subcultural members were positioned as ultimately reinforcing their subordination (Clarke et al. [1975] 2006). Haenfler (2006) believes that the practices of straight edge form a distinct challenge to mainstream society by rejecting norms of, for example, drug and alcohol use, and through being vegetarian or vegan and anti-sexist. In allowing members to have the social and cultural space in which to challenge norms and to create their own alternatives, the subculture "has real consequences for the lives of its members, other peer groups, and possibly mainstream society" (194). Leblanc (1999) suggests that we need to look beyond subcultural behaviours to include 'discursive' and 'symbolic' acts as also providing resistant potential (18).

In advancing his understanding of 'resistance', Williams (2011) developed a multi-dimensional mapping of the concept (92–105). He uses three axes (although suggesting that there may be more), postulating that subcultural—and individual—resistant acts (including thoughts, feelings and behaviours) range from passive to active, micro to macro, and covert to overt.

> A young person who identifies with the punk subculture may engage in relatively passive acts of resistance, such as buying punk music or a punk T-shirt, yet reading the CD-insert or song lyrics may lead her to engage in more active forms of resistance. She might hide her subcultural affiliation from her parents, but proudly display subcultural paraphernalia in front of peers or other adults. The resistant actions in which she engages may involve criticizing her peers in a personal diary or participating in a social justice demonstration with thousands of other people. In other words, one member of a single subculture may engage in many different types of resistance in their everyday lives, each with its own (set of) consequences. (Williams 2011: 105–106)

In including a range of possible resistant activities, Williams certainly takes a number of 'everyday', sometimes highly individualised actions, but all of these are related specifically to subcultural lives. However, it remains important to retain a wider lens on individuals' *whole* lives (Pilkington and Omel'chenko 2013) and a full range of potentially resistant practices.

In widening my own lens beyond subcultural lives, in Chap. 6 I also shift the researcher's gaze from subcultural resistance to everyday political activities. As Leblanc (1999) argues, "resistance is primarily [...] a form of political behaviour" (18). Given that 'resistance' is so interlinked with subcultural activities (Clarke et al. [1975] 2006; Haenfler 2006; Leblanc 1999; Williams 2011), it is necessary to extend the understanding of which activities might have political importance, in order to better understand the way in which punk and punks are culturally embedded in wider society (see Chap. 6 for this discussion).

Authenticity

In spite of the problems with Hebdige's (1979) discussion of the importance of originality in punk, authenticity remains a strong discourse within subcultural literature: particularly that focused on punk (Williams 2011).

Early conceptualisations of authenticity argued that subcultural forms were diffused and defused by the mass media. Whilst Muggleton (2000) may have critiqued the CCCS's work on subculture, he does not develop their understanding of authenticity beyond being tied to mass media practices. Instead he queries 'subculturalists' relationship to the media, arguing that it is less passive than the CCCS believed.

Later work on authenticity as a concept developed in two directions: practices and identity. Moore (2004) viewed punk as having two distinct periods: the 'culture of destruction' found in early US and UK punk, and the 'culture of authenticity' found in the 1980s US hardcore scenes. Authenticity, for him, was linked to punk's economic practices.

> The 'culture of authenticity' [...] developed as young people attempted to insulate themselves from the culture industry and consumer lifestyles in their search for expressive sincerity and anticommercial purity. Those who embraced the do-it-yourself approach transformed media and consumer identities into independent networks of cultural production, which enabled a sense of local community, allowed spectators to become participants, and created a space for public debate and dissent. (Moore 2004: 323)

Wallach (2008) saw that punk authenticity in Indonesia was tied to quite rigid practices of significations. Punks would employ a narrow range of markers, practices, and styles, which were drawn quite explicitly from originator scenes. Authenticity was therefore claimed by replicating other 'authentic' markers.

The idea that authenticity might be tied to identity was developed by Widdicombe and Wooffitt (1990), whose work indicated that authenticity was linked to strength and length of commitment to a particular subculture. Williams (2006) added that different subsections of subcultures might have different standards regarding how to acquire authenticity.

Williams (2011) critiques the CCCS's realist approach to subcultural identity and proposes instead a social constructionist understanding in which authenticity is made real through subcultural interaction. "Authenticity may be seen as some sort of ideal, highly valued and sought by individuals and groups as part of the process of becoming. Alternatively, authenticity may be something strategically invoked as a marker of status or method of social control" (140). We see that authenticity can be understood as tool in the creation and maintenance of individual (or group) identity, based on intersubjective understandings of what markers are needed to claim authenticity.

If viewed as an identity or a marker of status, it is important to understand the importance of 'subcultural capital' to the acquisition of authenticity. Thornton's (1995) coining of 'subcultural capital' (drawing on Bourdieu's (1984) hierarchies of cultural capital) did not explicitly address authenticity in terms of identity formation. However, if "[s]ubcultural capital confers *status* on its owner in the eyes of the relevant beholder" (Thornton 1995: 11, emphasis added), then we see there is a relationship between this concept and that of authenticity. The relativistic nature of the conferring of both subcultural capital and authenticity, according to the norms and practices of the subculture in question, mean that the acquiring of subcultural capital can contribute to an individuals' authenticity, just as being authentic can count towards gaining subcultural capital.

Geographical Contexts

The rise of theories of globalisation led to a recognition that we could no longer talk of locally bounded subcultures (if ever we could). The post-subcultural turn also marked the point at which theorists grappled with placing their groups into their local and global contexts. A number of models have been proposed, including centre/periphery, glocal and translocal.

Debates over the nature of global/local influences on culture have often drawn on globalisation theories relating to the relationship between 'centre' and 'periphery' (Shils 1975; Wallerstein 1974). Within punk scholarship the United States or United Kingdom's scenes are often seen as the most influential around the world; the US/UK are thus positioned as the 'centre' to the rest of the world's 'periphery'. As discussed earlier, this stems from a problematic focus on notions of authenticity that is derived from an emphasis on originality in subculture (Hebdige 1979). Whilst the persistence of punk and its spread to new locations has erased the usefulness of viewing 'authenticity' as directly related to the original punk scene, there remains an uneven balance of power towards 'core', originator scenes.

Wallach (2008) discusses how bands such as the Exploited, the Ramones, and the Sex Pistols dominated discussions of punk in Indonesia. Similarly Crass and The Clash are the most regularly cited bands by research participants in this study of Dutch punk. This highlights how punks around the world still claim subcultural capital through demonstrating knowledge of these 'authentic' bands. Such practices reinforce hierarchies of 'core' centres and 'other' peripheries.

In discussing the punk scenes of Mexico City and Barcelona, O'Connor (2004) extend the centre/periphery model to include three tiers, with the United States positioned as the centre, Europe as semi-peripheral, and Latin America as peripheral (176). He seeks to uncover how global cultural signifiers are utilised in the creation of new, local, scenes. O'Connor recognises that local forms can affect the global but also that structural inequalities can limit this. He gives examples of the inequalities in the 'flow' of punk between Spain and Mexico, with Spanish bands more likely to be known in Mexico than the reverse. This recognises that the 'flow' of cultural influence is more complicated than a simple centre/periphery model suggests. With these arguments O'Connor advocates against Appadurai's (1996) earlier break from discussions of centre/periphery, in favour of a model of the global flow of culture.

'Glocal' was first applied to (post-)subcultural theory by Mitchell (1998) in a discussion of Australian hip hop. This form of hip hop draws on global influences, particularly from the United States and distils these through local experiences, marking it out as 'glocal'. Sydney's western suburbs form the historical centre of Australian hip hop; underprivileged and with a wide ethnic mix of migrant cultures, they are positioned as the Australian version of the American 'ghettos' from which hip hop emerged. Artists draw influences both from mainstream American hip hop and more marginalised Spanish-language hip hop and use these to reinforce their own 'otherness' in Australian society. "Although US rap was the inspiration, the local scene caught fire on the fuel that was already there" (4). Different global forms of hip hop interact with locality to produce Australian hip hop.

'Glocal'—in relation to youth cultural practices—was further developed by Pilkington (2004). She situates 'glocal' within a model of centre/periphery and argues that 'glocal' allows a more accurate depiction of subcultural affiliations on the periphery. Her work notes that conceptualisations of a globalised youth culture in which practices on the periphery reflect those of the centre were not applicable in Russia. Different structural positions of young people enable some to draw on global cultures, whilst constraining others who therefore focus more on the local. "[T]he 'global' and the 'local' are resources drawn upon, differentially, by young people in the process of developing youth cultural strategies that manage 'glocal' lives" (132). 'Glocal' therefore usefully highlights the structural influence on different global or local cultural influences.

'Translocal' illuminates a different interplay between the local and global. It argues that numerous local scenes have come to be constructed along similar lines, thereby connecting "groups of kindred spirits many miles away" (Bennett and Peterson 2004: 8–9). Hodkinson (2004) applies 'translocal' to his research on the UK goth scene. He understands this to be a "singular and relatively coherent movement whose translocal connections are of greater significance than its local differences" (144). Issues of identity and taste were shaped by translocal media formats, consumer trends, and the latest subcultural fashions. Participants often travel for their scenic participation, such as to gigs, clubs, shops or festivals, and yet the day-to-day experiences and infrastructure of the scene remained based around local social connections.

Bennett and Peterson (2004) discuss three other applications for 'translocal' in terms of popular culture; transregional music, the music festival, and the music carnival. Transregional music refers to global forms of culture, diffused by mass media, which have now been appropriated by many diverse local scenes; they give hip hop as an example. Music festivals serve as a 'local' scene that draws bands and attendees from all over the world together for an event that facilitates communication of *ways* of *doing* cultural participation. 'Music carnival' is a label given to a group of a band's fans who follow them on tour, for example, the Grateful Dead's Deadheads. The 'superfans" presence at each performance "energize[s] local devotees", facilitating the communication of fandom at a translocal level (Bennett and Peterson 2004: 10). Understandings of 'translocal' provide a more nuanced view of complex patterns of cultural flow. However, it hints at a translocal parity that privileges the role of the 'centre', and therefore does not adequately consider the specificity of 'peripheral' experiences of subculture.

Webb (2007) highlights the complex interplay between local and global in his study of Bristolean trip hop. He argues that this cultural form could only have emerged in Bristol; the music's genre-mixing was a result of the mingling of communities in the city alongside other factors such as the well-developed local music scene. In the 1980s many of Bristol's musicians were engaged in hip hop of a style taken directly from New York, but a desire to do something different led to the instigation of a new 'Bristol sound'. Trip hop did not remain local for long, with London and the rest of the United Kingdom quickly noticing and emulating the style. Thus cultural influences are drawn globally (from a cultural 'centre') and take root in 'peripheral' Bristol, arguably situating Bristol as a *new* centre for trip hop.

In Chap. 4, I build on the theoretical work that has attempted to situate subcultures as part of a wider global whole. I investigate the way in which connections and mobility, both everyday and subcultural, have helped shape the Dutch punk scene and members' understandings of its local/global position.

Historical Contexts

In addition to regrounding debates by emphasising both the whole lives of participants and the wider cultural context in which subcultures operate, it is important to avoid (post-)subcultural tendencies towards ahistoricity.

In critiquing theories of detraditionalisation and individualisation, Smart (2007) highlights Beck and Beck-Gernsheim's (2002) ahistoricism;

> Whilst the idea of tradition is evoked, no specificity is provided so the reader cannot be sure if this passage refers to the pre-industrial era, the Victoria era or the early twentieth century. The idea that during this vague period people slavishly followed the prevalent rules and dominant beliefs is accepted without hesitation. A special moment in history having been created, that moment can then be compared with the present which, by dint of such a contract, looks challengingly different. But the past in this representation is little more than a straw man devised for the sake of argument. (Smart 2007: 18)

This argument is equally applicable to other theories that posit the role of individual agency and fragmented fluid (post-)subcultures as particularly 'new' (Bennett and Kahn-Harris 2004; Chaney 2004; Malbon 1999; Muggleton and Weinzierl 2003). In noting Shildrick and MacDonald's (2006), J. Clarke et al.'s ([1975] 2006), and Fine and Kleinman's (1979) understandings of the fluidity that was possible in subcultural membership, we see that the post-subculturalists' claims of this fluidity as an element of postmodern consumer culture are over-emphasised.

We can see echoes of Williams' (2011) and Pilkington and Omel'chenko's (2013) proposition to embed subcultural life in wider cultural life in Smart's (2007) call to understand individual agency as "embedded in culture and history, with these qualities manifesting themselves through forms of everyday behaviour which are not radically different to action in the past" (26). We therefore need to take a more grounded historical approach to understanding subcultures and can do this by uncovering everyday and subcultural practices in their historical context.

REGROUNDING PUNK

Punk in 1977 in London was not the same things as punk in 2007 in Atlanta (or even in 2007 in London). And while the label 'punk' is readily affixed to people and practices in both places/times, the meaning of punk has been interpreted differently as it spread around the globe. (Williams 2011: 39)

Over the last forty years, punk has spread over the whole world. Countless new musical subgenres have emerged, as well as other movements based on practices (for example, straight edge [Haenfler 2004, 2006]) or politics (for example, riot grrrl [Downes 2012]) or anarcho-punk (Cross 2010; Dunn 2011). As the label 'punk' comes to encompass more and more, it becomes harder for academics to pinpoint what punk might mean. Indeed, it is not only academics who struggle with defining punk but also punks themselves (see Chap. 5).

Yet there have been many attempts to answer the questions posed by Pilkington (2012); "why, thirty-five years on [do] we continue to talk about 'punk' when it is hard to find a punk who looks like a punk, sounds like a punk or describes him or herself as a punk"? (262). This section will discuss a number of the ways in which punk has been understood in the wake of the subcultural debates.

Economic Practices and DIY

In discussing the various developments of punk, Thompson (2004) gives an overview of seven distinct periods and places in which new punk scenes emerged: the New York Scene, the English Scene, California Hardcore, Washington, D.C. Hardcore, New York Hardcore, Riot Grrrl and Berkeley Pop-Punk. In discussing each of these it becomes clear that in his understanding these various punk scenes are bound by an ideological position in relation to economic practices. Like Laing (1985) Thompson discusses the DIY record labels that—he argues—are crucial to each scene. He makes it clear that an anti-capitalist and anti-commercial ideology is a prerequisite for punk.

Alternative economic practices, DIY practices and anti-capitalist ideologies, form the basis of a number of punk studies, including Gosling (2004), Dale (2012), Dunn (2012) and O'Connor (2008). There is a great deal of debate over the potential that DIY may—or may not—offer in order to resist corporate cultural hegemony within both subcultural literature (O'Hara 1999) and academic writing (Dale 2008, 2012). Ventsel (2008) located the economic practices of punks and skins within their wider everyday lives by uncovering networks of reciprocity in an informal, underground and semi-legal economy.

Similarly, Moore (2010) situates punk historically in wider economic contexts and suggests that punk, as a DIY movement, is an expression of post-Fordist alienation.

> [Punks] had been left with scant opportunities to find creative fulfillment in their day jobs, no guidelines for transforming a culture of consumption into meaningful existence, and unable to participate in the spectacles of mass media as anything but spectators. […] [They] sought to take control over what they consumed, transformed passionate consumer tastes into a basis for cultural production, and created a scene they could call their own. Doing it themselves, they made the ephemeral world of consumption into grounds for durable identities and participatory community. (Moore 2010: 62)

Social Practices

A number of ethnographic studies have emerged that focus particularly on the social practices of punk. In these works, punk as a subculture emerges through the actions, interactions, practices and understandings held by participants. In grounding the subculture in these practices we can better understand punk's place within punks' lives.

An important addition to the punk canon is Leblanc's (1999) *Pretty in Punk* which gives voice to—often marginalised—punk women. She furthers the discourse of punk as a resistant identity, focusing particularly on the ways in which women use punk to fight normative femininity, although this struggle often takes place within a masculine-coded subculture, complicating matters.

Haenfler (2006) focuses on the straight edge subgenre of punk, investigating how subcultural practices provide conflicting gendered experiences for 'edgers' both male and female and how practices and identification with the scene changes as participants age. The importance of straight edge is portrayed both in its guise as a social movement *and* as an individual identity, guided by the straight edge philosophy.

Whereas both Leblanc and Haenfler focused primarily on punk scenes in the (central) United States, Gololobov et al. (2014), O'Connor (2002, 2003, 2004) and Wallach (2008) have contributed ethnographic studies that take in various other (more peripheral) punk scenes. O'Connor's work focuses primarily on the experience of punk in Mexico. He contrasts this with punk in other locations (Barcelona, Washington, D.C., Austin, Texas, and Toronto) in order to understand punk's relationship with globalisation. Wallach uncovers the social experiences of punk in Indonesia and the opportunities it provides for self-expression. Gololobov (2014), Steinholt et al. (2014) and Pilkington (2014b) explore punk in various locations in Russia—Krasnodar, St. Petersburg and Vorkuta (respectively)—seeking to understand what unites very different formulations of punk. They conclude that "[p]unk exists not as discrete formation, politics or aesthetics, but as a set of non-exclusive and unfixed transnormative cultural practices and in the affective bonds generated in the process of their enactment" (Pilkington et al. 2014: 211).

CONCLUSION

This chapter has served to provide a brief overview of the historical development of 'subculture' as a theoretical framework and of 'punk' as an object of analysis. 'Subculture' has had a contentious history with a great many theorists adding to, developing, or sometimes even rejecting it as no longer of use. The trajectory of academic work on punk is intertwined with the 'subculture debate', with a number of theoretical developments relating to subculture drawing upon studies of punk for their empirical basis. It is therefore vital to locate where this book sits in relation to these debates.

This book adds to the work of Williams (2011), Bennett (2011) and Pilkington and Omel'chenko (2013) in seeking to 'reground' subculture. The post-subculturalists' critiques of structural determinism in the foundational work by the CCCS were often rather overstated, and therefore sometimes fell into the trap of arguing vociferously for an equally problematic opposite: an exaggerated emphasis on individualism. Rather than furthering an argument on 'subculture' versus 'post-subculture', this book will draw on the positive developments that have been made towards a more theoretically rich understanding of subcultures. With a recognition that subculture as a concept has had a complex past, I choose to continue to use this terminology. I thereby root this book within the trajectory of the many attempts to uncover the complexities of the subject positions of punk individuals within wider culture.

In order to do so, this book places its punk participants at the foreground of refining our knowledge of what punk—*and*—subculture can mean. In focusing on participants' discourse and their practices it gives centre stage to their punk subjectivity. This book does not delineate punk from the mainstream but instead embeds punk as a part of whole lives and punk subculture as part of wider culture. It unpicks the ways in which individuals are agents in the intersubjective creation of subcultural meaning whilst locating them as (active) subjects (in the maintenance and adaption) of complex structural factors.

Subculture cannot be disentangled from culture. Punk practices, people, lives, places, values, resources and so on cannot be understood in isolation from wider society. Subcultural groups are bound by social structures, just as they help create and reinforce them. Historical contexts shape individual, subcultural, and cultural trajectories. Individuals draw on subcultural—as well as cultural—resources in forging their own, meaningful, lives. Drawing boundaries, be they historical or spatial, around subcultures is therefore problematic. Instead I propose a holistic approach in which a deeper conceptualisation of subculture is attained through viewing the connectedness of individuals and their subcultural practices.

REFERENCES

Anderson, B. [1983] 2006. *Imagined Communities: Reflections on the Origin and Spread of Nationalism*. London: Verso.

Appadurai, A. 1996. *Modernity at Large: Cultural Dimensions of Globalization*. Minneapolis: University of Minnesota Press.

Bauman, Z. 2000. *Liquid Modernity*. Cambridge: Polity Press.

Beck, U. 1994. The Reinvention of Politics: Towards a Theory of Reflexive Modernization. In *Reflexive Modernization: Politics, Tradition and Aesthetics in the Modern Social Order*, ed. U. Beck, A. Giddens, and S. Lash, 1–55. Cambridge: Polity Press.

Beck, U., and E. Beck-Gernsheim. 2002. *Individualization: Institutionalized Individualism and Its Social and Political Consequences*. London: Sage.

Bennett, A. 1999. Subcultures or Neo-Tribes? Rethinking the Relationship Between Youth, Style and Musical Taste. *Sociology* 33 (3): 599–617.

Bennett, A. 2005. In Defence of Neo-tribes: A Response to Blackman and Hesmondhalgh. *Journal of Youth Studies* 8 (2): 255–259.

Bennett, A. 2006. Punk's Not Dead: The Continuing Significance of Punk Rock for an Older Generation of Fans. *Sociology* 40 (2): 219–235.

Bennett, A. 2011. The Post-subcultural Turn: Some Reflections 10 years on. *Journal of Youth Studies* 14 (5): 493–506.

Bennett, A. 2012. Dance Parties, Lifestyle and Strategies for Ageing. In *Ageing and Youth Cultures*, ed. A. Bennett and P. Hodkinson, 95–104. London: Berg.

Bennett, A., and P. Hodkinson. 2012. *Ageing and Youth Cultures*. London: Berg.

Bennett, A., and K. Kahn-Harris. 2004. *After Subculture: Critical Studies in Contemporary Youth Culture*. Basingstoke: Palgrave Macmillan.

Bennett, A., and R.A. Peterson. 2004. *Music Scenes: Local, Translocal and Virtual*. Nashville: Vanderbilt University Press.

Blackman, S. 2005. Youth Subcultural Theory: A Critical Engagement with the Concept, Its Origins and Politics, from the Chicago School to Postmodernism. *Journal of Youth Studies* 8 (1): 1–20.

Bourdieu, P. 1984. *Distinction: A Social Critique of the Judgement of Taste*. London: Routledge.

Chaney, D. 2004. Fragmented Culture and Subcultures. In *After Subculture: Critical Studies in Contemporary Youth Culture*, ed. A. Bennett and K. Kahn-Harris, 36–48. Basingstoke: Palgrave Macmillan.

Clarke, J., S. Hall, T. Jefferson, and B. Roberts. [1975] 2006. Subcultures, Cultures and Class. In *Resistance Through Rituals: Youth Subcultures in Post-war Britain*, 2nd ed., ed. S. Hall and T. Jefferson, 3–59. London: Routledge.

Clarke, G. [1982] 2007. Defending Ski-jumpers: A Critique of Theories of Youth Sub-cultures. In *CCCS Selected Working Papers*, vol. 2, ed. A. Gray, J. Campbell, M. Erickson, S. Hanson, and H. Wood, 230–255. Abingdon: Routledge.

Cobley, P. 1999. Leave the Capitol. In *Punk Rock: So What? The Cultural Legacy of Punk*, ed. R. Sabin, 170–185. London: Routledge.

Cohen, A.K. 1955. *Delinquent Boys: The Culture of the Gang*. New York: Free Press.

Cohen, P. [1972] 1997. Subcultural Conflict and Working Class Community. In *Rethinking the Youth Question: Education, Labour and Cultural Studies*, ed. P. Cohen, 48–63. Basingstoke: Macmillan.

Critcher, C. [1975] 2006. Structure, Culture, and Biographies. In *Resistance Through Rituals: Youth Subcultures in Post-war Britain, Second Edition*, ed. S. Hall and T. Jefferson, 139–144. London: Routledge.

Cross, R. 2010. There is No Authority but Yourself: The Individual and the Collective in British Anarcho-Punk. *Music and Politics* 4 (2): 1–20.

Crossley, N. 1996. *Intersubjectivity: The Fabric of Social Becoming.* London: Sage.

Crossley, N. 2008. Pretty Connected: The Social Network of the Early UK Punk Movement. *Theory, Culture & Society* 25 (6): 89–116.

Dale, P. 2008. It Was Easy, It Was Cheap, so What? Reconsidering the DIY Principle of Punk and Indie Music. *Popular Music History* 3 (2): 171–193.

Dale, P. 2012. *Anyone Can Do It: Empowerment, Tradition and the Punk Underground.* Farnham: Ashgate.

Davis, J. 2006. Growing Up Punk: Negotiating Aging Identity in a Local Music Scene. *Symbolic Interaction* 29 (1): 63–69.

Downes, J. 2012. The Expansion of Punk Rock: Riot Grrrl Challenges to Gender Power Relations in British Indie Music Subcultures. *Women's Studies* 41 (2): 204–237.

Dunn, K. 2011. Anarcho-Punk and Resistance in Everyday Life. *Punk & Post-Punk* 1 (2): 201–218.

Dunn, K.C. 2012. If It Ain't Cheap, It Ain't Punk: Walter Benjamin's Progressive Cultural Production and DIY Punk Record Labels. *Journal of Popular Music Studies* 24 (2): 217–237.

Fine, G.A., and S. Kleinman. 1979. Rethinking Subculture: An Interactionist Analysis. *American Journal of Sociology* 85 (1): 1–20.

Fogarty, M. 2012. "Each One Teach One": B-Boying and Ageing. In *Ageing and Youth Cultures,* ed. A. Bennett and P. Hodkinson, 53–65. London: Berg.

Giddens, A. 1991. *Modernity and Self-Identity: Self and Society in the Late Modern Age.* Cambridge: Polity Press.

Giddens, A. 1994. *Beyond Left and Right: The Future of Radical Politics.* Cambridge: Polity Press.

Giddens, A. 2000. *The Third Way and Its Critics.* Cambridge: Polity Press.

Gillespie, A., and F. Cornish. 2010. Intersubjectivity: Towards a Dialogical Analysis. *Journal for the Theory of Social Behaviour* 40 (1): 19–46.

Gololobov, I. 2014. Krasnodar: Perpendicular Culture in the Biggest Village on Earth. In *Punk in Russia: Cultural Mutation from the 'Useless' to the 'Moronic',* ed. I. Gololobov, H. Pilkington, and Y.B. Steinholt, 99–142. London: Routledge.

Gololobov, I., H. Pilkington, and Y.B. Steinholt. 2014. *Punk in Russia: Cultural Mutation from the 'Useless' to the 'Moronic'.* London: Routledge.

Goodman, P. 1960. *Growing up Absurd: Problems of Youth in the Organized System.* New York: Random House.

Gosling, T. 2004. "Not for Sale": The Underground Network of Anarcho-Punk. In *Music Scenes: Local, Translocal, and Virtual,* ed. A. Bennett and R.A. Peterson, 168–186. Nashville: Vanderbilt University Press.

Haenfler, R. 2004. Rethinking Subcultural Resistance: Core Values of the Straight Edge Movement. *Journal of Contemporary Ethnography* 33 (4): 406–436.

Haenfler, R. 2006. *Straight Edge: Clean-Living Youth, Hardcore Punk, and Social Change*. New Brunswick, NH: Rutgers University Press.

Haenfler, R. 2012 "More Than Xs on My Hands": Older Straight Edgers and the Meaning of Style. In *Ageing and Youth Cultures*, ed A. Bennett and P. Hodkinson, 9–23. London: Berg.

Hall, S., and T. Jefferson. [1975] 2006. *Resistance Through Rituals: Youth Subcultures in Post-war Britain*, 2nd ed. London: Routledge.

Hannerz, U. 1992. *Cultural Complexity: Studies in the Social Organization of Meaning*. New York: Columbia University Press.

Harris, K. 2000. "Roots"? The Relationship Between the Global and the Local within the Extreme Metal Scene. *Popular Music* 19 (1): 13–30.

Hebdige, D. 1979. *Subculture: The Meaning of Style*. London: Routledge.

Heelas, P. 1996. Introduction: Detraditionalization and Its Rivals. In *Detraditionalization: Critical Reflections on Authority and Identity*, ed. P. Heelas, S. Lash, and P. Morris, 1–20. Cambridge, MA: Blackwell.

Hesmondhalgh, D. 2005. Subcultures, Scenes or Tribes? None of the Above. *Journal of Youth Studies* 8 (1): 21–40.

Hodkinson, P. 2002. *Goth: Identity, Style and Subculture*. Oxford: Berg.

Hodkinson, P. 2004. Translocal Connections in the Goth Scene. In *Music Scenes: Local, Translocal and Virtual*, ed. A. Bennett and R.A. Peterson, 131–148. Nashville: Vanderbilt University Press.

Hodkinson, P. 2011. Ageing in a Spectacular "Youth Culture": Continuity Change and Community Amongst Older Goths. *The British Journal of Sociology* 62 (2): 262–282.

Hodkinson, P. 2012. The Collective Aging of a Goth Festival. In *Ageing and Youth Cultures*, ed. A. Bennett and P. Hodkinson, 133–145. London: Berg.

Hollows, J., and K. Milestone. 1998. Welcome to Dreamsville: A History and Geography of Northern Soul. In *The Place of Music*, ed. A. Leyshon, D. Matless, and G. Revill, 83–103. New York: The Guildford Press.

Honneth, A. 1995. *The Struggle for Recognition: The Moral Grammar of Social Conflicts*. Cambridge: Polity Press.

Laing, D. 1985. *One Chord Wonders: Power and Meaning in Punk Rock*. Milton Keynes: Open University Press.

Leblanc, L. 1999. *Pretty in Punk: Girls' Gender Resistance in a Boys' Subculture*. New Brunswick: RutgersUniversity Press.

Maffesoli, M. 1996. *The Time of the Tribes: The Decline of Individualism in Mass Society*. London: Sage.

Malbon, B. 1999. *Clubbing: Dancing, Ecstasy and Vitality*. London: Routledge.

Marcus, G. 1989. *Lipstick Traces: A Secret History of the 20th Century*. London: Faber and Faber.

Massey, D. 1993. Power-Geometry and a Progressive Sense of Place. In *Mapping the Futures: Local Cultures, Global Change*, ed. J. Bird, B. Curtis, T. Putnam, G. Robertson, and L. Tickner, 59–69. London: Routledge.

McRobbie, A. 1990. Settling Accounts with Subcultures: A Feminist Critique. In *On Record: Rock, Pop and the Written Word*, ed. S. Frith and A. Goodwin, 55–67. London: Routledge.

McRobbie, A., and J. Garber. [1975] 2006. Girls and Subcultures: An Exploration. In *Resistance Through Rituals: Youth Subcultures in Post-war Britain*, 2nd ed., ed. S. Hall and T. Jefferson, 177–188. London: Routledge.

Mitchell, T. 1998. Australian Hip Hop as 'Glocal' Subculture. Available from http://www.snarl.org/youth/tonym2.pdf. [14/05/2015].

Moore, R. 2004. Postmodernism and Punk Subculture: Cultures of Authenticity and Deconstruction. *The Communication Review* 7 (3): 305–327.

Moore, R. 2010. *Sells Like Teen Spirit: Music, Youth Culture, and Social Crisis*. London: New York University Press.

Muggleton, D. 2000. *Inside Subculture: The Postmodern Meaning of Style*. Oxford: Berg.

Muggleton, D., and R. Weinzierl. 2003. *The Post-subcultures Reader*. Oxford: Berg.

Nehring, N. 1993. *Flowers in the Dustbin: Culture, Anarchy, and Postwar England*. Ann Arbor: University of Michigan Press.

O'Connor, A. 2002. Local Scenes and Dangerous Crossroads: Punk and Theories of Cultural Hybridity. *Popular Music* 21 (2): 225–236.

O'Connor, A. 2003. Punk Subculture in Mexico and the Anti-globalization Movement: A Report from the Front. *New Political Science* 25 (1): 43–53.

O'Connor, A. 2004. Punk and Globalization: Spain and Mexico. *International Journal of Cultural Studies* 7 (2): 175–195.

O'Connor, A. 2008. *Punk Record Labels and the Struggle for Autonomy: The Emergence of DIY*. Lanham: Lexington Books.

O'Hara, C. 1999. *The Philosophy of Punk: More Than Noise!* Edinburgh: AK Press.

Pilkington, H. 2004. Youth Strategies for Glocal Living: Space, Power and Communication in Everyday Cultural Practice. In *After Subculture: Critical Studies in Contemporary Youth Culture*, ed. A. Bennett and K. Kahn-Harris, 119–134. Basingstoke: Palgrave Macmillan.

Pilkington, H. 2012. Punk—But Not as We Know It: Punk in Post-socialist Space. *Punk & Post-Punk* 1 (3): 253–266.

Pilkington, H. 2014a. Punk, But Not as We Know It: Rethinking Punk from a Post-socialist Perspective. In *Punk in Russia: Cultural Mutation from the 'Useless' to the 'Moronic'*, ed. I. Gololobov, H. Pilkington, and Y.B. Steinholt, 1–21. London: Routledge.

Pilkington, H. 2014b Vorkuta: A Live Scene in a "Rotting City". In *Punk in Russia: Cultural Mutation from the 'Useless' to the 'Moronic'*, ed. I. Gololobov, H. Pilkington, and Y.B. Steinholt, 143–195. London: Routledge.

Pilkington, H., I. Gololobov, and Y.B. Steinholt. 2014. Conclusion. In *Punk in Russia: Cultural Mutation from the 'Useless' to the 'Moronic'*, ed. I. Gololobov, H. Pilkington, and Y.B. Steinholt, 196–211. London: Routledge.

Pilkington, H., and E. Omel'chenko. 2013. Regrounding Youth Cultural Theory (in Post Socialist Youth Cultural Practice). *Sociology Compass,* 7 (3): 208–224.

Pries, L. 2005. Configurations of Geographic and Societal Spaces: A Sociological Proposal Between 'Methodological Nationalism' and the 'Spaces of Flows'. *Global Networks* 5 (2): 167–190.

Redhead, S. 1990. *The End-of-the-Century Party: Youth and Pop Towards 2000.* Manchester: Manchester University Press.

Robertson, R. 1995. Glocalization: Time-Space and Homogeneity-Heterogeneity. In *Global Modernities,* ed. M.L. Featherstone, S. Lash, and R. Robertson, 25–44. London: Sage.

Sabin, R. 1999. Introduction. In *Punk Rock: So What?: The Cultural Legacy of Punk,* ed. R. Sabin, 1–13. London: Routledge.

Savage, J. 1991. *England's Dreaming: Sex Pistols, Punk Rock, and Beyond.* London: Faber and Faber.

Shank, B. 1994. *Dissonant Identities: The Rock'n'Roll Scene in Austin, Texas.* Hanover, NH: Wesleyen University Press.

Shildrick, T., and R. MacDonald. 2006. In Defence of Subculture: Young People, Leisure and Social Divisions. *Journal of Youth Studies* 9 (2): 125–140.

Shils, E. 1975. *Center and Periphery.* Chicago: University of Chicago Press.

Smart, C. 2007. *Personal Life: New Directions in Sociological Thinking.* Cambridge: Polity Press.

Stahl, G. 2004. It's Like Canada Reduced': Setting the Scene in Montreal. In *After Subculture: Critical Studies in Contemporary Youth Culture,* ed. A. Bennett, and K. Kahn-Harris, 51–64. London: Palgrave.

Steinholt, Y.B., I. Gololobov, and H. Pilkington. 2014. St. Petersburg: Big City—Small Scenes. In *Punk in Russia: Cultural Mutation from the 'Useless' to the 'Moronic',* ed. I. Gololobov, H. Pilkington, and Y.B. Steinholt, 49–98. London: Routledge.

Straw, W. 1991. Systems of Articulation, Logics of Change: Communities and Scenes in Popular Music. *Cultural Studies* 5 (3): 368–388.

Straw, W. 2001. Scenes and Sensibilities. *Public* 22 (23): 245–257.

Thompson, S. 2004. *Punk Productions: Unfinished Business.* Albany: State University of New York Press.

Thornton, S. 1995. *Club Cultures: Music, Media and Subcultural Capital.* Cambridge: Polity Press.

Ventsel, A. 2008. Punx and Skins United: One Law for Us One Law for Them. *The Journal of Legal Pluralism and Unofficial Law* 40 (57): 45–100.

Wallach, J. 2008. Living the Punk Lifestyle in Jakarta. *Ethnomusicology* 52 (1): 98–116.

Wallerstein, I. 1974. *The Modern World-System.* New York: Academic Press.

Wan, C. 2012. Shared Knowledge Matters: Culture as Intersubjective Representations. *Social and Personality Psychology Compass* 6 (2): 109–125.

Webb, P. 2007. *Exploring the Networked Worlds of Popular Music: Milieu Cultures*. New York: Routledge.

Whyte, W.F. [1943] 1955. *Street Corner Society: The Social Structure of an Italian Slum*. Chicago: University of Chicago Press.

Widdicombe, S., and R. Wooffitt. 1990. "Being" Versus "Doing" Punk: On Achieving Authenticity as a Member. *Journal of Language and Social Psychology* 9 (4): 257–277.

Williams, J.P. 2006. Authentic Identities: Straightedge Subculture, Music, and the Internet. *Journal of Contemporary Ethnography* 35 (2): 173–200.

Williams, J.P. 2011. *Subcultural Theory: Traditions and Concepts*. Cambridge: Polity Press.

Willis, P. 1972. *Pop Music and Youth Groups*. PhD thesis, Centre for Contemporary Cultural Studies, University of Birmingham, Birmingham.

Willis, P.E. 1977. *Learning to Labour: How Working Class Kids Get Working Class Jobs*. Farnborough: Saxon House.

CHAPTER 3

Punk Lives On: Generations of Punk and Squatting in the Netherlands

The Dutch punk scene has developed characteristically strong associations with political activity. This chapter maps the particular development of the scene, especially highlighting the ways in which its trajectory is entwined with that of the Dutch squatters' movement. It suggests that this particular cultural context has had a lasting impact on punk in the Netherlands, tracing the ebb and flow of the Dutch scene alongside the rise (and fall) of the squatters' movement. It further argues that we cannot understand the contemporary Dutch punk scene without interrogating its relationship with squatting; one that has not always been comfortable.

In charting Dutch punk from its origins to the contemporaneous scene, this chapter shows that punk is most evidently not 'dead' in the Netherlands. Instead the punk scene has gone through fluctuating periods of size and activity. As younger generations become excited by punk, their activity provides an upswing for the scene as it expands (and fragments) to accommodate their 'new' ideas. Whilst their involvement is not static, and some individuals do leave the scene, the persistent involvement of others even during 'low' periods of activity ensures the continuation of the punk scene.

This chapter marks out various points at which new generations bring about 'highs' of Dutch punk, as well as providing an insight into what 'older' punks do if they remain involved in the scene. It ends with a discussion of how the presence of various generations of punks affects the

© The Author(s) 2017
K. Lohman, *The Connected Lives of Dutch Punks*,
Palgrave Studies in the History of Subcultures and Popular Music,
DOI 10.1007/978-3-319-51079-8_3

61

contemporaneous scene, in terms of both tension and solidarity between punks of all ages.

INTRODUCING THE SCENE

The punk scene that I encountered during fieldwork was by all accounts experiencing a 'lull'. However, whilst participants described the scene as 'small' and 'fragmented', it also contained a large number of committed and enthusiastic individuals. Many different groups were organised around different styles of punk. Different towns had multiple groups of punks, bounded by genre and/or generation who were more likely to know other punks across the country than those in other groups in their own town. Whilst the crowd at gigs was often small, there were a healthy number of active bands and promoters ensuring that events occurred regularly; perhaps too regularly (see Chap. 4).

Alongside the old guard of punk bands who were still active (such as The Ex) there were new bands being formed by punks of all ages. Teenagers just discovering the music, fashions and practices associated with punk were making them their own. There was a well-organised and nationally connected group of hardcore bands and fans in their mid-to-late twenties and early thirties. 'Middle-aged' squatter punks who remembered the 1980s heyday of Dutch punk were still around, as were some of the 'art school' punks of the 1970s who could talk of the days before anyone yet knew what punk was.

For too long academia has framed discussions of subcultures such as punk in terms of spectacular *youth* practice. Whilst Bennett (2006) and Bennett and Hodkinson (2012) have initiated analyses of the presence and experiences of older people within subcultures, there remains little work uncovering the ways in which the presence of multiple generations can affect a particular scene. This chapter maps out the way in which different generations tend to cluster together and also the establishment of cross-generational relationships. Moreover, forms of tension and solidarity caused by a multigenerational scene will be teased out, with particular reference to the sharing of subcultural knowledge between older and younger punks.

Whilst the Dutch scene was largely *existing* rather than growing at the time my research was conducted, this did not mean that those involved cared any less for it. As Owens (2009) argues in relation to the squatter movement in Amsterdam, such periods will often intensify the identities of those still involved. This was expressed through participants' sense of being 'active' punks (see Chap. 5): being involved in organising and maintaining elements of the scene by (for instance) playing in bands and running or attending gigs. It could also been seen in other aspects of their lives, such as the ways in which punk intersected with choices including those around work, housing, and their political activities (see Chap. 6).

Punk has a long-standing (and complex) relationship with political engagement, a subject discussed in depth in fanzines, scene literature and in academic work on punk (O'Hara 1999; Worley 2012) as well as later in this book (see Chap. 6). In the Netherlands this relationship and the nature of the punk scene as it exists today is shaped by its history; particularly important to this history is the development of the squatting movement. Punk, politics and squatting go hand-in-hand for many of those interviewed for this project. Throughout punk's history, gigs have been held at squats, bands have used squats' practice rooms, and punks have lived in squats. Activist campaigns are developed in squatters' bars and cafes, political literature is disseminated through the squats and activists are recruited in squats.

This is not unique to the Netherlands. Squatting and politics are intertwined with punk all over the globe: see O'Connor's (2004) discussion of Mexico City and Barcelona, Shaw's (2005) comparison of Berlin and Amsterdam, and Mudu's (2004) report on the Italian scene. However the specific cultural and political context in which the Dutch squatters' movement developed led to shifts in practices of squatting that had global implications. Tensions between squatters and the state in the 1980s, compounded by factionalisation within the squatters' movement, led to the development of large 'cultural' squats. These culminated in autonomous alternative villages within cities, an approach that provided an ideal that punk communities and squats around the world could use as the basis for their own projects.

Developing out of this, Dutch punk has become part of a globally connected scene rooted in complex networks of cultural flow. In order to appreciate how and where the Dutch scene fits as part of a bigger whole, we must understand how transnational connections are formed, a theme that will be highlighted throughout this chapter. Chapter 4 will situate the Dutch scene geographically as part of a global whole. However, this chapter will provide the necessary groundwork by contextualising the Dutch punk scene within its specific localised history, mapping how the contemporary scene came to be.

This chapter is based primarily upon interview data; it is led by the stories of research participants of all ages who have been involved at various times through punk's forty year history. These stories, which illustrate the trajectory of Dutch punk, are told against the backdrop of squatting both as linked to punk and as a distinct movement with an important place in late twentieth century Dutch social history. Wider literature in these areas remains patchy; a few (non-academic) books—upon which I also draw—focus particularly on the early years of Dutch punk, whilst studies of Dutch squatting focus primarily on the Amsterdam scene. The interview data gathered for this research project spans both a wider period and geographic area and will therefore present a more comprehensive picture of the intersection of punk and squatting in the Dutch context than we have to date.

This chapter, whilst arranged as a chronological narrative, does not aim to be an all-encompassing history of the Dutch punk scene. Where 'important' people, bands or places have been mentioned by my participants, they form part of the narrative, but this story can only ever be partial and many important actors in Dutch punk history may not feature.

A NOTE ON THE HISTORICAL CONTEXT OF THE RESEARCH

On 1 October 2010—roughly halfway through the fieldwork period for this research—a ban on squatting came into force. This was an important moment for the squatting movement and all those invested in squatting, such as activists, students and punks. A number of protest events occurred both prior to and following this change in the law, and discussions of squatting were prevalent in national media. It is important to note that this was, therefore, a topic of heightened resonance in Dutch society at the time that the interviews were conducted.

There was also a shift in cultural consumption towards practices of nostalgia—bands reuniting and re-releasing records to mark significant anniversaries. This was a particularly prevalent trend at the time of this research project. It is useful to note that a number of participants were actively engaged in practices of 'remembering' and 'narrativising' their past, shaping the stories that they foregrounded in the interview setting. Participants who were old enough tended to focus on the early 1980s—the period that was coming up for 20th anniversary releases—and they skipped more quickly over the 1990s. Whilst there is a consensus that the 1980s marked a particularly high point for Dutch punk (Jonker 2012), it is important to recognise that contemporary discourse and the construction of the past are interlinked.

DUTCH FORBEARERS OF PUNK

As much as punk discourses tend to claim that the emergence of punk represented an explosive new form that marked a distinct break from everything that had gone before—tired stadium rock, artistic endeavour as unattainable to most, 'culture' devoid of any meaning or political impact—punk was instead embedded in a far more complex process of cultural change. Its antecedents can be found musically in 1960s American garage rock bands such as MC5 and The Stooges, and in 1970s UK pub rock, which saw a number of bands cross into punk when it came along. Artistically, the heritage of punk in Dada and the Situationists has been well documented,[1] something that Menno says he recreated unintentionally when he formed the Rondos in Rotterdam in 1978.

In Amsterdam in 1965 the Provo movement was established. Provo combined the rhetoric of the Situationist International and 'happenings' of the early 1960s Abstract Expressionist movement, with '*nozems*' (a provocative Dutch teenage subculture akin to British Teddy Boys) and a more militant anarchist political aim. Provo called for the revolution of the 'PROVOtariat': "beatniks, *nozems*, provos, students, artists, criminals" (van Stokrom 2002: 41) and implemented the 'white plans'. These included 'white bicycles', which were left unlocked on the street and available for anyone to use. They hoped that this would ease traffic congestion and enable a ban on cars in the city centre. There was also 'the white house plan', which was designed to combat the housing shortage in Amsterdam and involved painting doors of empty properties white to indicate their availability for squatting. And there was a further proposed 'white chicken plan' in which the police force would be reutilised as unarmed social workers (for more on the Provos, see Kempton 2007).

A major element of Provo activities were the 'provocations': 'happenings' designed to rile the police and authorities. These were held every Saturday at the *Lieverdje* statue on Amsterdam's *Spui* and included events at which bicycles were painted white and 'presented' to assembled crowds and symbolic burnings, for example, of the statue itself or effigies of the Queen. Provo "received considerable national and international attention for their public hijinks" (Blom and Lamberts [1999] 2006:

454). This culminated in protests that took place during the celebratory procession through the streets of Amsterdam for the marriage of Princess Beatrix and Claus von Amsberg on 10 March 1966. Provo planted as many as 5000 protesters amongst the crowds of well-wishers, armed with smoke bombs to set off as the procession passed (Kempton 2007). There were echoes of this protest during Beatrix's later coronation procession in 1980, an important event for squatters and punks alike, which I will discuss later in this chapter.

Provo disbanded in 1967, with ex-members later going on to form the Kabouters in 1970. The Kabouters continued the heritage of political activism but worked within the establishment, winning seats on city councils nationwide. They built on the 'white house plan', not only by drawing attention to empty buildings but also by taking an active role in squatting them (Kempton 2007). This sowed the seeds for the foundation of the squatters' movement.

Provo and the Kabouters form a distinct cultural link in the Netherlands between the Situationist pre-history of punk and punk itself. When punk appeared, the groundwork had already been laid for a movement that combined shocking aesthetics and political anti-establishment aims. The manner in which both Provo and the Kabouters fed into the burgeoning squatters' movement provided a precedent for the combination of politics, cultural practice and the creation of spaces in which to organise, to live, and to create that would go on to have a crucial impact on both the Dutch and wider Western European punk and squatters' scenes.

THE SQUATTERS' MOVEMENT

Rights for squatters were enshrined in Dutch law in 1914. Throughout the twentieth century there were various times, such as the economic crisis of the 1930s, when squatting was a popular and very necessary means by which people could secure a place to live. Many of Amsterdam's buildings fell into disrepair after World War II. There was an influx of young people to the city throughout the 1960s, and the rise of housing speculation led to a housing crisis ('*wooningnood*') in which adequate housing was in short supply whilst many decrepit buildings lay empty. Owens (2009) argues that at this time squatting was largely an 'individual' practice rather than the organised movement it would later become. However, the spotlight that Provo shone on the '*wooningnood*' crisis in

Amsterdam, and the politicisation of this matter, led to a cultural shift that saw the establishment of collectively organised squatters' groups such as the '*Wooningburo de Kraker*'[2] (WdK), established in 1969. A 1971 court case ruling in Nijmegen made it easier for squatters to establish their rights to squat unoccupied houses. There emerged the role of the 'full-time' squatter who made up the core of the emerging squatters' movement (Owens 2009). They would put in the bulk of the work that went into locating, squatting, and repairing buildings. Full-time squatters attained more cultural capital than the 'part-timers', a divide that persists to the present day and was reported on by participants such as Marieke.

Throughout the 1970s the squatters' movement grew and strengthened. Many more people started to live in squats: most notably students, artists and musicians. Squatters' aims started to shift away from their focus on housing provision towards the need for other forms of space. Squats became places in which artists had studios and musicians had practice rooms.

THE FIRST GENERATIONS OF DUTCH PUNK

When punk first arrived in the Netherlands it was as an imported medium from the UK. For those participants who remember the earliest days of punk, their recollections involve first encountering punk through the music media: TV, radio or magazines. Sem first heard punk in 1976, "on the radio. On [the station] 'Nederland 3' there was a radio show with Pete van Bruggen where, I think every Sunday, they played an hour of just punk" (Sem). Jonker (2012) notes that in addition to this radio show, a magazine called *Oor*[3] published reviews of early punk records. For Menno it was the magazine *Panorama* that first made him aware of punk; "I saw a picture in Panorama [...] in 1976 or so I think. There were two punks in it and a short caption 'young people in London' and then I thought 'that is good music' I'd never heard it! Very strange!" (Menno).

When Jan travelled to New York in 1975 on business for the record shop he worked for he witnessed the burgeoning punk scene there, seeing The Heartbreakers and Blondie, amongst others. He returned to Amsterdam and said to his colleagues: "boy oh boy, your whole world is going to turn upside down. [We] might as well stop with the rubbish we're doing—The Eagles or whatever—because it's happened, there's something else coming" (Jan). But it was not until after punk had arrived in the Netherlands by other means that Jan would realise his dream: he opened his punk record shop 'No Fun' in 1977.

For most participants, punk in the Netherlands 'started' when the Sex Pistols landed in January 1977, although not all were immediately taken in by them; "I think it was January 1977, and I saw the Sex Pistols on [...] Dutch television. We had a programme called 'Disco Circus', and they had the Sex Pistols on. And I could [...] see like Johnny Rotten in front, throwing chairs and looking like he was completely on speed or whatever, going crazy, and I was just like 'what a bunch of idiots'" (Theo). Suzanne and Jacob also first encountered punk on British and German television (respectively).[4] Even those participants who were too young to appreciate punk themselves in 1977 mark the Sex Pistols' arrival as the date punk came to the Netherlands; "I was literally only like ten years old, [...] my daddy was a bit of an old beatnik [and] he actually went, here in Groningen, to see the Sex Pistols and The Ramones and everything and he bought the records" (Bram).

At this point, punk in the Netherlands was not the underground subculture that it would later become. It was instead the latest popular craze, with famous international bands playing sizeable venues; the first Sex Pistols gig in Amsterdam took place at the 1500-capacity Paradiso, a venue initially set up as a squat (Pruijt 2013). Indeed, the explosion of punk in the Netherlands is seen to have reinvigorated this failing venue, which was given a new lease of life as the city's main punk centre (Jonker 2012). Paradiso looms large in many participants' recollections of this time:

A lot of people gathered in Rotterdam and Amsterdam at the weekends, because that was where the concerts were. Of course you couldn't always go because you couldn't afford to travel. When you're young you have to do it from your allowance, or, you know, go on a train and not pay for the ticket, which we used to do. And to get in we would stand behind Paradiso, or wait for the vans to come with the band and help them with their equipment and [...] then usually they'd let you in for free cos you'd helped out. (Henk)

Despite being a sizeable venue, many of even the first generation of Dutch punk bands played their early gigs at Paradiso, often supporting international touring bands. There is no consensus on what the first

Dutch punk band was. However, Goossens and Vedder (1996) suggest that Ivy Green and Flyin' Spiderz—both of whom were pub rock bands that predated punk—shifted to playing music that was more ostensibly recognisable as punk during 1977. In this way the 'first' Dutch punk bands have a similar trajectory to many early UK punk bands such as The Stranglers (Jonker 2012).

Throughout 1977 and 1978, punk became more established in the Netherlands. Whereas throughout 1977 most Dutch punk bands had switched to punk from other genres, by 1978 new *specifically* punk bands formed. There was an overlap at this time between punk and artistic circles in the Netherlands, as in the UK, especially in regards to the spaces that they spent time in. Jonker (2012) points to two important 'centres' for Dutch punk during this period; Rotterdam's Huize Schoonderloo and Amsterdam's Zebrahuis/Gallerie Anus.

Menno's band the Rondos started in 1978 and grew out of their artists' collective based at Rotterdam's art college: "at some point a teacher asked us [....] 'do you have a band?' And [my friend] said, 'yes, we do'. Then [the teacher] said, 'can you do a gig on Friday?', 'yes', then [the teacher] said 'that's great'. We didn't have [a band] at all, we didn't have any music! So then, within a week, we had cobbled together a set of cover songs" (Menno).

Soon after this, the band decided to move in together to a building where they could have their own studio: Huize Schoonderloo. The tight-knit nature of the punk community meant that this house soon became something of a punk 'centre'; "a lot of bands also practiced at ours, because there weren't a lot of practice rooms. [...] Under the house [there] was a sort of bomb shelter [...] so we had a very good practice room. It was really in use throughout the week by all sorts of bands. Artists came [round] too, and also left wing anarchists, and [...] also people from the neighbourhood" (Menno).

Amsterdam's punk centre similarly came out of artistic circles based around two key figures; the poet Diana Ozon and artist Hugo Kaagman. They opened a punk club, DDT 666 (later renamed Gallerie Anus), in their squat, the 'Zebrahuis'. For Johan, also an artist who had long been involved in hippie and freak culture, it was Gallerie Anus that 'converted' him to punk;

Galerie Anus [...] in the Sarphatistraat in the 'Zebrahuis', that was a squat that was painted all over with zebra stripes, a beautiful building. And one

day I walked in, because they had a gallery there, and there they made and
sold the first punk leaflets produced in the Netherlands. I got talking to the
people there and they heard who I was, because people know my work, and
they immediately went like 'wow'. I was looking for a place to live, and [...]
could move in there. That is how [punk] actually started [for me]. (Johan)

The Zebrahuis is one example of a squat that also provided practice
spaces, studios, bars, and even a gig venue in addition to housing. In
1978 a large office building on the Keizersgracht was squatted; the
Groote Keijser also had space for punk gigs. The Groote Keijser and the
proliferation of these other large 'cultural' squats over the next couple of
years cemented the relationship between squatters and the punk scene.
However, at the same time, the government started to lose patience with
the squatters' movement (Owens 2009). Tensions between squatters and
the police rose, and the Groote Keijser became the powder keg that initiated the radicalisation of the squatters' movement.

Huize Schoonderloo and the Zebrahuis are examples of the overlapping worlds of art and punk at an underground level in the growing
Dutch punk scene. In this sense early Dutch punk had many similarities to the early UK scene. The spectacular and subversive styles are certainly present with Dutch art punks, placing them in a lineage with the
Sex Pistols and The Clash (Savage 1991; Nehring 1993). Menno and
Henk commented more noticeably on their stylistic choices than many
respondents from later generations: "[it was] dressing yourself up like a
Christmas tree, I guess, it looked completely ridiculous, I mean for the
first years of punk everybody looked ridiculous and that was the point I
guess" (Henk).

There was a tendency amongst these first generations of Dutch punks
to follow developments in UK punk. There were garage bands who
started to play punk, following The Stranglers' lead, and there were also
crossovers between art schools and punk. This all suggests elements of
'peripheral' mimesis of 'core' punk scenes (O'Connor 2004). However,
it is important to note the particular local influences that shaped Dutch
punk. The avant-garde history of Provo and the Kabouters, and the position of squatting within these movements, contributed to a stronger
political strand throughout Dutch punk. Indeed, the Rondos considered
themselves activists over artists.

Opinions of these 'early' forms of punk were contentious amongst
Dutch participants. Whilst Menno and Henk found the stylistic and

artistic expressions liberating, others such as Theo and Lotte were less enamored with this form of punk. Even in these very early days, when punks' political potential was debatable, Dutch punks tended to prefer the more politicised posturings of The Clash or Crass.

THE SQUATTERS' RIOTS

Whereas the mid-1970s had been relatively prosperous for young people in the Netherlands, especially in comparison to the economic problems in the UK that had fuelled punk, by the late 1970s and into the 1980s the Dutch economy was less secure. The impact of this featured in a number of participants' interviews, including those with Henk, Menno and Jacob.

Youth unemployment was high, and this would persist for much of the 1980s (Blom and Lamberts [1999] 2006). Certainly most interviewees who were young punks in the early 1980s recalled themselves and many of their acquaintances as being unemployed (see Chap. 6). The poor economy would be a major factor in the squatters' movement and the punk scene, drawing them especially close. With unemployment high, squatting was a necessity for many young people. It drew many punks (members of a subculture already predisposed to such life strategies) closer to a more politicised squatting scene, forging links that would shape the Dutch and European scenes.

Moreover, Daan recalls how international as well as domestic politics caused great concern to him: "on my fourteenth birthday I was at the anti-cruise missile demonstrations. There were forty-eight American nuclear missiles to be stationed in the Netherlands, [there were] massive demonstrations [...] I went there with my mum, there were over half a million people".

> The late 1970s were not an optimistic time for young people in the Netherlands as elsewhere. Threats materialized everywhere. The Cold War was experiencing heightened tensions; the threat of nuclear war felt very real, particularly in Western Europe. Nuclear war, however, was only the tip of the iceberg. Environmental devastation, economic troubles, and political inefficacy all combined to create a strong sense of 'No Future' for Amsterdam's young people. (Owens 2009: 92–93)

This unease and unrest formed the backdrop of the period in which the Squatters' Movement reached its height and saw its most violent confrontations with Dutch authorities.

The Groote Keijser was threatened with eviction in 1979. This came shortly after a severe police beating of squatters during another eviction. This time the squatters decided that they should fight back. The Groote Keijser was barricaded and those who did not want to be involved in fighting moved to other squats to leave only those prepared for a violent confrontation (Owens 2008). However the authorities, strategically, left the Groote Keijser alone and targeted a squat on the Vondelstraat instead. The squatters there barricaded the whole street in an attempt to save the squat and declared it the 'Vondel Free State'. They held out for a few days until the government sent in tanks on 3 March 1980.

Whilst the eviction of the squat on the Vondelstraat was eventually successful, the government's actions were contentious. The use of excessive force, in particular the use of tanks against civilians, turned public opinion against the government and served to further radicalise the squatters' movement (Owens 2009). As Owens writes, the "shared experience of radicalization brought squatters together, providing the movement a source of power, supplying an identity, a strategy, and an ideology. Radicalization strengthened the movement; radicalization secured the movement" (45).

Furthermore, these events cemented Amsterdam's position on the international squatting scene. Since the days of Amsterdam's Abstract Expressionist happenings, the city's squats had provided shelter for international countercultural tourists. This tradition was retained by many punk and wider cultural squats as well as Huize Schoonderloo, which developed a reputation as a meeting place for international punks (Menno). The events at the Groote Keijser and the Vondelstraat gained the Dutch squatters international notoriety and led to invitations to visit squats across Europe, particularly in Germany. As Owens writes; "[t] he summer of 1980 was a busy one for Amsterdam's squatters. [...] Through travel they forged stronger ties with their German 'fellow travellers.' In May and June, they paid visits to Cologne, Hamburg, and Münster, followed by trips to Darmstadt, West Berlin, and Nürnberg in the months that followed" (2013: 197, see also Andersen and van der Steen 2016; Owens 2016). The connections that were forged amongst these squatters and punks proved key to the international punk scene. For further discussion of how the connections and mobility of Dutch punks are crucial to the scene and how links with Germany are especially important, see Chap. 4.

On 30 April 1980, the coronation celebrations for Queen Beatrix were held. In line with tradition for such royal events, there would be a parade through the streets of Amsterdam. Squatters saw this as a perfect opportunity to gain attention for their cause and the whole of the month of April was set aside for a wave of squatting actions. This culminated in demonstrations during the parade itself, under the slogan '*geen wooning, geen kroning*' ('no house, no coronation'). During the parade rioting broke out with mass violence between protesters and the police, reminiscent of the unrest that had occurred at Beatrix's wedding in 1966. It was an event that would prove a crucial landmark for both the squatters and the punks. Participants in this project, reminisced about being there—or expressed a desire to have been there—and reflected on how important the protests had been for them: "the coronation was imminent, those were massive riots. [...] There was really enormous police violence going on around us. [...] So it really became radicalised very quickly. [...] Within no time you were really more [an] activist than [a] musician or [an] artist" (Menno). Just as with the Vondelstraat squat eviction, violence bred a more radical squatting—and punk—identity.

The 'coronation riots' cemented the punks' commitment to the squatters' movement and to political activism, and invigorated the punk scene. They held a special place in the memory of Dutch punks. However, some in the squatters' movement were critical of the violence that had taken place, aware that what had happened had lost them some public support. These squatters blamed the punks' involvement in the protests for the violence, initiating further tension between 'full-time' squatters and others (Duivenvoorden 2000).

Over the following few years, both the Dutch punk scene and the squatters' movement were at a height. Clashes with the government over squat evictions in Amsterdam or further afield occurred every few months. In reaction to this, squats became bigger and ever more ambitious. This culminated in the Wijers complex; a huge squat which had previously been the site of a large factory. It had 100 residents in addition to the following facilities:

A restaurant, bar, café, cinema, performance spaces, night store, art gallery, convenience store, acupuncture clinic, theatre groups, rehearsal studios for musicians, artist studios, printing press, nursery, skateboard park, theatre, music electronics workplace, wood recycling centre, fine wood dealer, two woodworking studios, guitar builder, piano restoration, wind energy workplace, bicycle repair, ceramics workplace, audiovisual workplace with a school, taxi collective, delivery service, cargo bicycle rental, silk screening, photography collective, repair services for electronics and clothing, an environmentally friendly store, recycled products store, architecture firm, press bureau, accounting office, book store and printer, Aikido school, tea and herb store, windmill services, first aid services, and information offices for environmental and activist groups [as well as a radio station]. (Owens 2009: 136–137)

With the Wijers, the squat scene had not only a cultural centre but also a complex akin to a small village, a model of squatting that persists today with examples including the ADM in Amsterdam, Køpi in Berlin, and Karlo Rojc in Pula, Croatia. There was a deliberate tactic on the part of the squatters to focus on building self-sufficient communities for themselves. Menno commented; "when I came to Amsterdam, the squat scene was really a city in itself. At that point there was something like five thousand squats. [Some] normal family homes, but also large buildings, and the crazy thing was that you could really live completely within the squat scene if you wanted" (Menno). Whilst punk is only part of the Wijers' history, it is certainly present. The practice rooms were important and the venue hosted many punk nights. However, the size of the premises meant that it was valuable not only to the squatters. The hotel chain Holiday Inn also wanted the premises, and their bid was supported by the government. This prompted a two-year-long 'battle' for the Wijers from 1982–1984, ending in the squatters' defeat.

In 1985 another event shook the squatters' movement. A mother and daughter were evicted from their squat after negotiations with the authorities broke down. This contravened an unspoken agreement whereby the authorities did not evict squats with children during the winter. The eviction caused protests at which a number of arrests were made. One of those arrested was Hans Kok, a squatter and the bassist in the punk band Lol en de Eilendelingen. Kok was found dead in his cell the following day; the squatters accused the police of foul play and there were further waves of protest.

In 1987, following the defeat of the Wijers and the death of Hans Kok, the tensions that had been brewing for years within the squatters' movement bubbled over as factions turned on one another. On one side were the 'politicos' who proposed a more militant and political approach to squatting, and on the other were the 'culturellas': squatters and punks who saw value in promoting squatting to support the cultural life of the city. The politicos formed the Politieke Vleugel van de Kraakbeweging[5] (PVK) who proposed eradicating the cultural squats. The PVK made death threats against other squatters, and battles between the cultural and the political squatters were waged both in words and on the streets. At its most extreme, the PVK kidnapped and threatened to torture a 'cultural' squatter. Many squats and squat cafés responded by excluding the PVK from their venues (including the renowned punk venue, Vrankrijk). Eventually the PVK were defeated, and its leaders left Amsterdam (Owens 2009). The culturellas' model of squatting, in which punks most certainly had a place, was left to become dominant in the scene.

These conflicts were discussed by Menno who, in his time playing with The Ex, felt they had been able to occupy a middle ground between the warring factions: "squatters sometimes got fed up with the sorts of punks who were far wilder and more radical [and] harder in the squat-riots too, so there were definitely conflicts at times. Well, generally speaking the Ex was in both, sort of a bit in between" (Menno). The punks thus occupied multiple positions in this conflict. The political squatters placed them firmly within the cultural camp; however, there were tensions between punks and cultural squatters. Punks' interactions with the squatting movement had radicalised them, but there were also those who emphasised partying and chaos above squatting.

The 'Death' of Punk and Its (Subsequent) Golden Period

By 1978 punk had been pronounced officially 'dead' in Britain. Academic understandings of punk had focused on the subversive potential of the style, and as knowledge of punk spread, it diminished punk's potential to shock and offend. When punk hit the mainstream in 1977, its days were numbered. Indeed Savage (1991) claimed the demise of the Sex Pistols as the death of punk.

As discussed in Chap. 2, this understanding takes away the possibility for punk to exist either historically or spatially beyond early UK punk, indeed, "the great majority of subculturalists are inauthenticated and marginalized because they do not measure up to this (actually very particular and partial) definition" (Muggleton 2000: 152). A move away from focusing on early UK punk to punk's development in other times and places has allowed for a broadening of understandings of punk.

Clark (2003) claims that "punk faked its own death" in the mainstream in order to allow underground punk to flourish (234).

Whilst the 'punk is dead' discourse persists and with the claiming of subcultural capital still weighted towards 'originality', these subsequent shifts in the discourse of what punk *is* (see Chap. 2) have enabled conceptualisations in which it becomes possible to view the Dutch scene *as* punk with its own specific trajectory.

In 1978 the punk scene was thriving in the Netherlands. Led by the approach of the punks who had come out of the Dutch art world, this generation was based firmly within squat culture and the DIY ethos. The period between 1978 and 1980 is marked by Goossens and Vedder (1996) as the second generation of Dutch punk, and spawned bands such as The Ex and the Boegies alongside the Rondos. Far from the second generation marking the 'death' of the first, this later stage of Dutch punk had arguably found its own more local, 'authentic' approach, garnering more subcultural capital than those first garage bands.

Indeed, this model of the Dutch scene reflects understandings of punk's wider developments. Davies (1996) argued that the politically empty first wave of UK punk (not wholly applicable to the Dutch context as outlined earlier in this chapter), paved the way for more political punk post-1978. These later 'waves' took as inspiration anarcho-punk in Britain led by Crass (Berger 2008; Glasper 2006), and hardcore in the United States, first in California and then across the country (Moore 2004; Tsitsos 1999). In the Netherlands, both of these forms were important to the development of Dutch punk. This was perhaps unsurprisingly given the heightened political aspects of both anarcho-punk and hardcore and the importance of a DIY approach.

In 1980 the Dutch punk scene hit an apex. According to Jonker (2012), this was the year that more underground DIY records were released by Dutch bands than in any other year. However, this golden age brought with it some tensions.

Menno disliked the direction that punk was heading as it became, in his view, less an artistic statement and more a fashionable 'subculture'. The Rondos disbanded. However, rather than declaring punk 'dead', he realised instead that it was shifting and no longer a place for him. The possibility of punk to shift and mutate is key to Daan, who points out that whilst *what* punk is may shift, it still, for many people, *is*. Mark adds, "in [19]77 punk really meant something else than in 1981, and then now, [in 2011, it's] completely [different] again" (Mark).

For those who remained or became involved in punk through the 1980s, there were still 'good' times to be had. Commenting on when he first got involved with punk (in the early 1980s), had left home and was first living in a squat, Jacob said: "that was in itself a nice time. Chaotic as well, it was really one long party—and making a bit of music" (Jacob). As Berkers (2012) argues, the groundwork had been laid by the squatters' movement to provide the 'infrastructure' for punk to continue to blossom in the Netherlands. Whilst some involved in the conflicts within the squatters' movement may have become more tied up with the fighting between factions, the strong culture of squatting in the Netherlands meant that more and more large cultural squats were still being set up, such as the WNC (Wolters-Noordhoff Complex) and the ORKZ (Oude Rooms Katholieke Ziekenhuis) in Groningen.

> Yes, it's absolutely a good thing that squatting exists, and that it's linked to punk. So in the Netherlands that's not so surprising, because of course in the 1980s punk was at its peak and with the anarchistic tendency that it still had, and the political angle of it, it was of course quickly linked to squatting and they found each other. [...] Obviously it doesn't have to be something that goes together, squatting and punk, but well, squatting, yes, I'm very positive about it. (Jeroen)

Bram: The end of the 1980s was like *the* period here when you had all the squats going. There was about 5 different squats in town where you could play. Some of the squats were huge [and] they had this thing called the WNC complex. [...] They had like a concert hall and they had a pub and [... a] café and a record store and a restaurant and they had like some feminist womens' café thingy and a book store and it was like tons of people living there and it was right slap bang in the middle of the centre.

Kirsty: yeah, and you lived there as well?

Bram: I didn't live there but it's where we practiced, it's where we put on all the shows and just everything.

But these squats remained insecure. Major protests and a prolonged eviction battle occurred over the WNC. For punks in Groningen this was a defining moment in their histories, with this conflict featuring in interviews with both Jacob and Wim, as well as Bram who described it as a "huge fucking riot, it was a two day riot and something like 150 people—of our side—got arrested for that and most of them were in jail for a month or more" (Bram). For Groningen punks, this was a key event in their living memory (Mah 2010) that they foregrounded, just as the coronation riots had been *the* event for punks in Amsterdam.

Some other squats avoided the eviction process by applying to become 'legalised'. The legalisation process, by which either the squatters themselves purchased the buildings or the city council did so on behalf of the squatters, ensured that some of the large cultural squats gained a degree of stability. Duivenvoorden (2000) reported that between the early 1980s and 2000 some 200 squats were legalised in Amsterdam alone. In Amsterdam important punk gig venues such as OCCii and Vrankrijk were legalised, and in Nijmegen the Grote Broek and Doornroosje venues went through the same process. Punk-squat bar Molli in Amsterdam, and the anarchist bookshop Het Fort van Sjakoo also became 'legal' squats (Pruijt 2012). This enabled the punks to have access to more stable underground venues and practice spaces, no longer at risk of eviction.

In addition to the *physical* space that the squats offered punk was also the *nonphysical* space: the possibilities offered by the freedom, connections and mobility. Punks who squatted and did not have work commitments had more freedom to travel. Connections with other punks and other squatters internationally meant that in the 1980s the Dutch punk scene was exceptionally mobile (see Chap. 4).

Whilst drugs had been present in the punk scene since its early days, in the Dutch context they are particularly associated with the 1980s. For some, this was part of what they enjoyed about the 1980s: "ah good times you know, there was a lot of partying, a lot of drinking, an *outrageous* amount of drugs!" (Bram).

For others the spread of drug use within the scene brought with it negative changes. The things that were important for them about punk (such as DIY, politics, and culture) were supplanted by those seeking a hedonistic lifestyle (see Chap. 5 for a greater discussion on the varied meanings ascribed to 'punk' by participants).

> I just find it a shame that quite a big group in the Netherlands, in my opinion, fucked it up badly. That is, when you squat somewhere I want to live there and I keep it tidy and I don't turn it into a tip, I want to have a working front door, I want this and I want that, everything must function. [But] there are a lot of people who don't want that, or want it but

don't manage [it], and that is just a pity that it is just wrecked for parties. In a squat it's fine to have a band play but don't wreck it and leave it tidy. And that is of course also inherent with the drink and drug use in the punk scene. Look in the 1980s there was of course a lot of booze and glue sniffing or whatever and that was because, probably, everyone was a bit disillusioned, in those days. (Jeroen)

The problem of drugs in the punk scene was not restricted to the Netherlands. In the United States a new scene emerged specifically to counter pervasive drug use in punk: straight edge. 'Edgers' have a variety of understandings of what it means to be straight edge, but generally they do not drink, smoke, take drugs, or have casual sex, and are often vegetarian or vegan (see Haenfler 2006). The first straight edge scene originated in Washington, D.C. as early as 1979. The 'second' scene, also known as 'Youth Crew', emerged in New York in 1986 (Thompson 2004). It was this second wave that proved most influential in the Netherlands. Straight edge caught on in the mid-to-late 1980s with punks such as Daan and his group of friends in Amersfoort; the bands Profound (later Man Lifting Banner) and Lärm (later Seein Red) also came out of this scene.

Straight edge was not the only new subgenre of punk; it was part of a trend from the mid-1980s, when many new types of punk emerged:

I've seen all these generations of punks, like you can actually set dates; 1977 to 1980 there was a special group, and then around 1980 'til 1985 there was also like [another]. I think if you could make a timeline you'd see all these generations. After 1985 I kind of lost track of it because everything got so divided, you got so many completely different kinds of punks. Like before 1985 everybody would go to a punk show, like if there was a punk show *everybody* would go, but like if you look at what happened after that, [...] if you now have a straight edge concert, only the straight edge kids will go there, and they will not show up at other punk concerts or whatever. [...] You have that with a lot of differences, you have the crusties, and you have got the skate kids, and all, it's all so different. (Theo)

The lack of cohesion in the punk scene of the late 1980s to early 1990s meant that there was less of a sense of an overarching punk community. This caused further tensions, especially within the very spaces that were integral to punk, and which previous generations of punks and squatters had fought for. Participants who helped out in venues saw the extent of this, with both Jacob and Mark complaining how some newer generations of punks had no respect for the venues or the equipment within them. Jacob complained that the atmosphere at Simplon in Groningen became unpleasant with punks dealing drugs, smashing bottles and trashing the venue. Mark caught punks pissing on the PA speakers at Amsterdam's OCCii. Both participants, when they attempted to challenge this type of behaviour, found themselves accused of 'fascism' by other punks.

Punk had become fragmented in the Netherlands, as it had done elsewhere. Liptrot (2014) argues that the greatest divide was between political and non-political punks, but divides were far more complex. With the emergence of each new subgenre of punk, came new sets of 'right' and 'wrong' ways to do punk and new tensions.

The developments of new subgenres were just one element of the fragmentation of punk. As highlighted by Theo (earlier in this chapter), generation also played a part. For Mark this was a distinct factor by which he defined himself; "I was kind of the second generation two years later. [...] Obviously you know I'm terribly old, but still too young to have [seen] the whole beginning, you know?!" (Mark). Furthermore, Ruben also used this to categorise himself as distinct from others from the earlier 1980s who were "from the older scene" (Ruben).

Where punks remained involved over a period of years, their generation was often supplanted in punk discourse by a new one (this is particularly seen in Thompson 2004). But the older generations and their forms of punk did not cease to exist, nor were they subsumed within newer trends. Some older punks would get involved with newer forms of punk, others were only involved in their own older forms of punk, and some did both. Moreover, as will be shown later in this chapter, as more punks joined the ranks of the 'older punk', practices of nostalgia became present on the punk scene. We see how even within punk subculture, individuals can hold a number of different positions or 'communication interlocks' (Fine and Kleinman 1979, see Chap. 2). The multiple subject positions within the punk scene would occasionally cause tensions, particularly between different generations who might believe 'their' punk to be more original or more authentic than others.

Daan related this period's hedonism and lack of activism within punk to the wider social context at the time: "of course in the eighties, there was little [in the way of class] struggle. In 1991 I joined the International Socialists and there were maybe two demonstrations a year? The left was in disarray". The breakup of the Soviet Union further consolidated this crisis amongst left-wing movements in Western Europe (Bull 1995; Sassoon 1996). In the Netherlands this was compounded by the squatting movement imploding with its intra-faction fighting. For Daan, this explained why punk had become more oriented around parties, drugs and hedonism than around DIY and activism.

THE 1990S AND BEYOND: NEW GENERATIONS, NEW FORMS OF PUNK AND PUNK NOSTALGIA

The dawn of the 1990s, participants agreed, was a 'low' period for Dutch punk. The fragmentation of punk styles, the spread of drug use, the lack of respect for 'punk spaces' and the hedonism that supplanted activism all contributed to a smaller, less committed scene. Meanwhile, the economic troubles of the 1980s had passed and employment was on the rise. The 'no future' sentiment that had fuelled youth disaffection in the UK in the 1970s and the Netherlands in the 1980s had waned. These factors all contributed to a 'lull' in punk in the 1990s.

Daan and Sander both complain of the musical quality of the bands that were active at this time; a number of hardcore bands had begun experimenting with a new, metal-influenced direction. Lotte says that in around 1993 punk in Groningen "started to go backwards" (Lotte). Bram elaborated on this, suggesting that the riots following the eviction of the WNC were the catalyst:

That kind of signalled the start of a *really* bad time here because that riot got so out of control and so out of hand like everybody in the city here, like the politicians, the cops, the regular citizens they all were like "oh squatting we can't let that happen, ever again," you know! So [...] you couldn't squat anymore, it was really repressive you know, we [would] basically just walk in the street and you [would] just randomly get beaten up by some students and stuff. [...] Cops they knew us by name, you know, so a cop car would drive by and they would actually just like open the window and shout your name out of the window, like "oh we're going to get you". [...] So it was a really bad time actually. At that time I think a lot of people moved away. (Bram)

Being a punk at this time in Groningen was difficult; not only were punks subject to persecution but many of the spaces in which gigs had taken place had gone. With the WNC evicted and the atmosphere at Simplon less welcoming, the punk scene shifted to Café Vera; never solely a punk hangout but certainly a venue where punk bands played regularly.

This dip in the early 1990s was not limited to Groningen but was present elsewhere too. Luka also complained of 'nothing going on' in Amsterdam.

Whilst this was a quieter time, the scene was still active: bands were still forming, playing, recording and touring, and zines were still being written. Owens (2009) discusses this as a phenomenon of 'decline' in the context of the squatters' movement, suggesting that "[e]ven as the movement enters its decline, activists take refuge in their own activist identity to get them through the period between movements" (17). A similar process happens by which punks continue to bolster the scene even in a low period.

It was not too long, however, before the next generation became involved, attracted by the pop punk craze that hit the mainstream in the mid-1990s. The commercial success of bands such as Green Day, The Offspring and Bad Religion, along with Dutch band de Heideroosjes, put this music onto radio stations, television channels and computer games, and made punk—in this guise—available to a younger generation.

> The first bands [I listened to] were [...] Nirvana, also Green Day, Bad Religion. [...] And then discovered some other bands, you know the Heideroosjes? They are a really big band for when you are sixteen, haha! A lot of people nowadays think they are '*jaah* [(negative)] a popular shitty band', but still when you are sixteen and first listen to a band and feel the energy at the shows—because it's always a big party at their shows—it was for me like '*wooow*' it was cool, I want to do this. (Larry)

The rise of pop punk—specifically its commercial success—was not entirely welcomed by other, older generations of punks, who often either reject or negate it in their narratives. Jacob remembers a young Green Day touring Europe and begging for gigs in Groningen so that they could afford the petrol to the next venue, he described his subsequent shock when later the same year they signed to a major label and appeared on the MTV awards. Jacob argued that pop punk "is actually more pop music" (Jacob), whilst Jaap commented that, "all that poppy punk stuff, or hardcore poppy punk stuff: I think it's idiot music" (Jaap).

Whilst these tensions emerged generationally, they draw on wider and long-running debates over commercialism and authenticity in punk. As such, pop punk has become a key sphere of derision within the punk scene. The discourse that pop punk isn't 'real' punk, either because it's too commercial or because the music is too accessible, has become a common refrain, even amongst those who (previously) liked it. Pop punk therefore becomes either a past mistake, excusable only as a 'gateway' to 'real' punk or a 'guilty pleasure' to be indulged in, mitigated by excuses given in order to avoid losing subcultural capital (Thornton 1995). This is highlighted by the way in which Larry, aware of the subcultural context, feels he must defend his musical taste.

Pop punk was therefore framed as a common entry point to the punk scene by participants in their mid-twenties and early thirties. Many later broadened their interests to other genres of punk. Once their interest was piqued, they sought access to the structures that underpinned the rest of the underground punk scene. Alongside youth centres, squats were still providing spaces for punks to gather, socialise, attend and run gigs, and practice with their own new bands. In time, this new generation of punks helped to rejuvenate the Dutch scene. "[T]here was this explosion of bands here, new kids came and [...] new places got opened, new squats [and] new shows" (Luka).

Meanwhile, there were similar resurgences in the hardcore scene. This was particularly notable in the case of straight edge, which enjoyed a particularly popular period across Europe from the late 1990s to the early 2000s: "at a certain point [...] everybody started playing straight edge hardcore, and then a couple of years later everybody dropped the 'edge'" (Larry). Many of those who became aware of punk through pop punk in the mid-1990s moved into hardcore. This certainly was the case for Lisa, Larry, Andre and Bart.[6]

The Dutch straight edge scene shrunk dramatically following its high in the late 1990s. This was part of a global trend caused by a backlash against the scene, which had become increasingly rigid in its definitions and militant in maintaining boundaries (Haenfler 2006). In the Dutch context many individuals and bands often remained part of punk but dropped the straight edge label, with many also dropping the practices of abstinence. A few individuals, including those four participants (Larry, Luka, Maxim and Daan) who had previously identified as straight edge maintained the lifestyle but dropped 'straight edge' as an identity. By the time of my fieldwork there was consequently little in the way of a straight edge 'scene', more a handful of individuals who remained connected through the wider punk scene.

However, there were new developments in other Dutch punk and hardcore scenes around the dawn of the millennium. Some of the bands who were prominent in the scene at the time of this research project, and who were mentioned by participants as of particular interest, were established around this time. Nijmegen's Antillectual began playing in 2000 and built their fan base throughout the 2000s, and Gewapend Beton formed in 2003. Vitamin X, who started out as a straight edge band in 1997, received cross-over support from the hardcore scene even after straight edge dwindled and they continue to tour.

Gewapend Beton were part of a notable new generation in the mid-2000s Dutch punk scene. When they got involved with the scene they were considerably younger than other active punks. They used this to define themselves as the 'embryo punk' generation.

Sander: We we started to listen to punk and started to go to punk pubs it became obvious that we were the very youngest, we were fourteen or fifteen, so that's certainly quite young. The next youngest were called the 'baby-punks', [...] we asked ourselves "what's younger than a baby?" [...] we called our demo tape "embryo punk", and then we wrote a song with "embryo punk" in the chorus, and then we started calling ourselves [and] our friendship group [embryo punks]. Actually, we wanted to call our whole generation of punks 'embryo punks'.

Kirsty: In Amsterdam, the Netherlands, or the whole world?

Sander: The Netherlands, Europe, it doesn't matter. If we play a gig and we play the song with 'embryo punks' in the chorus, then there is really the feeling that this is for today's generation of punks, you know? Becuase there's a lot of people who are hung up on what went before, but "embryo punk" is more about what people are doing with [punk] now.

The embryo punks were particularly prominent in the scene between late 2007 and early 2009, when they opened a squat (De Baarmoeder,[7]) notable for hosting many gigs. It was not just members of the 'embryo' generation who remember this period fondly. Maxim, a few years older and originally part of Amsterdam's straight edge scene in the late 1990s, named the time spent in this squat as the most important period for his experience of Dutch punk:

> I think really for me personally the peak was when there was a squat, [...] the Baarmoeder which was run by Gewapend Beton. [...] They really had a lot of really good shows going on there and they had a really great festival, [...] they called it the "abortion festival" when they were getting kicked out of that squat. That was [a] really *really* good scene going on there. (Maxim)

Members of the older generations were still around and active throughout this period. By the late 2000s the Dutch punk scene was made up of multiple intersecting groups, divided as much by generation as by subgenre. This seemed to be especially true of Groningen, where the scene is more isolated from the rest of the Netherlands and where there were high levels of activity amongst older punks. Interviews with Groningen punks indicated that there were distinct generations of punk, each with their own scene. This theme was reinforced by fieldwork observations in which a younger crowd did not seem to have much contact with older punks. Commenting on the younger generation, Bram said, "I know some of them, but actually it's a separate little scene" (Bram). However, in other places such as Amsterdam, generations were more mixed. Ultimately, though, the fragmentation of punk in terms of both genre and generation had opened up the potential for members to be part of multiple social groups *within* punk.

Whilst older punks often played in contemporary bands—some of which had existed for a long time (e.g., The Ex and Yawp!), and others of which were new (e.g., Indifferent Suns)—there was a notable trend for punk nostalgia at the time of this project. This trend could be seen in the organising of reunion gigs and the re-releasing of old recordings. Punk nostalgia in the Netherlands is reflective of a wider trend of old 'greats' reuniting and re-releasing material, as highlighted by the Sex Pistols tours of 1996, 2002, 2003, 2007 and 2008, and the 35th anniversary edition of 'Never Mind the Bollocks, Here's the Sex Pistols' in 2012, alongside many other bands' and individuals' practices of 'punk nostalgia' (McLoone 2004).

Man Lifting Banner reunited in 2008, played new gigs and released the double album 'The Revolution Continues' in 2012. This featured a number of new songs as well as re-releases of previous EPs. The sleeve art draws parallels between their earlier political thought and more recent revolutionary developments, such as the Arab Spring. This placed their nostalgia in a contemporary continuum, highlighting links between old and new. The Rondos took a more distinctively retrospective approach, releasing their 30th anniversary box set in 2009 accompanied by a bilingual biography, a 226-page photo-booklet, lyrics, and a Red Rat comic strip in which the main character revisits the collective-living lifestyle of the Rondos in the 1970s.

The punk nostalgia trend was boosted by the growth of social media. One participant described Facebook as the catalyst for a large reunion of Groningen punks that took place in May 2011. Excitement and anticipation for this event was present during my time in Groningen.

> There is now also one of these reunions of a bunch of people. [...] Last year I had a girlfriend and she wanted to know—on Facebook—"show us some photos with [you when you had] hair". So I post a few and then a couple of people saw that and [also] put old pictures up, and then somebody went "great, we should do a reunion". [...] I am not so much one to look back but [...] I find it fun because I'll be seeing a lot of people I haven't seen in ages and that's always nice, people who live in France now or something. (Jacob)

When the fieldwork for this project was conducted in 2010–2011, the scene, according to many participants, was again 'quiet'. They stressed that Dutch punk was not as active as it had been. Lotte commented that, "the scene has shrunk", and Sander expanded on this: "it isn't that you see something on every street corner or that something is being organised everyday by the people, yes, it's quite small, that's for sure" (Sander).

However this, again, certainly did not mean that there was not an active scene. Gigs happened regularly (there were many punk gigs per week listed across the Netherlands), and those I went to were well-attended. There were many active musicians, bands, promoters, activists and others who helped support the scene in multiple ways. Indeed, there were complaints that there were 'too many' gigs, with multiple events occasionally run within travelling distance of one another either within a city or a few hours' travel away (this phenomenon is further discussed in Chap. 4). This highlighted the manner in which scene participants (especially) in 'quiet' periods are willing to travel further to attend a gig. Moreover, a higher proportion of those who are part of a 'quiet' punk scene are 'active' within the scene, putting on gigs and/ or playing gigs. Just as in the other intervening 'quiet' times between 'golden' periods, the scene continued to exist and develop, with a core of people invested in it.

A few participants discussed a more general cultural shift that mean that young people might now be less likely to identify as strongly with punk. "Young kids are [...] more open minded, they think less in 'hokjes'[8] we call it in Dutch" (Ruben). However, this concept of 'hokjes' as related to age is complicated by older participants' who also invoke 'thinking outside hokjes' when describing the widening of their *own* subcultural interests over time. Indeed, Haenfler (2006) also talks about older members "refusing to be compartmentalized into a tidy stylistic or ideological box" (160) as they age. The process by which people move beyond or reject 'hokjes' reflects shifts outlined in Chap. 2 towards postmodern, fluid, subcultural identities. There was a worry amongst some participants that this would impact the continuation of the Dutch punk scene, as there were less invested individuals willing to participate heavily.

A few participants, however, found positive aspects in the diminishing punk scene. They suggested that after earlier fragmentation, different factions were reuniting in an effort to keep things going. Lotte observed that historic rivalries between different subcultures had also been set aside, and Bram confirmed this:

> Well if you go to the bars here where we hang out, or the gigs, you [now] get a lot of different people you know. It's not just [the] punks, it's also [...] the metal guys, and rock and roll, rockabilly, [...] even the proper normal looking people, middle age[d] people. [...] It's not always like that but it has been perhaps for the last ten to fifteen years. And I like that. It's also because the subcultures are getting smaller so it mixes a bit more. (Bram)

For most, the contemporaneous 'lull' was seen as temporary, as all past lulls had been. Jeroen was quietly optimistic that in the contemporaneous context of a poor economy and state repression of squatting, a change would soon come. "I think we're now at a point, in the Netherlands anyway, that things will go downhill [... but] then something new may come along" (Jeroen).

SQUATTING AND THE ACTIVIST SCENE: 1990s TO 2000s

Whilst the Dutch punk scene went through ups and downs in the 1990s and 2000s, the squatting movement similarly saw highs and lows. After the 'defeat' of the PVK at the hands of the now dominant 'culturellas', the scene shifted towards the Wijers model of squatting. As Owens (2009) notes: "During the 1990s, squatting became associated more with large-scale squats that served the cultural needs of the community and less with pitched battles against the police" (229). Poldervaart (2002) argues that this shift cemented the squats as the location for 1990s 'utopian' political projects to take place; with the battles won, the squatters were able to focus on something other than the movement itself as its own political end.

Van Stokrom (2002) discusses the many different aspects of the 'radical action movement' that grew out of the Dutch squats from the 1990s onwards. This included the anti-globalisation movement that targeted the World Bank, the International Monetary Fund and the European Union. Moreover, the squatters' movement continued to build on the trans-European connections fostered throughout the 1980s that had proven so crucial to international connectivity in punk. One such initiative was the 'European caravan': a travelling 'info shop' that set out from Leiden in 1991 and passed through 12 other countries in Europe. The concerns of the squatters' movement became global, with squatters and activists from the global south recruiting those in Europe and the Netherlands to take part in the Global Days of Action and Zapatista solidarity. One participant, Wouter, recruited the embryo punks to run fundraisers that provided financial support to protesters travelling to Scotland for the G8 summit in 2005.

In 1998, Amsterdam's mayor realised that squats could be a valuable asset to Amsterdam's burgeoning tourism economy. Many of those seeking to experience the 'real' Amsterdam would visit the large public squats for the latest artistic and cultural innovations. Owens (2008) notes that: "[Mayor Patijn's slogan] 'No culture without subculture' became a catchphrase of the new Breeding Grounds Policy, the product of an apparent convergence of the goals of the city council, the squatters' movement, and tourists. Begun in late 1998, the program was intended to maintain and recreate the cultural functions previously performed by large squats" (54). Whilst the 'Breeding Grounds' policy was controversial amongst squatters—with many suspicious of the state's attempts to co-opt them—a number of squats benefitted, including OT301, which had an art studio, cinema, bar and restaurant, and a large gig venue.

During this time, older generations of punks who had lived in squats during the 1980s started to drift away from squatting. They cited various reasons, such as health problems or the desire to bring up children in more secure environments. Younger generations did continue the tradition, including Luka, who lived in squats in the 1990s, and Sander and Tom who set up new squats in the 2000s. Predominantly, however, the squatting scene and the punk scene came to be less entwined during this period. This was partly due to shifts in the structural position of young people in the Netherlands, especially compared with the 1980s. Unemployment had dropped, and even punks were expected to work. Access to unemployment support was restricted, and squatting became more difficult than it had been in the 1980s, requiring a greater commitment from those who did chose to squat.

The 1990s also brought with it a new underground techno scene, which benefitted from squatting in the same ways that punk had before it. From the 1990s onwards, the subculture most often associated with squatting became techno rather than punk: "I mean you've got a lot of young kids who are really active at squatting and then they are into techno and stuff but punk not so much, back in the days it was squatting and punk [... that went] hand in hand" (Ruben). This did not, however, mean that punk was pushed out. The large cultural squats and the many hundreds of smaller squats presented a diverse range of opportunities both cultural and political for punks and others to get involved. Punk was still considered part of the various political/cultural aspects of the squat even though the links were less strong than in the past:

Lots of contacts also developed internationally and that's why since the nineties people talk about 'The' movement consisting of a network of all kinds of diverse (left-radical) protest groups who collaborated. This doesn't quite include the punk movement [... But] at the same time punks and squatters are so much intertwined that, nevertheless, you can consider punks to be part of 'The' movement. (Poldervaart 2002: 23)

1 October 2010

On 1 October 2010, the law on squatting in the Netherlands changed. Since 1994 there had been no punishment for occupying a building that had lain empty for at least one year. Now, squatting *any* building became illegal, carrying with it a two-year prison sentence. Whilst the squatting movement had been largely peaceable throughout the 1990s and 2000s, the passage of this law saw a period of heightened protest from squatters. Evictions were resisted and violence broke out at protests. Pruijt (2013) suggests that the ban, coming after decades of tolerance for squatters, was part of a wider attack on left-wing ideals led by right-wing populists such as Geert Wilders.

Some participants were planning to continue to fight against the ban; Mark was searching for legal loopholes to save his squat, and Tom was organising with other squatters in order to 'fight' with direct action strategies. Jeroen, Mark, Marieke and Tom all agreed that times ahead would be more difficult. Marieke reported that by November there had already been arguments between the 2000 squatters left in Amsterdam over whether there should be a more militant approach or not, echoing the problems of the 1980s. She suggested that those who lived, worked, and created art in squats would likely end up having to find alternative spaces, whilst the movement would become dominated by those willing to invest their time into squatting as political activism. Menno, pessimistically, suggested that "maybe it is indeed the end, something else has to happen" (Menno).

RELATIONS BETWEEN GENERATIONS IN THE CONTEMPORANEOUS SCENE

At the time of my research, the Dutch punk scene was made up of multiple groups of people of all ages. The interactions between generations, and in some cases the lack thereof, have shaped the development of the scene historically. These relationships characterise a distinct facet of the punk scene as it was at the time of my fieldwork, leading to both solidarity and tensions between various groups in the scene.

Whilst punk is often still framed in academic debates as an example of a 'youth subculture', there has been a move towards addressing this. A number of recent studies have discussed various aspects of aging as a member of a subculture, including the commitments that come with mainstream adulthood and embodied aspects of aging. Bennett (2012) investigates those who both maintained and built a career alongside participation in the electronic dance music scene, and Hodkinson (2011, 2012) discusses goth parents dealing with the demands of childcare. Fogarty (2012) focuses on the way in which older bodies restrict the physical demands of subcultural involvement, whilst Haenfler (2012) and Hodkinson (2011, 2012) both explore the way in which subcultural style alters with age. Davis (2006) frames different approaches to aging as a punk as either successful or unsuccessful.

In most discussions, older cohorts are examined in isolation from the rest of their respective scenes. However, Fogarty (2012) and Schilt and Giffort (2012) take broader approaches by framing the experiences of older members alongside their relationships with younger members, specifically in the form of instances of sharing knowledge. The final section of this chapter will unpick how relationships between generations have played out in the Dutch punk scene.

Tensions

As discussed earlier in this chapter, the relocation of punk to the Netherlands removed the connection between the discourse of authenticity and the first generation of punk. However, age and generation are still used as tools for claiming scene hierarchy within Dutch punk. Tom experienced older generations claiming greater subcultural capital with the phrase, "I was a punk before you were a punk" (Tom).

This is reflected in other criticisms between generations. From their 'misguided' interest in pop punk to a more general ignorance of youth, participants from older generations often criticised those who came to punk later (than them). However, this criticism can be laced with a fondness and an understanding, as with Bram's account, which is based upon his own personal trajectory. "[S]ome of these young [kids], like with the mohicans and all the fucking studs and stuff—not all of them, but some—when they first came in[to the scene] like a year [or] two years ago, they were all like really ignorant. Which I suppose is okay—we all started out ignorant!" (Bram).

Ruben also criticised his younger self for only hanging out with his own generation; "[I was] very naïve with a lot of things and I wouldn't do it like that these days. Yeah. I was young, I couldn't blame myself. [… I]f you only hang out with the same kind of people you hear the same kind of ideas all the time" (Ruben). Bram and Ruben's criticisms of younger punks fits with those noted by Haenfler (2006) who discusses tensions between straight edge generations.

Both Bram and Ruben believed that if younger generations remain involved for long enough, perhaps mixing with older ('wiser') generations, they will turn out okay. It is on this basis that Bram's stronger criticisms are reserved for those who would not stay involved: "you still see that with American bands coming over. It's just basically young kids fucking [around] between going to high school and going to college or something. They take like a year off to 'be punk rock' or something! And then they go on to have careers and make a load of money and stuff" (Bram).

Some tensions were exacerbated by judgements around which generations had faced more obstacles. For example, Theo was resentful of how much easier it had become to acquire musical equipment. The development of cheaper instruments, perhaps coupled with greater parental support, meant that;

> bands now they just, […] they can get a backline quite easily, […] a bunch of youngsters and all of a sudden they've got three guitars and a big Marshall amp or something. But I had to work like for almost two years to be able to buy my first guitar. […] We used an upside-down trash bin for drum kits, and I smashed all my Kiss records: used them as cymbals! [… And] I would plug my guitar into my stereo, and it had a low gain microphone input so it would like get a distorted sound through that, and I had some old electric guitar, just like the framework of an electric guitar and we put some bass strings on it and we had a bass guitar! (Theo)

A few participants mentioned that 'being punk' is less risky now that it is no longer as new or as 'shocking':

> It's completely different nowadays, which I think is a good thing though. I'm not jealous or whatever, I'm not envying them, it's just like, I think there's a difference between how you can be a punk [now and …] in the old days [when] you'd be beaten up on the street, people would look at you. […] Like here in Holland we had problem with [the] 'discos' especially. I think in England it was mainly skinheads—we had some problems with skinheads but not as much as the 'discos'—they were after us and would like beat us up, and if they could catch you they would throw you in the canal. Yeah, well it was their fun, their way of fun, it was kind of stupid. […] It was like that in those days, actually being a punk, demands something from you. (Theo)

Some discussions brought up the alienating qualities of the Internet as a challenge to the punk scene. It was viewed as a double-edged sword for the contemporaneous scene. Whilst punks were able to make and maintain relationships and develop mobility (see Chap. 4), the Internet also shifted non-gig engagements off the streets and into bedrooms, changing the solidarity amongst punks, altering the nature of the scene, and exacerbating its fragmentation.

> Wim: That's also the thing; yeah I mean it's not as easy any more. I think there's still like a lot of people but most are sitting now behind the computer [...] that's probably also a problem of this time.

> Bram: Well I think you had it as well in the past like in every strange city that you came into you just saw some guy with a Mohican on the street you just walked up to him and say, "hey man I come from here and here and here, do you know where the punks hang out?" And they would just tell you where the punks would be hanging out, you know, and that's where you would go, and you would always have a place to sleep. And that is obvious now you can walk in major fucking cities and never even meet anybody that's into punk [...] because they're all sitting at home.

Wim and Bram also discussed a number of structural societal changes that they saw as affecting younger generations of punks:

> Wim: Without sounding too like an old fart or something, but they can't be young in a way that we were young. [...] I see it with my own kids you know?

> Bram: Well they have a lot more responsibilities now, they can't fuck off like we did.

> Wim: Like if I want to shave a Mohawk, I shave a Mohawk, for me it was available when I was ten years old like it was possible to have a Mohawk.

> Bram: No, but that's another big difference is that when we were young we could just like drop out of school, go to the squats whatever, do that kind of thing, whatever. They can't do that now, like they only get student grants for a couple of years.

> Wim: They are much more trapped in the system now then we were!

> Bram: They don't get like social security or anything like when they are out of school you know. We used to get it all. Most of us already were on the dole since we were like sixteen [or] seventeen, whatever. But all these kids now they all have to work, they all have to find jobs [...] they still have to be responsible.

Changes to social welfare and societal expectations of young people affect the way in which they might be able to engage with punk. This has altered the make-up of the modern scene, with even the young punks having to balance their commitments. Most of the younger punks in this study were studying, working, or both, a sharp contrast to the 1980s where unemployment dominated the scene.

Therefore, whilst older punks critiqued younger punks, this was often through a lens of hindsight and understanding: innocence is excused and external reasons for changes to the scene are sought. These levels of acceptance only break in the face of 'fake' punks who don't have the commitment to stay in the scene beyond a brief period of teenage rebellion (such as the American punks Bram criticises). In this we see older punks reifying long-term commitment as a necessary attribute of a 'real' punk, as noted by Widdicombe and Wooffitt (1990).

Relationships

Whilst there are multiple divisions within the Dutch punk scene, and many of these are along generational lines, there are also examples of cross-generational relationships.

One of the key sites in which different age groups come together to form close relationships is within bands. Some bands, like Gewapened Beton and their wider embryo punk group, formed initially through school-based friendship and thus have retained a membership with a close age range. However, many more punk bands form *through* the scene itself, and as such, age divisions need not be as much of a factor.

Vitamin X's current lineup came about through Amsterdam's straight edge scene of the late 1990s; when a member left the band in 1999, Maxim was invited from the younger generation of punk kids to join the band. Similarly Yawp! have been through a number of lineup changes with new members often being younger than those they replace.

Bram discusses how this has occurred throughout Dutch punk's history. When he was younger he played in bands with older members: "I was always playing with the people who were a lot older than me. [...] I was seventeen and I suppose the one who was closest to my age was [my bandmate] who was about twenty then or something, but all the rest were already near thirty at that time you know, so they were like old bastards! And I was the little kid bastard!" (Bram). Now, Bram finds that this has reversed; "I'm the oldest [(forty-four)], and then you get there's a guitar player that's about ten years younger than me, and then we got a bass player [who] is like [in their] early twenties" (Bram). This practice is particularly prevalent in places with small, cohesive scenes. This was also noted by Pilkington et al. (2014) where the tight-knit punk scene in Vorkuta, Russia, had a great number of bands with overlapping and cross-generational membership.

Gig-going often becomes a less regular occurrence as participants age (Haenfler 2006; Hodkinson 2011), with participants having to prioritise work or children over their leisure pursuits. Gigs are still attended by older punks, however, and thus they *do* still form a point of contact between different generations.

> Oh yeah, definitely I mean we hang around [with] those kids. [...] The people from [... the Gewapened Beton] crew, the embryo punk generation you know, like they're still around at every show, [or at least] most of the shows. [There are] even some younger kids [as well]. It's a small scene here and they all know each other and we all going to the same shows, so it's not like really, "I'm like fifteen years older than them so I don't care what those kids are doing". It's not awkward. It's all together (Luka).

Some participants view the punk scene as cohesive with sub-groups that are more age-based; others recognise a degree of mixing but perhaps would not see younger punks as 'close' friends. Theo says: "I also hang around with these guys, well not *hang around* with—it's not [that] we visit each other regularly—but I mean, it's like I do hang around with [a member of] Gewapened Beton, for example. I don't really care about age" (Theo). In this sense, despite some mixing between the generations, age does remain a factor in dividing the punk scene into smaller groups.

Sharing Knowledge Between Generations

Schilt and Giffort (2012) and Fogarty (2012) both discuss the importance of intergenerational relationships for subculture in terms of opportunities provided for sharing knowledge. Schilt and Giffort (2012) discuss formalised 'rock camps' for new generations of girls to learn from old riot grrrls, whilst Fogarty explores informal mentoring relationships in B-Boy culture. This form of mentoring is viewed as being of both subcultural and political importance: "the phrase 'each one teach one' means that if you have had the opportunity to learn, you are obliged to teach another what you have learned" (Fogarty 2012: 58).[9] The sharing of knowledge is therefore positioned in a positive light for subcultures as a whole.

Relationships between generations may serve the purpose of reinforcing practices related to subcultural capital, as discussed in Chap. 2 in terms of the intersubjective creation of punk meaning and identity formation. Daan discusses the way in which older members 'fostered' him and taught him the difference between 'good' and 'bad' punk: "I was brought up by [his friends, members of the band] Lärm and [another member…]. They really tried hard to get me off The Exploited" (Daan). Both Daan and his friends share the assumption that one should aim to listen only to 'good' punk. Whilst initially they differ on the specifics of what that might be (namely, The Exploited), Daan ultimately shares the understanding that for greater subcultural capital, he should avoid (or avoid mentioning) The Exploited.

For others, subcultural sharing was knowledge as well as artefacts;

> I've known [Menno] forever. I didn't really know him, [but] when I was eighteen years old and my house got burnt down [by Nazi punks] and my whole record and book collection was gone, I didn't know him personally then but [through mutual friends] he let me have […] a big box of amazing books and records […] Because he was really [affected] […] by the fact that somebody had that happen. So after that I've always been a bit in awe! […] I'm quite eager about certain things and he's always trying to teach me, so I really see him as my occult master. […] It's just kind of funny that he's in mid-fifties or something and I feel like a kid, because I still act like a kid but I know I'm no longer a kid. (Mark, age 38)

Both Mark and Daan, then, have benefitted from intergenerational relationships in ways similar to those outlined by Fogarty (2012), Haenfler (2006), Pilkington et al. (2014) and Schilt and Giffort (2012). The sharing of knowledge remains a key element by which older punks have "assumed the role of informal educators, filling the gaps in younger punks' knowledge" (Bennett 2006: 229).

In some cases younger punks have been left disappointed when older generations have not been forthcoming with guidance. "If the younger punks […] have a question for the old punks [they're sometimes told] 'it's your turn now', you know. […] They forget themselves where they started off" (Tom). The younger punks referred to by Tom specifically look to their 'elders' for advice, but in this instance the older punks take a more hands-off approach than any of the punks that Daan and Mark knew or critique younger generations (see earlier in this chapter, and also Haenfler (2006) and Pilkington et al. (2014)).

A lack of guidance and the desire on the part of younger punks to emulate their 'elders' could cause further tensions between generations when it was felt that younger punks were internalising the more negative aspects of punk history. Jeroen complained about the way in which some of the youngest punks were attempting to emulate the drug problems of the 1980s:

> It's nearly become fashionable [...] at punk gigs I see boys of sixteen taking speed and then I think "yeah what is this really all about?" That is a fashion that's crept in and, unfortunately is difficult to shake, but that ruins it a lot. [...] Speed, drugs, alcohol and punks—what do I know— the destructiveness, yeah that's a shame. Yes everything is fucked, but [then] you might as well just give up and scream "cunt, cunt, cunt, cunt". (Jeroen)

The sharing of knowledge between generations can therefore have both positive and negative effects upon both individuals and the scene, bringing back problems that caused fragmentation in the 1980s. The mixing of different generations and informal 'tutoring', as well as the tensions and divides between generational groups, has certainly affected the development of the Dutch punk scene.

CONCLUSION

This chapter has traced the development of Dutch punk from the cultural groups that preceded it to the contemporaneous scene that formed the basis for this research project. It has described various active groups within the scene and foregrounded the importance of Dutch squatting history to the development of Dutch punk.

Punk has continued to transform and mutate as new generations become involved. Each new generation brought new ideas and new forms of punk, whilst also learning from interactions with older generations. The persistent involvement of some of the oldest punks in the Dutch scene, both alongside younger generations and in their own separate spheres, contributed to the character of the scene at the time of my research.

This chapter has also examined the manner in which the Dutch punk scene has gone through better and worse times and explored the systems that underpinned the activities of the scene, even during a 'lull'. In particular, the squatting scene provided physical space and (international) connections for all kinds of cultural experimentation.

When the fieldwork for this project ended in early April 2011, it was unclear how the squatting ban would affect the future of the punk scene, the future of other creative scenes in the Netherlands and the future of the squatters' movement itself. However, many participants were optimistic. Those who had talked about the history of Dutch punk in terms of cycles or waves with highs and lows and all of those who had presented the contemporary scene as rather 'quiet' looked forward to the next upswing: all *expected* the next upswing.

With the economy thrown into disarray and a new wave of state repression of squatting (much like in the 1980s), Jeroen hoped that a new generation would be radicalised. Participants such as Johan look to the future with excitement; "I think something new will come along, it won't be as big, but punk is certainly not dead anyway. Maybe at the moment it's comatose, and has been for a while, but it's not dead, it's starting again, starting to recover, a little" (Johan).

NOTES

1. Marcus (1989) and Savage (1991) focus particularly on the influence on Malcolm McLaren and the Sex Pistols and Nehring (1993) on the persistence of this influence.
2. Squatter's Housing Office.
3. Ear.
4. The Netherlands television network features domestic and international stations.
5. Political Wing of the Squatters' movement.
6. It is worth noting that the foregrounding of the hardcore scene over others (such as pop punk) in this narrative is in part due to the way in which snowballing recruitment for participants will give prominence to the particular subgenres in which participants are involved.
7. The Uterus.
8. Boxes. '*Hokje*' is both used to represent 'thinking outside the box', or as a synonym for 'being pigeonholed'.
9. See Chap. 6 for a further discussion of the political importance of education.

REFERENCES

Andersen, K., and B. van der Steen. 2016. Introduction: The Last Insurrection? Youth, Revolts and Social Movements in the 1980s. In *A European Youth Revolt: European Perspectives on Youth Protest and Social Movements in the 1980s*, ed. K. Andersen and B. van der Steen, 1–21. Basingstoke: Palgrave Macmillan.

Bennett, A. 2006. Punk's Not Dead: The Continuing Significance of Punk Rock for an Older Generation of Fans. *Sociology* 40 (2): 219–235.

Bennett, A. 2012. Dance Parties, Lifestyle and Strategies for Ageing. In *Ageing and Youth Cultures*, ed. A. Bennett and P. Hodkinson, 95–104. London: Berg.

Bennett, A., and P. Hodkinson. 2012. *Ageing and Youth Cultures*. London: Berg.

Berger, G. 2008. *The Story of Crass*. Oakland, CA: PM.

Berkers, P. 2012. Rock Against Gender Roles: Performing Femininities and Doing Feminism Among Women Punk Performers in the Netherlands, 1976–1982. *Journal of Popular Music Studies* 24 (2): 155–175.

Blom, J.C.H., and Lamberts, E. [1999] 2006. *History of the Low Countries: New Edition*. New York: Berghahn Books.

Bull, M.J. 1995. The West European Communist Movement in the Late Twentieth Century. *West European Politics* 18 (1): 78–97.

Clark, D. 2003. The Death and Life of Punk, the Last Subculture. In *The Post-subcultures Reader*, ed. D. Muggleton and R. Weinzierl, 223–236. Oxford: Berg.

Davies, J. 1996. The Future of "No Future": Punk Rock and Postmodern Theory. *The Journal of Popular Culture* 29 (4): 3–25.

Davis, J. 2006. Growing Up Punk: Negotiating Aging Identity in a Local Music Scene. *Symbolic Interaction* 29 (1): 63–69.

Duivenvoorden, E. 2000. *Een voet tussen de deur: geschiedenis van de kraakbeweging 1964–1999*. Amsterdam: De Arbiederspers.

Fine, G.A., and S. Kleinman. 1979. Rethinking Subculture: An Interactionist Analysis. *American Journal of Sociology* 85 (1): 1–20.

Fogarty, M. 2012. "Each One Teach One": B-Boying and Ageing. In *Ageing and Youth Cultures*, ed. A. Bennett and P. Hodkinson, 53–65. London: Berg.

Glasper, I. 2006. *The Day the Country Died: A History of Anarcho Punk 1980 to 1984*. London: Cherry Red Books.

Goossens, J., and J. Vedder. 1996. *Het Gejuich Was Massaal: Punk in Nederland 1976–1982*. Amsterdam: Stichting Popmuziek Nederland.

Haenfler, R. 2006. *Straight Edge: Clean-living Youth, Hardcore Punk, and Social Change*. New Brunswick, NH: Rutgers University Press.

Haenfler, R. 2012. "More than Xs on My Hands": Older Straight Edgers and the Meaning of Style. In *Ageing and Youth Cultures*, ed. A. Bennett and P. Hodkinson, 9–23. London: Berg.

Hodkinson, P. 2011. Ageing in a Spectacular "Youth Culture": Continuity Change and Community Amongst Older Goths. *The British Journal of Sociology* 62 (2): 262–282.

Hodkinson, P. 2012. The Collective Aging of a Goth Festival. In *Ageing and Youth Cultures*, ed. A. Bennett and P. Hodkinson, 133–145. London: Berg.

Jonker, L. 2012. *No Future Nu: Punk in Nederland 1977–2012*. Amsterdam: Dutch Media Uitgevers.

Kempton, R. 2007. *Provo: Amsterdam's Anarchist Revolt*. New York: Autonomedia.

Liptrot, M. 2014. "Different People with Different Views but the Same Overall Goals": Divisions and Unities in the Contemporary British DIY Punk Subcultural Movement. *Punk & Post-Punk* 2 (3): 213–229.

Mah, A. 2010. Memory, Uncertainty and Industrial Ruination: Walker Riverside, Newcastle upon Tyne. *International Journal of Urban and Regional Research* 43 (2): 398–413.

Marcus, G. 1989. *Lipstick Traces: A Secret History of the 20th Century*. London: Faber and Faber.

McLoone, M. 2004. Punk Music in Northern Ireland: The Political Power of "What Might Have Been". *Irish Studies Review* 12 (1): 29–38.

Moore, R. 2004. Postmodernism and Punk Subculture: Cultures of Authenticity and Deconstruction. *The Communication Review* 7 (3): 305–327.

Mudu, P. 2004. Resisting and Challenging Neoliberalism: The Development of Italian Social Centers. *Antipode* 36: 917–941.

Muggleton, D. 2000. *Inside Subculture: The Postmodern Meaning of Style*. Oxford: Berg.

Nehring, N. 1993. *Flowers in the Dustbin: Culture, Anarchy, and Postwar England*. Ann Arbor: University of Michigan Press.

O'Connor, A. 2004. Punk and Globalization: Spain and Mexico. *International Journal of Cultural Studies* 7 (2): 175–195.

O'Hara, C. 1999. *The Philosophy of Punk: More Than Noise!* Edinburgh: AK Press.

Owens, L. 2008. From Tourists to Anti-tourists to Tourist Attractions: The Transformation of the Amsterdam Squatters' Movement. *Social Movement Studies* 7 (1): 43–59.

Owens, L. 2009. *Cracking Under Pressure: Narrating the Decline of the Amsterdam Squatters' Movement*. Amsterdam: Amsterdam University Press.

Owens, L. 2016. Amsterdam Squatters on the Road: A Case Study in Territorial and Relational Urban Politics. In *A European Youth Revolt: European Perspectives on Youth Protest and Social Movements in the 1980s*, ed. K. Andersen and B. van der Steen, 53–66. Basingstoke: Palgrave Macmillan.

Pilkington, H., I. Gololobov, and Y.B. Steinholt. 2014. Conclusion. In *Punk in Russia: Cultural Mutation from the 'Useless' to the 'Moronic'*, ed. I. Gololobov, H. Pilkington, and Y.B. Steinholt, 196–211. London: Routledge.

Poldervaart, S. 2002. Inleiding: Het Levendige Linkse Activism Als Onderdeel van de Sociale Betrokkenheid van Velen. In *Leven Volgens je Idealen: De Andere Politieken van Huidige Sociale Bewegingen in Nederland*, ed. S. Poldervaart, 1–36. Amsterdam: Aksant.

Pruijt, H. 2012. The Logic of Urban Squatting. *International Journal of Urban and Regional Research* 37 (1): 19–45.

Pruijt, H. 2013. Squatting in Europe. In *Squatting in Europe: Radical Spaces, Urban Struggles*, ed. The Squatting Europe Kollective, 17–60. Wivenhoe: Minor Compositions.

Sassoon, D. 1996. *One Hundred Years of Socialism: The West European Left in the Twentieth Century*. London: IB Tauris Publishers.

Savage, J. 1991. *England's Dreaming: Sex Pistols, Punk Rock, and Beyond*. London: Faber and Faber.

Schilt, K., and D. Giffort. 2012 "Strong Riot Women" and the Continuity of Feminist Subcultural Participation. In *Ageing and Youth Cultures*, ed. A. Bennett and P. Hodkinson, 146–158. London: Berg.

Shaw, K. 2005. The Place of Alternative Culture and the Politics of its Protection in Berlin, Amsterdam and Melbourne. *Planning Theory & Practice* 6 (2): 149–169.

Thompson, S. 2004. *Punk Productions: Unfinished Business*. Albany: State University of New York Press.

Thornton, S. 1995. *Club Cultures: Music, Media and Subcultural Capital*. Cambridge: Polity Press.

Tsitsos, W. 1999. Rules of Rebellion: Slamdancing, Moshing, and the American Alternative Scene. *Popular Music* 18 (3): 397–414.

van Stokrom, R. 2002. Netwerken voor een rechtvaardige wereld. De wortels van de anders-globaliseringsbeweging in Nederland. In *Leven volgens je idealen: De andere politieken van huidige sociale bewegingen in Nederland*, ed. S. Poldervaart, 37–81. Amsterdam: Aksant.

Widdicombe, S., and R. Wooffitt. 1990. "Being" Versus "Doing" Punk: On Achieving Authenticity as a Member. *Journal of Language and Social Psychology* 9 (4): 257–277.

Worley, M. 2012. Shot By Both Sides: Punk, Politics and the End of "Consensus". *Contemporary British History* 26 (3): 333–354.

CHAPTER 4

Mobility and Connections: In and Beyond the Dutch Punk Scene

The Dutch punk scene is characterised by connectivity and mobility within and beyond artificial national borders. As we saw in Chap. 3, from the moment that punk began, Dutch punks have been drawing their influences from elsewhere; the UK, the United States, and Germany in particular. When the Netherlands started to produce its own bands and zines and established its own punk centres, these forms of culture began to feed into the now global flows of punk. This chapter will extend the historical mapping of the Dutch scene (Chap. 3) by situating it spatially.

The legacy of the Dutch punk and squatting scenes' historical connections around the world will be developed in this chapter, as punk participants' mobility is unpicked as a facet and instrument of global cultural flow. Mobility will be discussed in the context of day-to-day travelling for scene activities, of bands' touring practices, and of participants' resettlement both within the country and internationally. The structural factors that both enable and constrain this mobility and the power dynamics at play will be uncovered through these discussions.

The chapter sets out with the understanding that the Dutch scene is 'peripheral' to the 'core' original punk scenes of the UK and the United States. However, it further develops the multiple levels at which centre-peripheral relationships work. On a national level a centre-periphery hierarchy has developed between the cities in the well-connected central region and the more distant cities of the north. Furthermore, within the 'peripheral' north, a city such as Groningen is positioned as central to other smaller conurbations. On an international level the Dutch scene is

© The Author(s) 2017
K. Lohman, *The Connected Lives of Dutch Punks*,
Palgrave Studies in the History of Subcultures and Popular Music,
DOI 10.1007/978-3-319-51079-8_4

situated as part of a privileged North West European scene, which enjoys heightened connectivity in comparison to more 'peripheral' South and Eastern European scenes.

Moreover, the importance of personal relationships in making and maintaining the connections that help to enable mobility will be uncovered, with reference in particular to touring practices between the Netherlands and the United States.

Processes of mobility and connections feed into participants' own spatial conceptualisations of their scene. This chapter uncovers how heightened mobility might erase the idea of a local scene for some Dutch punk participants, whilst for others a centre-periphery hierarchy can reinforce a sense of pride in a local scene.

The chapter will begin by discussing theories of cultural flow, particularly in relation to mobility. It suggests a model of rhizomatic connectedness shaped by centre-periphery inequalities. These concepts will be applied to the discussions of mobility highlighted by Dutch punk participants and my own experiences of fieldwork in the scene.

CULTURAL FLOW: MOBILITY AND CONNECTIONS

In Chap. 2 we saw how subcultural research has focused on interactions between the 'global' and the 'local', and that this has given rise to a number of conceptual frameworks including 'glocal' (Mitchell 1998; Pilkington 2004) and 'translocal' (Bennett and Peterson 2004; Hodkinson 2004). However, in order to reground approaches to the geographical mapping of a scene, I will instead highlight how individuals' relationships to mobility and space create a sense of place. This chapter will therefore follow Crossley's (2008) and Massey's (1993) lead in highlighting individual instances of mobility and personal connections as important to understanding the transmission of subcultural practices and the construction of the spatial. The flow of culture is, here, embodied (Casey 1996) by these individuals and their movements, highlighting the way in which culture flows in a rhizomatically connected manner (Deleuze and Guattari [1987] 2003) but cannot be extricated from hierarchies of power in multi-levelled centre-peripheral relationships (Hannerz 1992; Massey 1993; O'Connor 2004).

The importance of mobility to shaping cultural flow in a globalised world was discussed in Chap. 2. Appadurai (1996) highlights the role of migration, whilst Massey (1993) widens this to include everyday instances of mobility. This chapter will discuss both of these aspects in respect to participants' mobility. Kennedy (2010) highlighted the multifaceted way in which local lives function in relation to globalised cultural flows. He argues that globalisation debates have not placed enough emphasis on the role of the local in affecting individuals' interaction with the global nor how this then impacts global flows. Individuals need to be recognised as micro-actors in both constructing and understanding their place in a local and in a global world. This chapter will therefore embed individuals' 'subcultural' mobility within, and not as distinct from, wider 'mainstream' mobility (Pilkington et al. 2014: 210).

In arguing against the centre-periphery idea of global cultural flow, Deleuze and Guattari ([1987] 2003) offer a concept based on connectedness (Smart 2007: see Chap. 2). They suggest a model of 'rhizomes', which "ceaselessly [establish] connections between semiotic chains, organizations of power, and circumstances relative to the arts, sciences, and social struggles" (Deleuze and Guattari [1987] 2003: 7). They argue that a rhizomatic model for culture, based on biological rootstocks, 'exposes' the hierarchical 'arborescent' culture (representing the centre-periphery model) for what it is: linear, binary and unidirectional in the manner of a family tree. The rhizome model can instead be understood on varying levels: allowing flow between different cultures, different forms of culture, and different understandings of one form of culture. There may be high levels of interrelatedness, whilst retaining the possibility of multiple individual iterations: "[t]he wisdom of the plants: even when they have roots, there is always an outside where they form a rhizome with something else" (11). A rhizomatic model allows for an in-depth understanding of the complexity of cultural interactions. However, this chapter suggests that breaking completely from the centre-periphery model problematically erases inequality in the 'flow' and production of culture (Massey 1993; Pries 2005). As such this chapter will draw out the rhizomatic connectedness of individuals and explore how this shapes cultural flow but will also highlight the ways in which centre-periphery inequalities remain and are maintained through these processes.

This understanding of cultural flow is particularly pertinent to the ways in which inequalities of mobility contribute to participants' understandings of their scene as either local or not. Shields (1991) wrote of how a *sense of place* is constructed by individuals, depending on the ways in which they interact with a location. Myths of place may build up over time through discourses of individualised senses. These discourses then shape the construction of the space and the sense of community. Massey (1993) considers this in the context of mobility. She argues that space is not only moved *through* but is also constructed *by* these movements and each individual's relationship to the sense of place. "The uniqueness of a place, or a locality […] is constructed out of particular interactions and mutual articulations of social relations, social processes, experiences and understandings. […] Instead then, of thinking of places as areas with boundaries around, they can be imagined as articulated moments in networks of social relations and understandings" (66). The multiplicity of individuals' construction of space will be highlighted throughout this chapter.

An important element of subcultural mobility, especially in regard to touring practices (see further in this chapter), is that of individual personal connections and relationships. Crossley (2008) has done some important work connecting this to mobility and the transmission of cultural practice. He attributed the development of the 'post/ punk' scene in Manchester to connections formed between individuals in London and Manchester. The first important moment came when Howard Devoto and Peter McNeish decided to travel from Manchester to London to check out a band (the Sex Pistols) that they had read about in the New Musical Express paper. In London they met Malcolm McLaren and promised to organise a trip to Manchester for the Sex Pistols. The resulting two gigs at the Lesser Free Trade Hall have a place in Manchester's punk folklore for being where a 'critical mass' of interested parties met, leading to the formation of the Manchester post-punk scene. Bands such as the Buzzcocks, Joy Division, and The Fall formed soon after these events. Crossley's work highlights the importance of personal connections within a scene, demonstrating that these can be formed between localities and that individuals' mobility can be key in the transmission and development of culture.

Crossley suggested that both of his network analyses of British punk (2008, 2009) provide crucial sociological understandings of the development of subcultural practices. He argued that networks of individuals are the basis on which the mechanisms that resulted in punk (and post-punk) operated (2008). Whilst this is valuable work towards grounding the production of culture in human interaction, the formulation of relationships into network analysis oversimplified what are inherently messy and individual instances of connection. His reliance on a limited selection of histories of the scene, with an over-representation of books centred on either the Sex Pistols (Sabin 1999) or The Clash, results in a perpetuation of these histories and the erasure of other key players in early punk[1] (Namaste 2000). Whilst Crossley's work does illustrate cultural flow based on individuals' movements and social relations, it doesn't interrogate the power relations in place/created by these processes, and moreover reinforces these power narratives within academia, unchecked. I therefore shall not adopt a network analysis but instead draw attention to the moments at which personal relationships have had particularly important effects on participants' mobility and the global flow of culture.

MOBILITY AND LOCALITY IN THE DUTCH PUNK SCENE

Structural Aspects of Mobility

Before discussing specific examples of how scene participants' mobility may affect the spread and development of punk, it is pertinent to consider the wider societal structures that enable this mobility. A specific location can greatly affect the scene that grows around it, as shown in work on Bristol trip hop (Webb 2007) and also in S. Cohen's (2007) discussion of the production of place through music (and music through place) in Liverpool. This section will highlight a number of factors that have had an effect on Dutch punk, but it does by no means constitute an exhaustive list. Instead it represents factors that have been raised as important by participants.

The Netherlands' punk scene has been affected by the geography of the country. Its small size and the short distances between neighbouring cities enable easy overlap between punks and bands from different locales. This is particularly true of the densely populated *Randstad* central-western area of the country where the 'big four' cities (Amsterdam, Utrecht, the Hague and Rotterdam) all lie around (or under) one hour's travel from each other. Gregor commented that this increased the regularity with which bands would meet up with each other: "any band who also play reasonably often and who are on tour a lot you're bound to know because you always bump into each other [...] but of course The Netherlands is really small" (Gregor). This feeds into other structural factors, which leads to a blurring of the boundaries of the 'local'.

The Netherlands is an affluent Western European country. At a state-level this has allowed for a well-integrated public transport system. Also of note is the country's exceptionally flat landscape and excellent national network of cycle paths. In other words, the day-to-day possibilities for participants to be geographically mobile are high in the Netherlands. The ease of mobility around the country was a common theme among participants. Comments included the regularity of travelling by trains between large cities (facilitated by trains running throughout the night), in addition to which participants would often cycle long distances or drive to gigs elsewhere. Utrecht, already in a central position, is a major rail network hub. The ease of travelling elsewhere from Utrecht is one reason Gregor chose to live there. Similarly, Bart chose Nijmegen as a home because it is only 45 min by train from Eindhoven and under 90 min from Amsterdam.

The mobility of the Dutch punk scene further extends beyond the borders of the Netherlands. This is facilitated by the country's membership of the European Union, and its participation in the Schengen Agreement. Residents of countries in the Schengen Area are able to travel freely across national boundaries, as there are no passport controls at their common borders. This enables much less complication for bands who are touring, as well as for scene participants to attend gigs and experience punk outside the Netherlands.

In the late twentieth century the Netherlands was a popular destination for migrant workers and their families, and for asylum seekers. The 1950s onwards saw successive waves of immigration particularly from former Dutch colonies, Mediterranean countries and former Socialist states (Siegel and de Neubourg 2011). As will be highlighted later in this chapter, this has resulted in a number of punk participants with backgrounds and scene connections in other countries. This affects their own experiences of punk but has also shaped punk itself both in the Netherlands and abroad (Lohman 2013).

These various geographical and socio-political structures inform the way in which participants relate to the spatial, thereby affecting the manner in which they create a sense of space, or myth of place (Shields 1991). Most notably this can be seen in how different locations in the Netherlands have different levels of access to processes of mobility, affecting the way in which participants understand the existence of a *local* punk scene. In the hyperconnected 'core' cities the ease of mobility has led to a breaking down of local boundaries as participants understand the space of their scene to be wide and porous. In the more distant north, participants' lower levels of mobility create a local identity in which they understand themselves as peripheral to the rest of the country. These findings will be further elaborated later in this chapter.

Travelling Participants

The structural factors previously outlined shape not only participants' sense of place but also the very nature of the 'Dutch' punk scene. The ease of mobility in a small and well-connected country has resulted in a great deal of movement between various locations for 'scene interactions', which will be outlined later in this chapter.

A number of participants talk of travelling regularly in order to attend gigs. On the Saturday prior to being interviewed, Theo had travelled from his home in Amsterdam to see TSOL play in Eindhoven. Sander also lives in Amsterdam but will go to, "Nijmegen, Utrecht, Tilburg, if it's a really big band, then we'll hop in the car or on the train, no problem". Lotte also says that she will regularly travel for a gig. Indeed this was a practice in which I participated during fieldwork.

Just as participants are willing to travel beyond their local area in order to attend a show, they will also on occasion travel to another country to see bands play. Although, "then it has to be something quite special, sometimes we'll go to Antwerp, or Oberhausen or something" (Sander). Jasper was at the time considering a gig trip to Hamburg and Bart an overnight trip to Berlin to follow a favourite band on tour.

Travelling outside one's local town in order to attend a gig is something that seems commonplace. However, it holds significance for theorisation of the nature of subcultural development. Traditional, locally bounded studies tend either to ignore this phenomenon or play it down, but such frequent gig trips play an active part in affecting the development of the scene, and furthermore contribute to the disintegration of the 'local'.

The role of travelling is discussed by Hodkinson (2002) with regard to UK goth. Travel to other places in the UK[2] happened primarily for big club nights. Goth gigs are a less frequent occurrence than is the case within punk, although when they do occur they also attract 'translocal' crowds. The culmination of this is the biannual Whitby Gothic Weekend: an event that is a key meeting place for goths from all over the UK (and abroad). These translocal goths are mobile in a different way to the Dutch punks for whom travel is more part of their regular subcultural activity. "Regular club nights [...] tended to attract a minority of travelling goths, but mostly from within their region. [... M]ore goths travelled greater distance for less-frequent events" (101–102). By contrast, even the smallest Dutch punk events may draw their audience from a variety of locations.

The mobility of the Dutch punk scene can further be seen in the way that some bands are able to draw members from across the Netherlands, or, indeed, beyond. When Planet Eyelash were formed, they were initially based in Groningen: three of the four members lived there, with one travelling to rehearsals from nearby Leeuwarden. But the members of the band all left Groningen and by the time they sought a fifth member, being from Groningen no longer mattered. All members would travel by train from their separate cities to meet in Zwolle once a week to practice.

Bart and Gregor's bands have similarly been 'national' groups. Bart travelled an hour from Nijmegen to Diemen for his band practices. When Gregor's band, began all of the members were based in Wageningen; they then spread out to Nijmegen, Utrecht and Amersfoort before finally all settling in Utrecht together. Vitamin X, considered one of the bigger and more successful 'Dutch' hardcore bands of the moment, has members who live in both the Netherlands and Germany. Whereas bands are often understood to be 'from' the town/city in which members live, these bands highlight how the link between band and place can be more complex.

Mobility changes the makeup of the audience at a gig, which brings into question the very notion of what constitutes the 'local'. Bart talks of the overlap in people who attend gigs in Eindhoven and Nijmegen: "[in Eindhoven] you actually bump into the same people as you meet in Nijmegen, well, the Netherlands are small, aren't they?" When asked about the scene in Utrecht, Gregor questioned the very notion of an *Utrecht* punk scene; "oh well, there are of course a few places where there is the occasional gig but in any case, you always get the same people coming and often [...] people from Nijmegen turn up and from Amsterdam and there is a sort of a solid base of people coming to the shows" (Gregor). For these participants it does not make much sense to talk of a *local* scene beyond the physical venues in which participation may take place.

The internal connectivity of the Dutch punk scene manifests itself, therefore, in a lack of identification with ideas of the 'local'. The lack of 'local' scenes creates a greater homogeneity in punk on a national level.

This puts the Dutch scene in contrast with the way in which punk has developed in larger, less well-connected countries such as the United States or Russia. In these places, there is much greater diversity between punk from different regions or even cities. The Unites States has, historically, produced many variations of punk, with very distinct forms of hardcore emerging in California (a first wave of stripped down, political, masculine music), in the (white) suburbs of Washington, DC (where collective and DIY approaches were foregrounded and straight edge first emerged), and in New York (where Washington, DC's brand of straight edge hardcore was combined with metal) (Thompson 2004). In Russia far-flung cities have bred very different scenes. Vorkuta (an ex-Gulag mining city in the Arctic north with rapid deindustrialisation and depopulation) has a small scene notable for the high levels of crossover between alternative subcultures. St. Petersburg (the economically strong ex-capital) has many vibrant 'subscenes' where various genres and activisms intersect. Krasnodar (a city in the south with a strong agricultural- and tourism-based economy) has a large alternative scene that has been strongly influenced by punk (Pilkington 2014a).

There is recognition amongst participants that this mobility is not always a positive feature of the scene. Mobility, coupled with highly active promoters, produces a number of drawbacks: "if you want to there's more than enough shows to go to, I just can't make all of them—unfortunately—[...] every night that you go out you spend money on the entrance and then after that you spend money on drinks and I can't afford it" (Theo). I regularly heard the complaint (coupled with the recognition of this as an inherently privileged 'problem') of there being 'too many gigs'. "[S]ometimes there is a [gig] in Amsterdam and in Nijmegen, [and one in] Utrecht and then [...] all those people who normally go to everything then have to choose and you'll end up having a lot of gigs with twenty [people] watching" (Gregor). The 'too many gigs' phenomenon is particularly problematic during a scene's 'lull' (see Chap. 3). More of those involved with punk at such a time are running and playing at the gigs themselves, leaving attendance scarce: particularly when attendees have so many options of gigs within travelling distance. This sets the scene in the geographically compact and well-connected Netherlands as rather different to many other places where there is a greater tendency towards local shows attended by local punks (Thompson 2004).

Peripheral Locality

As noted by Massey (1993) and Pries (2005) mobility is not evenly distributed. Instead mobility privileges the most connected cities, such as those in the centre of the Netherlands. This creates a phenomenon by which there still exist 'core' and 'peripheral' cities within an ostensibly rhizomatic Dutch scene. It was notable that in Groningen, which is two to three hours' travel from many other 'core' Dutch cities, there was a distinct feeling of isolation from the rest of the Netherlands. Whilst Groningen may be 'peripheral' to other Dutch cities, it also held a 'core' position within the northern region of the Netherlands, with punks from nearby Leeuwarden citing Groningen as their centre.

Lisa had lived in and participated in the punk scenes of both Nijmegen and Groningen and was able to compare how their locations within the country affected the scene. "Groningen is a bit more … isolated. […] I have the impression that for instance during the week there are not so many bands playing, just in the weekend. Here in Nijmegen there are a lot more, that's because you can travel here so easily from Arnhem or Utrecht or wherever" (Lisa).

This isolation has had a complex impact on Groningen; indeed, there is evidence that its peripherality has bred a greater sense of locality. It was the only place where I conducted fieldwork that participants felt there was a distinctly different scene from the rest of the country. Ruben, Lotte and Kosta all mentioned a distinct 'Northern'[3] or '*Groningense*' scene, with Bram commenting, "I think everyone here will tell you the same, [the] Groningen punk scene is nothing like the rest of Holland" (Bram).

Whilst it did not seem that participants based in Groningen were any *less* connected than those based elsewhere, their connections tended to be with others beyond—rather than within—the Netherlands (see later in this chapter). Moreover it was the only place where there seemed to be a much stronger day-to-day punk community. This was based around the punk and rock bar Crowbar (the crowd had only recently settled here, having moved from Simplon in the 1980s–1990s to Café Vera and then to Crowbar), where punks would meet many times a week. Participation seemed higher here than elsewhere in the Netherlands. In Groningen, a number of punks discussed the importance of supporting their *local* scene. In Groningen, therefore, there was a distinct *sense* of place (Shields 1991) in which locality—and pride in that locality—was emphasised.

Mobility therefore creates rhizomatic networks nationally across the country. However, hierarchies between 'core/centre' and 'peripheral' locations remain. Moreover, mobility affects participants' constructions of 'locally' bounded scenes, actively erasing the sense of the local where mobility is high and contributing to a stronger 'local' scene where it is not.

TOURING AND THE BUILDING OF RELATIONSHIPS

The mobility of punks is reflected in the touring practices of Dutch bands. This form of mobility is often founded upon personal translocal or transnational connections with other punks around the country, continent or globe. These practices form wider rhizomatic connections through which particular cultural practices may be intersubjectively developed. Hodkinson (2002) suggests that "travelling participants [of UK goth] were all liable to influence and be influenced by their counterparts in other areas of the country. [...] The national and sometimes international tours of even small goth bands provided further translocal influence" (106–107). Touring is therefore a key facet to cultural flow.

This section will describe international touring practices of Dutch bands. It will first highlight how structural similarities between scenes in North West Europe foster greater connectivity and mobility. It then unpicks how this feeds into and perpetuates a centre-periphery hierarchy that extends *across* Europe. A discussion of how touring practices extend *beyond* Europe will focus on the crucial aspect of personal global relationships between punks in order to facilitate tours and consider the implications for a *Dutch* scene that has such a globally connected position.

Touring in Europe

Touring bands in the Netherlands often find themselves playing outside the country very rapidly. This is partly due to the small nature of both the scene and the country; "Holland is too small [to do shows every weekend]" (Theo). Larry charts the rapidity with which his band played further and further afield: "[a]fter the first demo we started playing outside of our own town. And then after our first album we started playing all over the country and eventually we went to other countries"; "our first gig abroad was in Belgium in Oostende and we really did a lot of gigs in Belgium"; "we went to England, well we had some shows in France, [...] But we also went to Germany, Austria, Slovenia, Italy, Switzerland, Hungary, Poland, Romania [for] one gig, Slovakia, Norway and Sweden" (Larry). Larry's band started off playing a few 'nearby' international gigs before very quickly expanding to play gigs across a large portion of Europe.

The historical connections and communication between punks, rooted in the squatting scene's networks (see Chap. 3) mean that it is easy for punks to travel and for a 'young' band to get gigs abroad: "we had an attitude of 'yeah lets first focus on where we already have a base', mainly Benelux and Germany" (Sander). The sharing of international connections means that an overwhelming majority of the bands that feature in this project have toured—at the very least—in North West Europe. Even a small, short-lived band such as Jolanda's first group, who never recorded their music, toured "once five days in the Netherlands and Belgium, and once we went to Germany for two days" (Jolanda). For some bands, dates played abroad were such a regular occurrence that they weren't seen as anything special. "We do odd days here and there too, but I don't really count those!" (Gregor).

Whilst Groningen is somewhat disconnected in the Dutch punk context, it is not disconnected from international networks. The scene in Groningen maintains especially close ties with Oldenburg in Germany, due both to historical connections and its proximity.[4] This foothold in Germany affects Groningen bands' touring opportunities. Compared to other Dutch bands, Groningen punks tend to tour internationally in Germany before they have toured much in the Netherlands itself: "you can compare [Groningen] a lot more with the German punk scene, which is not that weird because we're more or less on the border. [...] None of our bands played a lot in Holland either, we always went over the border straight away" (Bram). Bram notes not only how proximity affects touring chances but also how this affects Groningen punks' sense of place: as closer in identity as well as in distance to Germany's punks. Local identity and transnational connections both affect the rhizomatic network. Bram's observation was backed up by the regularity with which participants discussed touring in Germany and other neighbouring countries; Suzanne, Maarten, Jacob, Ruben, Jaap, Henk, Bram and Wim all discussed this.

Andre pointed out the importance of structural factors that help support punk and which also work to facilitate communication and homogeneity. He identifies a number of countries in North West Europe with similar traditions in regards to culture and live music: Germany, Austria, Switzerland, the Netherlands and Belgium. These countries, all of which Andre and his band have toured extensively, share similar traditions of government-subsidised art, culture, and youth centres. These youth centres are often run by young volunteers who regularly put on shows, giving new generations the skills needed to run events well. Moreover, the countries also share similar models of large cultural squats that are central to the punk scene in terms of providing living space and gig venues and enabling the mobility and connectivity that comes with touring.

The centrality of squats for live music and culture has also played a role in driving up the quality of non-squat facilities, which need to provide similar amenities in order to compete. Andre explains that: "Most venues [in Germany] also have somewhere to sleep, they have a backstage and they make sure you have free beer backstage and there is a kitchen" (Andre). This means that it is relatively easy for promoters to run events cheaply, something that is important in a subculture that has a complicated relationship with commercialism (O'Hara 1999) and where high ticket prices are frowned upon. Andre describes the squat history and state-sponsored youth centres as the 'two legs' that hold up the scene. The mobility of participants and bands throughout the Benelux and Germanic countries of North West Europe, coupled with some structural similarities has led to a well-integrated and well-connected scene in which new bands are able to very quickly become 'international touring bands'.

Andre notes the differences between the structures available to promoters in North West Europe compared with elsewhere in the continent. A less developed squatting movement, along with fewer subsidies to support culture, affects the punk scene. In France or Italy it is common for a small punk band to play in a bar as tailored venues are too expensive. The use of bars often means that whilst the promoter doesn't always have to pay for the gig space, the lack of extra facilities (such as bedrooms and kitchen space) leads to other costs for running events. This increases the financial risk of promoting punk events, ultimately impacting on the scene.

A number of research participants discussed their experiences of touring beyond the affluent North West of Europe. Andre noted the marked difference between gigs in Northern and Southern Italy in similar terms to the way a few participants (Gregor, Larry) talked about Eastern Europe: as the area was poorer, it was harder for a promoter to make money enough to pay bands to cover their travel cost. As a result, Dutch bands don't tour there as often.

This inequality does not just affect North Western bands' touring prospects but also impacts the bands that come out of these scenes. For bands from Eastern Europe, where the average income and cost of living is significantly lower than in the Netherlands, it is harder to cover the costs of touring even in North West Europe. During fieldwork I did not see a single band from Eastern Europe. Conversely, I saw a number of bands from other Benelux and Germanic countries, as well as from Scandinavia.

These structural inequalities set up another hierarchical relationship between an affluent 'centre' in North Western Europe, which has a good infrastructure to support the scene, and the 'peripheral' rest of Europe whose scenes do not have access to these resources. "For it does seem that mobility and control over mobility both reflect and reinforce power. It is not simply a question of unequal distribution, that some people move more than others, some have more control than others. It is that the mobility and control of some groups can actively weaken other people" (Massey 1993: 62). Uneven cultural flow actively affects both 'central' and 'peripheral' countries.

Conversely Dutch bands who *did* tour Eastern Europe tended to enjoy these gigs above others. The lower instance of gigs (especially featuring touring bands) meant that attendees were more likely to make a particular effort to enjoy their evening. Bands often received warm responses from the crowd; Maxim described the audience in Russia as 'wild' and 'enthusiastic'. For some participants this was reason enough to tour further afield, despite the financial losses. Larry commented, "you'll make a loss but you will really have a great time. People also really appreciate you take the trouble to come" (Larry).

Menno describes two illegal gigs with The Ex in Socialist Eastern Europe in the 1980s (at a time when punk was banned) as the best in his life; the energy surpassed anything he had ever experienced before or since. The crowd's enjoyment and his experience of meeting people living in the Communist Bloc was perhaps particularly influential for Menno, who had previously labelled the Rondos' politics as 'communist' (see Lohman 2013). We see therefore how cultural flow affects not just subculture but also other facets of life, such as political engagement (see Chap. 6).

Touring Beyond Europe

Touring beyond mainland Europe is more complicated due to the necessary extra preparations and travel costs. Although bands tour more distant countries less frequently, this still forms an important moment in the life of a band. The United States, in particular, is a draw for many of those involved in the Dutch punk scene. This may be due to the way that American punk has dominated the global scene for many years with various waves of hardcore and their dominance of pop punk. With such a mythological status, the United States becomes a highly desirable place to tour, therefore reinforcing its status as a 'central' punk scene.

The Groningen scene has well-established links with the Americas. Connections have been made, particularly with the United States, by Groningen-based individuals. One particular relationship has shaped both the touring opportunities for later generations of punks and particular musical forms that punk has taken in Groningen.

A connection with Portland's Dead Moon originated when those who worked at Groningen's Café Vera decided to bring them over for a special gig. In order to celebrate the city's 925th anniversary, money had been provided for cultural endeavours, giving those at Café Vera the freedom to indulge themselves with gigs that they would ordinarily not be able to afford to put on.

> We flew in Dead Moon, our most favourite unknown band, from Portland, Oregon [for the release gig]. They came to Europe for one gig only, and that was here. And since then they played about twenty times. [...] They always started the[ir] tour[s] in the cellar bar with like [a] free secret gig, but of course all the people... knew [about] it. It was always packed and sweaty and they [would] play for two and a half hours. And the last gig of the tour was [always] in the main hall. [...] They played like thirteen times in the main hall and about maybe nine times in the downstairs. (Jaap)

It was this musical connection that resulted in a transatlantic friendship between members of Dead Moon, the rest of Portland's "punk hearted" 'rock and roll' scene (Jaap), and individuals in Groningen. It facilitated visits and tours in both directions; and thereby enabled the creation of yet further networks of contacts.

In 1992 Jacob and Jaap travelled to America to play at their friends' (Fred and Toody from Dead Moon) 25th wedding anniversary party.

They then toured the USA's West Coast. Wim and Bram also discussed American connections stemming from a joint tour undertaken by Fleas and Lice and the Boycott in 1998. They started in Canada and travelled down America's East Coast before finishing the tour in Mexico.

The personal relationships that have flourished with these connections have further shaped the Groningen punk scene. The interest in Dead Moon's style of punk rock 'n' roll in Groningen meant that Café Vera also booked bands such as The Gun Club, who are mentioned by three participants as particularly influential to both their tastes and those in the wider local scene (Lotte). This heightened interest in rock 'n' roll-influenced punk was something that was particular to the Groningen scene when compared to the rest of the Netherlands. Indeed, this musical differentiation from the rest of the country was one of the markers by which Kosta noted the Groningen scene as particularly local. Its embeddedness in global cultural flows, and the specificity of important personal relationships helps to define Groningen's sense of locality. Moreover, we see an instance of how punk's meaning can shift by intersubjective sharing through different communication interlocks (see Chap. 2).

The contested importance of locality within globalized musical practices, and the relationship between a city and the production of and promotion of its 'sound', has been discussed in depth by S. Cohen (2007) in relation to Liverpool. These themes have been further explored in Lashua et al. (2014) book, *Sounds and the City*, which recognises that these localities affect global practice just as globality affects the local: "the increasing mobility of individuals, cultural practice, and ideas, and the emergence of global networks such as the Internet, made popular music places more common and yet more diverse. In this century, popular music has become a leisure form that seems to transcend borders and it has reshaped the postmodern city" (Lashua et al. 2014: 5).

Touring mobility becomes a form of rhizomatic cultural flow in which Groningen's local punk is shared globally, and punk from elsewhere shapes the Groningen scene in turn. Moreover, these historical connections impact later generations' touring opportunities. Whereas non-Groningen-based Andre commented that, "America is really hard to go to for a tour" (Andre), Jolanda reports that (for the Groningen bands that she knows), "there are very many bands who go on tour to America really quickly" (Jolanda). This difference highlights how transnational friendships can affect the touring opportunities in different locations.

Practices of touring are based on the intersection of structural factors that constrain and allow touring and the personal connections between individuals. As highlighted by the example of Groningen and the United States, opportunities to play abroad are often based on contacts that the scene has. These build up over time. Menno describes how, when he played with the Rondos in the 1970s, the Dutch scene was relatively isolated from the rest of the world, mediated only by the (punk) travellers that did pass through, letters to foreign bands, and imported LPs and zines. The Rondos played the majority of their gigs in the Netherlands. By the time Menno played with The Ex between 1985 and 1987, however, he only performed *outside* the Netherlands. He describes how the punk scene had become better connected throughout the world. This 'community' came into its own through looking after bands and putting on performances for bands worldwide. It seems therefore that global punk touring practices emerged after the 'first' wave of punk was over, and as punk became more rooted in squatting culture and DIY practices.

Processes of reciprocation feed into touring practices and the personal relationships and connections that develop. Many of the participants of this research not only are in bands that have toured abroad but also have acted as promoters who have brought foreign bands to play in the Netherlands. "I think there are also a lot of bands [...] from Nijmegen who tour abroad, so in that way they also make contacts. And then they set up a gig for a foreign band in the hope they can play somewhere else through [that connection]" (Lisa). Erik similarly took a very pragmatic approach to this:

> If people help me out then I'll help them out even if they aren't friends of mine. So if they do a show for [my band] Kensington Arms, I do a show for them, that's my policy. And of course when you are on tour with bands and you come back home you get a lot of emails from bands that you met on tour [...] and then it depends if I see the value in it. [If] they can do shows for me then I'll do it [...] but I have to get something from that too cos I want to have cos I want to let my own band grow too, that's the that's why I do it. (Erik)

Processes of reciprocation are therefore important in the punk scene, particularly amongst DIY networks. This can also be seen in Ventsel's (2008) work on reciprocation in the alternative punk economy in Germany.

Whilst accounts from my participants focused largely on the normality of travelling to events such as gigs, the travelling process of bands touring is more embedded in subcultural and social practices of affect. Hollows and Milestone (1998) discuss the way in which the Northern Soul scene in the UK is based around travel, with participants gathering infrequently for events at particular locations. This constructs the process of travelling as part of subcultural practice and the building of affective bonds between members.

This is further reflected in the number of participants who would spend extra time on tour with *other* bands, usually friends' bands, going along in any capacity in which they could. Gregor and Bart have gone on other bands' tours to help with the driving. Lotte toured for 10 years with Zeke and Motörhead selling merchandise and acting as band manager: "yeah, it's a good life" (Lotte). And Jeroen will fulfil whatever a touring band needs: "It depends; tour manager, driver, merch. It really depends on which band, that's maybe my 'thing' in punk [rather than playing in a band]. [...] MDC or GBH are bands with whom I have toured as well [...] you get to see all aspects of it" (Jeroen).

Some, such as Jeroen, enjoyed touring in order to see as many sides of punk and as many places as possible. Indeed, many participants, when asked about where they had toured, would reel off a list of countries they had 'collected', "I think I've had every country [in Europe], except Ireland" (Jeroen).

Primarily, however, respondents remarked upon the sociability of touring, of touring as being about building relationships. Jacob, for example, noted touring as an opportunity to spend time with other "like-minded people" (Jacob). Mark noted how much he enjoyed getting to the bottom of how 'punk' can be understood differently and why this was (see Chap. 5). Lotte described how important it was for her to have friends all over the world, borne out of connections from the Groningen punk scene.

That's the nice thing about the punk scene here, there are a lot of connections with England, Ireland, Scotland, a lot of people who know each other. [...] Many friends and from all over the place, also America and Germany. That's the nice thing about the punk scene; if someone drops by like "I am a friend of such and such and I need somewehere to stay", yeah it's a really nice scene. (Lotte)

Certainly these experiences suggest that in this sense the Dutch scene is similar to those in Russia where "[f]riendship is central to punk belonging; arguably it is the primary affective bond on scenes" (Pilkington et al. 2014: 200). Moreover, there's the *potential* of all the bonds that you have not yet made: the knowledge that punks you have not yet met are also your friends.

Touring and travelling for gigs, both nationally and internationally, forms an important part of subcultural activity for those involved in punk in the Netherlands. High levels of mobility are supported by a variety of factors, including the size and wealth of the country and its good transport connections. This feeds into the connections that are made on a personal level between participants in various locations. These relationships help aid further mobility, and thus affect the manner in which cultural practices spread and are shared across distances. Influences are drawn from an ever wider array of people and places, altering the nature of punk. Differences between 'centres' and 'peripheries' in some instances become less pronounced through the connectivity and mobility of the participants; however, structural inequalities can also foster greater divides.

RESETTLEMENT

An important part of mobility in a globalised world, beyond more mundane or everyday travelling practices, are processes of—and opportunities for—migration and resettlement. As discussed in Chap. 2, for Appadurai (1996) this was a key aspect to modern forms of globalisation. Whereas people's migration and the role of this in transporting and spreading cultural forms was nothing new, Appadurai argued that the level of it was. Much has been written on the effects of immigration on culture (Appadurai 1996; Hall 1990; Hannerz 1992); however, this has often focused on music (or other cultural forms) that reinforce migrant or diasporic identities, particularly in a new locale. For example, Hebdige (1979) discusses Rastafarian culture in the UK, and Dudrah (2002) focuses on British Bhangra.

Little research focuses on migrants who *don't* participate in cultural forms related to their heritage. However, a few exceptions show that this is a crucial area for further research. Miller (2010) studied migrants' adoption of blue jeans as a 'post-identity' expression of ordinariness rather than a staking out of their difference. Hall (1990) noted that cultural identity is rooted in past, present *and* future. Shared cultural roots may form one aspect of cultural identity (in the case of his study, that of the black diaspora), but crucial intersections with new positions and future possibilities place these migrant identities as open to change. Hall and Miller offer the opportunity to understand migrants' cultural identity as in flux and thereby open up the possibility of the adoption or adaptation of new cultural markers—or non-markers—after resettling. Migrants need not participate in cultural forms related to their heritage in order to bring new cultural understandings to bear on their new social worlds.

In further unpicking the role of migration and other forms of movement, it is crucial to understand the importance of the individual and their body to cultural formation. "To be located, culture also has to be *embodied*" (Casey 1996: 34). Culture is thus located as inextricably linked to the body. We therefore need to interrogate how these bodies move and carry culture between locations, shaping those locations as they enter them. An individual who was involved in punk in one country and relocates will bring with them alternative understandings of what punk can be, shifting and broadening the possibilities for punk intersubjectively with their new punk contacts. Moreover, if the individual in question retains links and relationships with those still residing in their former locations, that cultural flow may move in more than one direction (Lohman 2013). This section will uncover how processes of international and national resettlement have affected the Dutch punk scene.

Within the Netherlands

One of the most common reasons for resettlement amongst participants was in order to study. Discussion of this was especially prevalent amongst those participants who were in their mid-to-late twenties. The majority of participants of this age group had either been to—or were currently studying at—university. This reserves this form of mobility for those who tend to be from a more privileged background. For most this involved moving to their chosen university city. Indeed, many of the key locations for this research were also university towns. Andre discussed the impact of the university on Nijmegen's punk scene: "one way or another, because there is a university, lots of young people come here and that's good for a scene and a reason that people remain settled here" (Andre).

The importance of the punk scene in their university town was mentioned by a few of the research participants. Some, as Andre predicts, get involved and remain in the city for the scene. For others it is the scene itself that affects university choice.

Lisa had applied for her PhD study in three cities, but said, "I *did* think beforehand, 'Nijmegen, that has a lot of cool punk bands', and also because Nijmegen is politically far left I thought, 'that's surely a town where I will feel at home'" (Lisa). This was even more of an important factor in Lotte's decision; "I really came to Groningen for the music scene, for the *city*. Twenty years ago [...] I really wanted to study journalism but you couldn't [study that] in Groningen. But I really wanted to go to Groningen so I came to university here and studied Dutch language and linguistics [instead]" (Lotte). Andre, after studying in Maastricht, moved to Nijmegen due to band commitments. Basing these choices on punk highlights the commitment on the part of the participant to the scene, contributing to their authenticity, according to the markers developed by Widdicombe and Wooffitt (1990) (see Chap. 2). These decisions would impact the scene due to the new relationships and connections that would be created after each resettlement.

Those participants who were or had been part of the squatting scene were also particularly mobile. Squatting comes with a low level of housing security; even when squatting was legal in the Netherlands squats often had a short life span. The more permanent squats had revolving doors in terms of residents. As a result of this instability, squatters would relocate regularly. Whilst this was often within the same city, a lack of ties rooted in their choice to squat afforded individuals many more opportunities to relocate nationally or internationally. Luka, Wouter and Sander have lived in squats across the Netherlands. Marieke talks of the ease of moving to Amsterdam when she was already connected to the squat scene in Arnhem: "I just [hitchhiked] to the biggest squat in Amsterdam [...] and asked 'have you got room?' Haha! I knew people indirectly; someone had said 'well if you ask if so-and-so is at home then it'll be okay'" (Marieke). Similarly to Lotte, as previously shown, Marieke was able to rely on an extended friendship network of squatters and punks.

For Johan and Mark, their experiences of living abroad were tied up with their positions in the squat scenes. Johan had spent most of his adult life moving between squats, both throughout the Netherlands and beyond. Initially he was involved in the hippy counterculture before becoming a 'freak' in the 1970s. Just before discovering punk he was living in an artists' commune in Italy, keeping in contact with the Dutch cultural world via radio, newspapers and books. Mark also spent most of his life moving between squats, within the Netherlands, across Europe and also in the United States. In the early 1990s he spent two and a half years living in New York. During this time he was able to form many new connections, keen to learn from other participants how squatting and punk were differently interpreted in different places. "[It's always intrigued me that] all these things happen but they're all slightly different and people go about them differently. The codes in punk rock were slightly different [in different places]—and the aesthetics. In some places it's perfectly fine for the goths to hang out with the punks and in other cities that's unthinkable" (Mark). Punk had emerged differently within these different communication interlocks. However, in being mobile and able to resettle, these punks are able to forge embodied (Casey 1996) connections between scenes, becoming an added node through which intersubjective subcultural understandings emerge. They influence the cultural contexts in each new location they go to as new experiences interact with the old.

International Resettlement

The ease of migration within the European Union, as well as welcoming immigration policies for much of the twentieth century, meant that a number of participants had experiences of living in other countries for extended periods of time. Some, such as Johan and Mark, were Dutch citizens living abroad; others moved to the Netherlands. Each of these participants have had their experience and understanding of (punk) culture altered by these new influences, bringing new dimensions to their participation in the Netherlands.

For a couple of participants, the opportunity to live abroad was as part of their university studies. Lisa resided in Ghent, Belgium for 6 months, marking the occasion by organising her first punk gig as a leaving party. Daan talks about his study trip to Russia in 1991–1992 in terms of the way in which he felt his straight edge identity and politics were challenged (Lohman 2013). He returned home and told his bandmate (of the straight edge, communist band, Man Lifting Banner) that "straight edge is dead". Daan felt that such identity politics were fruitless in the face of real poverty and need in the former Soviet Union. Thus the shape of punk in the Netherlands was subtly altered by Daan's experience abroad.

Lotte's experience of living abroad came through her involvement in punk. After booking a tour for English punk band The X-Rays, she fell in love and began a relationship with a member of the band, moving to Nottingham as a result. During this time she got involved in the UK punk scene and solidified some of the links between Groningen and the UK.

Lisa, Daan, Lotte, Johan and Mark all talk of their time living abroad as having important influences on their lives. By reconnecting with the scene in the Netherlands on their return, these international influences permeate the Dutch scene.

There are also examples of individuals who have relocated *to* the Netherlands whose life trajectories have influenced their punk partici-pation. As highlighted earlier, much has been written on the effects of immigration on culture, but little attention has been focused on subcul-tural participation.

Maxim's formative experiences were in Russia, but he moved at the age of 13 and his teenage years were spent in Amsterdam. He attended a school for the children of migrants from all over the world to learn Dutch, and it was through this international group of friends that Maxim first discovered punk. As a group they became involved with the local Amsterdam scene.

Luka moved to Amsterdam during the break-up of Yugoslavia. He was 19 when he moved and had first discovered and become involved with punk seven years earlier in his home town of Belgrade. Thus, when he became involved in Dutch punk, he was drawing on years of expe-rience in participating, organising gigs and making zines. He talks of being disappointed to discover that when he first moved to Amsterdam there was relatively little going on compared both to Belgrade and to his expectations.

I kind of thought "oo Amsterdam, BGK and all those old bands were from here and with all the squats it must be like a lot of things happen-ing, a lot of shows, a lot of people going on in this music". When I moved here there was like nothing going on, there was a few people doing a few things, a few people from the older generations you know. Very few younger kids. (Luka)

However, within a few years he was part of a young and highly active punk scene in Amsterdam. Vitamin X, the band he formed with Maxim, has become one of the Netherlands' foremost straight edge hardcore bands.

Kosta, like Luka, was a little older when he left Serbia in 1991. He had been involved in punk in Serbia for twelve years before he left for a short stay in Berlin, followed by ten years in Groningen. He had been in Amsterdam for almost ten years again when this research was conducted. He also described encountering very different forms of punk upon moving to the Netherlands. The scene in Serbia in the 1980s was characterized by a wider state Socialist context in which openly displaying a 'punk identity' (or indeed any subcultural affiliation) carried with it a heightened risk that was not part of the Western punk scene. The threat of trouble with the authorities required a greater dedication on the part of those who were involved.

Nico first got involved with punk in Portugal. He moved to the Netherlands at the age of twenty-eight, ten years prior to the interview. He continues to apply a punk ethic to every aspect of his life (see Chap. 6).

For these participants, punk played a significant role in helping them integrate into their new community. For Maxim it was through his identity as a migrant learning the local language that he discovered punk and through punk that he got to know others with similar experiences, along with many others of all backgrounds. For Luka, Kosta and Nico, punk formed a constant in a time of upheaval, although all talk of marked differences between their experiences of punk in their countries of origin and their experiences of punk in the Netherlands. Having already acquired knowledge of 'how to be a punk', and therefore already possessing subcultural capital, they were quickly accepted into new social groups. These participants all became involved in the Dutch punk scene, bringing to it their own understanding of what punk is. This illustrates Deleuze and Guattari's ([1987] 2003) argument that cultural rhizomes allow for individually specific iterations of punk whilst drawing on a common 'root structure'.

The continued contact that participants maintained with people who remained in Russia, Serbia and Portugal adds yet another level of cultural connectedness. These contacts enabled Vitamin X's tours in Russia. Meanwhile, Kosta now regularly organises cultural exchanges between Serbia and the Netherlands, and has used his connections to promote transnational music and art events for the Anti War Action Foundation for Former Yugoslavia.

CONCLUSION

This chapter has argued for a more nuanced understanding of the ways in which cultural influence may 'flow' in a subculture such as punk. By drawing both on Hannerz's (1992) understanding of a centre/periphery and Deleuze and Guattari's ([1987] 2003) 'rhizome' model we are able to gain a better understanding of the complexity by which cultural practices are intersubjectively shared, whilst maintaining a view of the inherent inequality of the system.

The Dutch punk scene is situated as part of a global subculture in which mobility, connections and relationships are important to the communication and spread of punk ideas and influences. Mobility has been discussed in various formats, from the day-to-day movements of participants for scene interactions to the more exceptional experiences of touring to practices of resettlement. It has argued that the mobility of participants is a particular characteristic of the Dutch punk scene due to its geographical position and that historical connections developed through squatting as well as punk networks have further aided this mobility. All elements of mobility have been investigated in terms of the structures that allow or constrain them as well as the impacts that movement has on the Dutch punk scene.

The chapter also investigated how this mobility works to shape participants' understanding of the space that is 'their' punk scene: whether that is a porous, nationally connected core scene or a local, northern peripheral scene. It has further placed the Dutch scene as a whole in a 'central', privileged position in comparison to southern and eastern European countries. However, it maintains that whilst centre-peripheral relationships are inherently unequal and power imbalances are consistently reinforced, these are far from one-way relationships and that culture may also flow from periphery to core.

NOTES

1. Particularly women, queer people and people of colour.
2. Hodkinson (2002) does not discuss international travel, although he does mention British goth nights that are popular with visitors from abroad.

128   K. LOHMAN

3. For a discussion of Northern peripherality affecting locality in punk, see Pilkington (2014b) in relation to punks in Vorkuta, Russia.
4. That is, 130 km from Groningen to Oldenburg, compared to 180 km between Groningen and Amsterdam.

REFERENCES

Appadurai, A. 1996. *Modernity at Large: Cultural Dimensions of Globalization.* Minneapolis: University of Minnesota Press.
Bennett, A., and R.A. Peterson. 2004. *Music Scenes: Local, Translocal and Virtual.* Nashville: Vanderbilt University Press.
Casey, E.S. 1996. How to get from Space to Place in a Fairly Short Stretch of Time. In *Senses of Place*, ed. S. Feld and K.H. Basso, 13–52. Santa Fe, New Mexico: School of American Research Press.
Cohen, S. 2007. *Decline, Renewal and the City in Popular Music Culture: Beyond the Beatles.* Aldershot: Ashgate.
Crossley, N. 2008. Pretty Connected: The Social Network of the Early UK Punk Movement. *Theory, Culture & Society* 25 (6): 89–116.
Crossley, N. 2009. The Man Whose Web Expanded: Network Dynamics in Manchester's Post/Punk Music Scene 1976–1980. *Poetics* 37 (1): 24–49.
Deleuze, G., and F. Guattari. [1987] 2003. *A Thousand Plateaus: Capitalism and Schizophrenia.* London: Continuum.
Dudrah, R.K. 2002. Drum'n'dhol 1 British Bhangra Music and Diasporic South Asian Identity Formation. *European Journal of Cultural Studies* 5 (3): 363–383.
Hall, S. 1990. Cultural Identity and Diaspora. In *Identity: Community, Culture, Difference*, ed. J. Rutherford, 222–237. London: Lawrence & Wishart.
Hannerz, U. 1992. *Cultural Complexity: Studies in the Social Organization of Meaning.* New York: Columbia University Press.
Hebdige, D. 1979. *Subculture: The Meaning of Style.* London: Routledge.
Hodkinson, P. 2002. *Goth: Identity, Style and Subculture.* Oxford: Berg.
Hodkinson, P. 2004. Translocal Connections in the Goth Scene. In *Music Scenes: Local, Translocal and Virtual*, ed. A. Bennett and R.A. Peterson, 131–148. Nashville: Vanderbilt University Press.
Hollows, J., and K. Milestone. 1998. Welcome to Dreamsville: A History and Geography of Northern Soul. In *The Place of Music*, ed. A. Leyshon, D. Matless, and G. Revill, 83–103. New York: The Guildford Press.
Kennedy, P. 2010. *Local Lives and Global Transformations: Towards World Society.* Basingstoke: Palgrave Macmillan.
Lashua, B., K. Spracklen, and S. Wagg. 2014. *Sounds and the City: Popular Music, Place, and Globalization.* Basingstoke: Palgrave Macmillan.
Lohman, K. 2013. Dutch Punk with Eastern Connections: Mapping Cultural Flows Between East and West Europe. *Punk & Post Punk* 2 (2): 147–163.

Massey, D. 1993. Power-geometry and a Progressive Sense of Place. In *Mapping the Futures: Local Cultures, Global Change*, ed. J. Bird, B. Curtis, T. Putnam, G. Robertson, and L. Tickner, 59–69. London: Routledge.

Miller, D. 2010. Anthropology in Blue Jeans. *American Ethnologist* 37 (3): 415–428.

Mitchell, T. 1998. *Australian Hip Hop as 'Glocal' Subculture.* Available from http://www.snarl.org/youth/tonym2.pdf. [14/05/2015].

Namaste, V. 2000. *Invisible Lives: The Erasure of Transsexual and Transgendered People.* Chicago: University of Chicago Press.

O'Connor, A. 2004. Punk and Globalization: Spain and Mexico. *International Journal of Cultural Studies* 7 (2): 175–195.

O'Hara, C. 1999. *The Philosophy of Punk: More Than Noise!* Edinburgh: AK Press.

Pilkington, H. 2004. Youth Strategies for Glocal Living: Space, Power and Communication in Everyday Cultural Practice. In *After Subculture: Critical Studies in Contemporary Youth Culture*, ed. A. Bennett and K. Kahn-Harris, 119–134. Basingstoke: Palgrave Macmillan.

Pilkington, H. 2014a. Punk, But Not As We Know It: Rethinking Punk from a Post-socialist Perspective. In *Punk in Russia: Cultural Mutation from the 'Useless' to the 'Moronic'*, ed. I. Gololobov, H. Pilkington, and Y.B. Steinholt, 1–21. London: Routledge.

Pilkington, H. 2014b. Sounds of a "Rotting City": Punk in Russia's Arctic Hinterland. In *Sounds and the City: Popular Music, Place, and Globalization*, ed. B. Lashua, K. Spracklen, and S. Wagg. Basingstoke: Palgrave Macmillan.

Pilkington, H., I. Gololobov, and Y.B. Steinholt. 2014. Conclusion. In *Punk in Russia: Cultural Mutation from the 'Useless' to the 'Moronic'*, ed. I. Gololobov, H. Pilkington, and Y.B. Steinholt, 196–211. London: Routledge.

Pries, L. 2005. Configurations of Geographic and Societal Spaces: A Sociological Proposal Between 'Methodological Nationalism' and the 'Spaces of Flows'. *Global Networks* 5 (2): 167–190.

Sabin, R. 1999. Introduction. In *Punk Rock: So What? The Cultural Legacy of Punk*, ed. R. Sabin, 1–13. London: Routledge.

Shields, R. 1991. *Places on the Margin: Alternative Geographies of Modernity.* London: Routledge.

Siegel, M., and C. De Neubourg. 2011. A Historical Perspective on Immigration and Social Protection in the Netherlands. *UNU-MERIT Working Paper 2011–2014.* Available from http://papers.ssrn.com/sol3/papers.cfm?abstract_id=1949683. [13/06/2013].

Thompson, S. 2004. *Punk Productions: Unfinished Business.* Albany: State University of New York Press.

Ventsel, A. 2008. Punx and Skins United: One Law for Us One Law for Them. *The Journal of Legal Pluralism and Unofficial Law* 40 (57): 45–100.

Webb, P. 2007. *Exploring the Networked Worlds of Popular Music: Milieu Cultures*. New York: Routledge.

Widdicombe, S., and R. Wooffitt. 1990. "Being" Versus "Doing" Punk: On Achieving Authenticity as a Member. *Journal of Language and Social Psychology* 9 (4): 257–277.

CHAPTER 5

Punk Is...

Two questions were posed to nearly every participant in this research project: 'what is punk?' and 'are you a punk?' Whilst it may seem paradoxical that an individual involved in the Dutch punk scene might have difficulty with either of those questions, many did.

Punks, and those writing about punk, have always struggled with defining what punk is, perhaps more so than defining what it is not. Countless zines have debated it, and academics continue to suggest new conceptualisations. This chapter seeks not to define punk, per se, but to provide an overview of the myriad of ways in which punks themselves understand what punk may be. In doing so it will suggest that punk is not *one thing* that can easily be defined but is far more nebulous; definitions of punk shift over time, space, between scenes, and, crucially, between individuals. The attempt to impose a finite definition of punk is therefore in itself problematic.

This chapter will set out by providing an overview of the ways in which academic research on punk has grappled with understanding its own boundaries before grouping punks' own understandings into five categories: punk as music, the social position of punk, punk as social practice, punk as an ideology, and punk as individual practice. 'Punk is music' is the least contentious of punks' claims, although issues of what punk music *is* and whether punk is more than music provoke more debate. Some punks attempted to understand what punk might be by trying to locate their place within—or outside of—wider society; in doing so they set out their perspective on the 'subculture debate'

© The Author(s) 2017
K. Lohman, *The Connected Lives of Dutch Punks*,
Palgrave Studies in the History of Subcultures and Popular Music,
DOI 10.1007/978-3-319-51079-8_5

(Chap. 2). The final three sections contain other definitions of punk, punk as a set of social practices including partying and fighting, punk as an ideology including, for example, anarchism, or punk as an individual practice in which punks seek to set themselves out as 'different'. All have precedence within punk literature.

AVOIDING THE QUESTION

Before I was able to elicit an answer to the question 'what is punk?' most participants would attempt to evade it. Many of them found this a challenging question and expressed their frustration to me, perhaps in order to give themselves time to think: "that's an awkward question" (Tom), "that's definitely not a clear-cut matter" (Lotte). Others tried to sidestep the question: "umm ... you could write a whole essay on that!" (Andre). Whilst these Dutch punks were happy to talk *around* the subject of punk, *defining* it was another matter.

Participants certainly alluded to the nebulousness of punk: "punk? I find it difficult to put my finger on what that exactly is" (Jeroen). Many suggested that there was no *one* definition of punk; it was entirely possible that each individual would have their own ideas of what punk is. "It is something different for everyone, but, well, I don't know" (Andre). Furthermore it was accepted that punk need not have a set of rules that should be applicable to all: the multiplicity of punk possibilities is *part* of punk. Theo said there are "different scenes, all different groups, all different views on what punk really is. I don't think there's a definition of punk possible anyways!"(Theo). Mark suggested that this posed problems when punks with different ideas try to communicate or work together. When he went to New York he found that "all the details didn't mean the same things, people didn't go about it in the same way, and there was endless confusion, talking using the same words but feeling that the [meanings] don't connect" (Mark). Different locales further contribute to the multiplicity of punk.

For some, their own personal definitions had shifted over time. Bram answered the question with: "I don't know. You know, with punk rock I always—over the years—I had a lot of different definitions for it" (Bram). Mark said that whilst perhaps he could once have defined punk, "[now,] I dunno anymore" (Mark). As a younger punk he had more precise views of what did and did not count as punk, but now that was far more open.

Whilst, on the one hand, avoiding the question was a deflection practice to give respondents time to come up with an answer, on the other hand, it fitted into wider punk practices. Resisting being defined is a part of punk traditions, as punks attempt to set themselves apart from wider society and from one another (Steinholt 2012).

EXISTING DEFINITIONS OF PUNK

Punk has evolved, mutated, fragmented and shifted over the last four decades. Meanwhile, academic interest in subcultural activities has remained strong. Successive generations of academics continue to search for a workable definition with which to demarcate their field of study. In a similar way, the shifting nature of punk has meant that the academy has struggled to pin down what it *is*. Moreover, certain academic discourses (e.g., the predominance of work addressing the early punk scene) have persisted, affecting the way in which punk continues to be understood today.

This section will serve as a brief reminder of the development of the field of 'punk studies' first outlined in Chap. 2, highlighting how academic definitions of punk have changed in an attempt to keep up with the practices and understandings of punks themselves.

Academic work focused on punk can be divided into (at the very least) two main 'waves'. The first, spearheaded by Hebdige (1979), focused particularly on the stylistic practices of punks. This was based on a semiotic analysis of punk's clothing and attitude, a method also followed by Laing (1985). These two works took punk to mean the subculture based around London in the mid-1970s, encapsulated particularly by the Sex Pistols and The Clash. Three further important texts followed that maintained the focus on early UK punk, and in particular on the Sex Pistols' art school avant-garde lineage; Marcus (1989), Nehring (1993) and Savage (1991).

A second 'wave' was focused more on punk practices and tended towards ethnographic methods. These studies recognise punk in a variety of locations and guises and often search to understand what binds the many different forms that punk has taken. Within this group were those who presented punk as bound by an ideology (Clark 2003; O'Hara 1999), often focusing particularly on how this manifested itself in DIY and anti-capitalist or anti-corporate economic practices (Dale 2012; Gosling 2004; Moore 2004, 2010; O'Connor 2008; Thompson 2004).

Other researchers focused on the social practices of punk (Gololobov et al. 2014; Haenfler 2006; Leblanc 1999; O'Connor 2002, 2003, 2004; Wallach 2008).

There has also been some work on the idea of punk as an identity category (Widdicombe and Wooffitt, 1990), a discourse that will be developed throughout this chapter. There is a tension between viewing punk as a set of social practices and punk in terms of an individual identity. However, as will be demonstrated in this chapter, often when punks talk about identity formation, they draw on (group) markers by which differentiation from (mainstream) society is sought (Shank 1994). Through finding 'their' group they are able to express the difference they feel from 'others' (Haenfler 2006; Leblanc 1999; Williams 2011).

We see there has been a plethora of understandings of what punk might *be*: art, identity, ideology, cultural or social practice. We turn now to how participants of Dutch punk themselves attach meaning to 'punk'.

PUNK IS MUSIC

When attempting to articulate their own definition of punk, many participants started with the music: "punk is a musical genre" (Sander). Nico defined punk in terms of his own connection to it: punk is "my [...] favourite music" (Nico). For a few participants the music was the key to punk: "it's primarily the music" (Lotte). Music was prioritised as either the only or the most important element for defining punk. For Larry punk is "just music and having fun" (Larry), and for Ruben "punk is just a genre—just a music genre" (Ruben). Whilst most participants would have disagreed with Ruben, bringing in many other strands of what punk could 'be', the foregrounding of music justifies a discussion of how participants understand it and why they attach so much meaning to it.

Participants used a variety of adjectives in their attempts to explain what made punk, punk. "Hard", "loud", "heavy", "fast", all featured prominently. As did "angry", "violent" and "aggressive", although Andre wished to problematize the 'aggression' in punk: "I find 'aggression' such a negative word, I think 'energy' sounds better. At least, it sounds a bit more positive" (Andre). Others agreed that 'energy' was the key to the music; "in hardcore it's all about raw energy" (Sem).

Other adjectives highlight that there is a great deal of variation within punk; Sander thinks of punk as "just really catchy" (Sander), and Daan defends the "poppy" Descendents' right to be seen as punk: "if someone says to me that Descendents aren't a punk or hardcore band then I think 'you've got a screw loose'" (Daan).

Gregor, amongst others, points out the degree to which punk acts as an umbrella term for many types of music: "in punk there are of course a lot of sub-genres [...] like alongside punk you also have hardcore, beat-down, mosh, power violence, you've got a lot of these categories and yet more that emerge" (Gregor). Contemporaneous to this research, "in Amsterdam you've got the 'embryo punks', the 'baby punks', the 'beer punks', the 'political punks', etcetera etcetera" (Marieke). Certainly in the case of the specifically Dutch 'embryo' and 'baby' groups this tendency towards creating further subgenres can be read both as an attempt to differentiate themselves from others in a search for identity (Shank 1994) and as an 'evasion' of the predetermined categories that carry with them ideals to live up to (Steinholt 2012).

Gregor stresses, however, that punk should not be distilled down to its subgenres; there is an element that holds them together as punk: "in any case I think it shouldn't just be [viewed as] the sub-genres" (Gregor). Jacob suggests that; "as far as I'm concerned punk is just really direct, energetic music and it can be that in all kinds of ways, I mean it can stretch from super-fast to really trashy, or whatever" (Jacob). Both Gregor and Jacob therefore search for a *musical* quality that binds the subgenres of punk.

A few participants are drawn to the 'simplicity' of punk, both to listen to and to play. Ruben's first band started off playing punk after discovering that metal was too difficult. Sander thinks it is "pure genius in its simplicity, that you can play just three notes and find it's very catchy" (Sander).

The difference between punk and mainstream music is another attraction for many. "It was simply completely different from what we heard on radio. And I thought that was really cool" (Lotte). Again, we see evidence of punks differentiating themselves from the 'other'. This theme will be developed throughout this chapter.

Some participants expressed some rather more individual reasons for their liking of punk *music*. For Lotte punk music has a particular quality to it that she describes as 'sexy'. "I find the music [...] simply incredibly sexy music, [...] in particular garage-punk" (Lotte). For Andre the music—particularly because he discovered it through skateboarding—gave him an adrenaline rush that he likened to taking drugs.

Yes, drugs immediately sounds so heavy, I know, [but] if there was some cool music on, it always made me 'go' easier when skating. And that stimulated me to listen [to punk] and [even] if you weren't skating, then listening to the music then you [still] got this energy. [...] I don't know if that is a Pavlov reflex but [...] yes when I cycled to school I put it on as well and that then worked as well and when I walked through the school I also had it on. (Andre)

However, whilst there was all this emphasis on the music from the majority of respondents, there was also a general consensus that the music was just one facet of punk. For Jeroen, the importance of the music was due to its position as a 'gateway' to the rest of what constitutes punk, with which "you engage, of course, through the music" (Jeroen).

SOCIAL POSITION OF PUNKS

As discussed in Chap. 2, academic discourses about punk have dealt with the position of punks in relation to wider society by terming punk a *sub-culture*. These discussions are (in some cases) based on the social practices of those involved with punk but don't necessarily take into account the way in which those involved would position themselves in relation to wider society (Hebdige 1979, in particular). Whilst the 'subculture debate' may seem firmly rooted in academia and a world away from punk lives, there *is* some discussion of these issues amongst punks themselves.

A number of punks made references to whether or not their understanding of punk fitted within notions of what a subculture may be. For some, punk is definitely a subculture: "I like the idea of creating a subculture within the bigger culture that we live in and [in] creating a place for your own" (Jasper). In this understanding subculture is not a lesser entity but instead a smaller group within the rest of society. This can be compared to the CCCS's conceptualisation of subculture (Clarke et al. [1975] 2006); Jasper's description of punk as a means to 'create' a space can be read as resistant to normative cultural practices (see Chaps. 2, 6). However, there is disagreement over the structural position of subculture. Jasper claims that punk is equal but separate from wider culture whereas the CCCS would position subculture as subordinate to 'parent' culture.

Jasper's reading of subculture is also reflected in Bram's comment on the solidarity between different groups in order to support alternative spaces. "It's also because the subcultures are getting smaller so it mixes a bit more. You can't run a pub with just 10 fucking metalheads showing up, you know, you need to get all the other people in as well!" (Bram). Henk suggests that punks' fragmented subgenres form further, yet smaller, subcultures in themselves: "it's very tunnelled, you know all the little subcultures have their own little subcultures" (Henk). Again, this tendency towards fragmentation both from society and within a subculture itself can be read as a need for differentiation from others (Shank 1994). The smaller numbers of punks has led to greater connectedness with other subcultural groups.

Some participants have a more critical understanding of what denotes subculture and how this may—or may not—be part of what punk *is*. For Jaap, Tom, Henk and Menno, 'subcultures' are fashionable trends based around consumer-driven and normative social practices. This reading of subculture relies heavily on early understandings of punk based around stylistic practices (Hebdige 1979).

Punk may now have become 'possible' without 'style'; however, punks may still slip into the 'error' of feeling that they must dress and act in certain ways in order to be read as punk. Henk criticises contemporary young punks for wearing expensive skate clothing. For him, punk clothing is more about DIY practices: "[d]on't make other people rich by buying your subculture elsewhere, just make [it] yourself. Make your own stuff. Listen to music that you can make yourself. Don't idolise musicians cos they're not worth it!" (Henk). Jaap further develops this critique of 'fashionable' punk bands by discussing Café Vera's booking policy as in opposition to this: "the idea we had as a club is [that] we should go for good music and not for *subculture* or something" (Jaap, emphasis added). For Menno a punk 'subculture' was an oxymoron.

> At that time [(the late 1970s)] beautiful things developed without people realising it and at some point people become aware and then it turns into a sort of subculture and that really is something else I think. Then it is some kind of folklore, where people just do certain things, in the weekend they go to a gig, they adopt a certain look and say certain things and then it is really all cast in stone and that I really didn't find that interesting anymore. (Menno)

Henk explained his thoughts on subculture by discussing differing class structures between the Netherlands and the United Kingdom. For him, the theorising of punk as a subculture was distinctly linked to early UK punk's origins in working class (sub)cultures. In this understanding he mirrors the way in which Hebdige (1979) discussed early punk.[1] For Henk, the lack of a British-style class structure in the Netherlands negates the possibility of Dutch punk to be understood as a subculture:

> In England you had all these subcultures. No, in Holland [...] you know it wasn't really a subculture, not something that they considered a subculture. [...] I think because for one [thing] we didn't have much of a working class in Holland, we didn't even—we still don't—have the class system like you have in England so you, no sense in projecting that on[to] subculture in Holland. (Henk)

Other participants also discussed the way in which they conceptualised punk's position in relation to wider society. Bram and Menno both saw themselves as explicitly *not* part of general social structures and this was, for them, inherently part of punk. Whereas Menno, previously quoted, describes punk as ending when it became 'subcultural' (fashionable), punk did exist when it was a '*tegencultur*'; an 'anti-culture'. Punk is, in this conceptualisation, not a subgroup of wider society as Jasper proposed but set in opposition to wider society. For Bram this is integral to his punk identity and has real everyday implications for him. Bram is a punk *because* he is outside of societal and cultural norms.

> I kind of tried [... to] find like a job and [to] fill in my tax forms and stuff and I just found out I was completely clueless. I did not know how to do any of that. I fucking like [went] straight from living with my parents [...] into the punk scene, [and was] already at that time touring with bands, [I] never fucking had a job, [I] never had to do any official shit, you know? [I] lived completely more or less outside of society. [And] so at some point you try to get a little bit back into that, out of necessity, because the rules have gotten a lot stricter than they used to be. And you find out that you're absolutely clueless, you don't know how to handle yourself in that [world] at all, you know? You've been so used to being outside the whole fucking system and it's still like that so that's why I would say I'm still a punk, I'm always going to be a punk! I just find it way too hard to cope in the real world! (Bram).

These discourses of oppositionality and outsider status are found more widely amongst the participants in this research. For Lotte this approach to punk is based on maintaining her (and other punks') individual identity. A main requirement of being punk is "you shouldn't conform too much, that is important as well, that you can keep on doing your own thing" (Lotte). This discourse of individuality within punk will be further examined later in this chapter.

For Luka and Kosta punk was necessarily confrontational towards wider society in the manner of its opposition to normative cultural trends. "[I]t was a little bit of a provocative thing" (Luka). For Kosta this was specific to his upbringing in communist Serbia.

Kosta: my father was a communist and when I went to play with my band, he knew the lyrics and he was praying to god that I would come back home alive.

Kirsty: So it was dangerous?

Kosta: it was very dangerous.

Kirsty: ...fights?

Kosta: No, no it was the lyrics because you're singing against the government, against the cops. Because in a communist country, it was a risky business because they can arrest you, they can arrest your family, you're putting yourself how you say, in a very dangerous position. But we loved it—dreadful!

As we see, Dutch punks critically engage with ideas surrounding subcultural identity and their own place in relation to wider society; they variously position themselves as embedded within wider society, or as outside it. On the face of it this might seem to pose a challenge to conceptualisations of such individuals being embedded in communication interlocks that include wider society. However, we see that even Bram—who understands himself as completely *outside* of wider society—does so by positioning himself in relation to it. Based on his understanding of—and communications with—*others* his sense of himself as an outsider is intersubjectively created through negotiation and shared assumptions with the 'other', as much as with the 'punks' and/or others he identifies *with*.

Punk as Social Practices

For many, an important aspect of punk was its sociability. Meeting other punks, playing music together, going to gigs, having political discussions, and hanging about with other punks were all key punk practices. This section will discuss social activities that participants discussed (this is of course not exhaustive of punk in more general terms) as being an important part of punk or as constituting punk in itself. I will then go on to discuss how punk is organised socially and how this shapes what punk might be.

Many participants talked not just about their punk social activities but also in terms of how these intersect with their definitions of punk. Punk *is*, for some, about having fun; partying, drinking, and so on. It is "about having lots of fun and making fucking loads of noise with your mates" (Bram). Mark discusses punk as having a "sort of party element" (Mark). And for Marieke, it is this element of punk that she applies to herself: "you party hard, and, well, a lot of booze as well, and drugs and that sort of thing" (Marieke). Jan describes how his punk record shop became more a place where people came for the social aspect than to buy records. "[A]t one point it just became a social centre, people just came to drink beer" (Jan).

However, as we saw in Chap. 3, this partying aspect of punk was not welcomed by all. Some participants felt it made the scene less welcoming and that it was a contributing factor to the fragmentation of punk. "Plus that it always involves a lot of alcohol [...] and the next day I have another hangover and that, well, let's say I don't want that" (Wouter). So whilst for some punk is defined by partying and hedonism, for others it is not. "It hasn't got to do with either drink or drugs [...] as far as I'm concerned" (Lotte).

Beyond partying, participants mention other social activities that they understood as being part of punk. As discussed extensively in Chap. 3, the Dutch punk scene's proximity to the squatting scene is key to the development and nature of punk in the Netherlands. Whilst not interchangeable, it is important to consider the social nature of squatting practices in discussions of punk social practices. "To me the old punk rock mentality and the DIY squatting mentality were very similar and so to me growing up, those two together seemed really natural" (Mark). The highly organised social side of squatting (weekly '*kraakspreekuur*',[2] VoKus and squatters bars or cafés that were open daily) all form meeting places for punks and squatters alike; squatting as a sociable activity has helped shape and define punk in the Netherlands (Uitermark 2004, see also Chap. 3).

Punk has a long history of violence, most notably in terms of fighting practices between punks and other subcultural groups. In the Dutch scene this seems largely historical, with many older punks recounting fighting stories from, especially, the 1980s and 1990s, whereas few of the younger punks had similar tales. Punks' rivals in the Netherlands have included: 'farm kids', *gabba*[3] fans, football hooligans, skinheads and 'discos'. Dutch punks position themselves as always under attack and never the aggressor, similar to some of the Russian punks discussed by Steinholt et al. (2014) and Pilkington (2014a). Theo discussed the extra risks—of ending up in a canal—posed by fights in Amsterdam, and Jacob talked about fights with the Z-side group of football hooligans in Groningen (see Perasović 2012 for a discussion of the complex relationship between punk and football fans). These experiences could often help foster punk solidarity and strengthen the group's affectual bonds, as demonstrated by Bram:

> We'd be in the squat with like a hundred people waiting for them to show up, [and] they would, every fucking Friday and Saturday night. Like two [or] three hundred people would show up in front of the squats and try to fucking fight us you know? Throw rocks at us and whatever and yeah that [was] mainly kind of led by hooligans and skinheads but most of the kids were just drunken farm kids who went along for the fun you know, and we had to always fight them. And you get this weird kind of like Asterix and Obelix situations you know where basically you get a huge mob attacking the squat, and then all of a sudden the door of the squat opens and like fifty of us would come running out with fucking baseball bats and like motorcycle helmets on and homemade fucking shields made with traffic signs [...] that you [... modify with the] inner tube of a bicycle so you keep it in front of your face and just fucking go after them! And it was always like that here, you know. It was a bit of a rough life but in a good way cos also really cemented the scene. That's one [good] thing at that point cos you had a really clear common enemy. (Bram)

For Luka, fighting formed part of his experience of punk as an oppositional identity. Being a punk in Serbia resulted in a lot of bullying, fighting, and being kicked out of many schools. In punk he found a "group where [...] I could belong" (Luka). Being punk, being a target of violence, and having a group to fight back *with* are all tied up in many participants' experiences. In Dutch punks' fighting practices, solidarity seems to be attained through fighting side-by-side against other groups (similar to some Russian punks, Pilkington 2014a).

The importance of sociability in participants' discussions of punk experiences results both *in* and *from* the way that punk is organised. A number of participants discuss the existence of a 'punk network', which may operate on a local, national or global level (see Chap. 4). For Daan, punk *is* a "world-wide network". In this network punks are able to provide and share resources, knowledge and solidarity amongst themselves.

These networks shape the experiences of punk for many of those involved. Larry comments that punk *is* "the atmosphere within the audience, I always experienced it as the same—there is kind of a solidarity" (Larry). For Wouter the unity and solidarity of the local punk and squat network empowered him, personally and politically:

> The first time I squatted I was only fifteen [...]. It was a complete failure. I did it with a friend and we got [...] three days [of] solitary confinement. We were caught red-handed and we sort of let the police talk us out of it [(the squat)]. And I said to them like: "you know, dear policeman, *this* time you nick me", but I did promise that I'd come back with my fifty punk friends and just stir up a lot of shit. And the second time, that's what I did. I invited fifty punks from Rotterdam at the *kraakspreekuur* and then we set up a squat and that was unheard of in Vlaardingen. Such a dull, really Christian village, suddenly you've got fifty weirdos on the doorstep. So we were laughing our heads off, of course. [...] Let's say it gives you a sense of power, especially when you're fifteen, to manage to get such a crowd of people together when you organise something. (Wouter)

For Wim and Bram, global punk solidarity allowed them to travel more easily, using the connections and relationships discussed in Chaps. 3 and 4. Even in a strange city they knew they could ask directions from anyone who looked like a punk to the nearest pub or squat where they might be able to stay.

However, for Mark, the social practices of punk had their negatives. He found that, especially amongst younger punks, social practices bred a cliquey atmosphere of conformity. He felt that there were "more conservative restrictions of what is punk rock and what isn't and why" (Mark), and that the scene became dominated by "a bunch of drunken idiots who completely dictate the atmosphere for too long so other people don't want to go there anymore" (Mark). Punks' tendency to delineate between insiders and outsiders, as discussed earlier in this chapter, sometimes led to more rigid and even militant enforcing of conformity to punk; an issue also experienced in straight edge (Haenfler 2006).

Furthermore, complaints came from participants that punk was, and continued to be, male dominated. This was especially a problem in the 'social' sphere of punk: the drinking and fighting practices and the gig spaces. Larry and Luka both described punk as "a man's world" (Larry) and "a male dominated scene" (Luka). And Lisa, Lotte and Jolanda discussed how this impacted them as some of the few women in the scene. Lotte said that being marked out for her gender "feels *kut*"[4] and described how she's been termed as "not punk" because she's female. Lisa has had experiences of her—all female—band being mistaken for groupies when backstage at a gig. Jolanda gave up playing in all-female bands as she was sick of being treated differently from other bands. These experiences reinforce many of the difficulties that Leblanc (1999) terms a 'double-bind' for women in a subculture that is structurally coded as masculine (Fig. 5.1).

Fig. 5.1 "Yes, we *are* the band" (Lisa). Photo taken by author, 17 September 2010

PUNK AS AN IDEOLOGY

A significant strand of research into punk has focused on defining punk in terms of a guiding or binding ideology. Many Dutch punks would agree, it seems. The discourse of punk *being* an ideology or a set of moral or political rules was prevalent amongst participants in this research. However, opinions on what punk ideology could be varied greatly. Most agreed that politics have a definite role within punk, but there was variation on how important the relationship was; some argued that it could not be punk without politics, others said that punk was simply a gateway to politics, whilst yet more believed that was separate from politics. Various specific ideological positions were also displayed in relation to punk practices (i.e., DIY approaches) or ideals (e.g., anarchism). Whilst Chap. 6 will discuss the prevalence of politics in many punks' lives, this section will focus on how politics is part of punk itself.

For many participants a hugely important aspect of punk was the political opportunity it afforded them. When asked about punk, Daan often steered the conversation to politics. Bram commented that: "when I first got into punk rock, I really just thought it was just about the politics you know" (Bram). And for Andre being punk is being inherently political: "[y]ou view things critically, I think that is a bit of a punk attitude, sort of, that you're critical towards your surroundings and what happens and not just accept things from others, take things for granted. [...] I think that is the most comprehensive summary of being punk" (Andre).

However, for most respondents, politics was simply one of many aspects of punk. Indeed, Andre immediately goes on to say: "for me it's [politics], [but] for others it just means getting hammered at the weekend and not to have to think too much about work or something. But that's not how *I* define it or [...] how *I* imagine punk to be" (Andre). Others such as Marieke talk of the "political *side*" of punk. Larry says that whilst it is political for him, punk "doesn't have to be [political]" (Larry). Opinions on how *far* punk and politics are related vary.

Wouter recognises that there are apolitical punks and criticises this as a modern trend in punk. He believes that punk has become less political and even those who *do* wish to effect change might get lost in a movement that no longer prioritises political action. "What I *do* think is a fact is that punk has become very apolitical. Yes. And that has always bothered me enormously in punk, [...] or at least after a few years it really bothered me enormously. That actually they talk an enormous amount but in the end do very little, and parties are more important than [...] say, *doing* things" (Wouter). For Wouter punk should be about more than political posturing.

However, when Jeroen mentions "apolitical punks", he does so in a way that suggests he believes the 'a' to be more akin to 'anti-political', and therefore, by extension, political: "the political punks, or the apolitical punks, whatever you want to call it..." (Jeroen). In this sense his view can be compared to those of Tsitsos (1999) and Phillipov (2006) who discuss apolitical punks (or 'drunk punks') as engaged in inherently political practices of rebellion by dint of being punk. All view apolitical punks *as* political.

Some discuss punk's ideology in even broader terms, evoking 'ideas', 'ideals', 'theories', or the Dutch term '*boodschap*', which broadly translates to a 'message' or a 'mission'. The idea that punk is based around such sets of ideas can be integral to how individuals relate to punk: "I do like punk rock, I do like a lot of the ideals behind [it]" (Nico), and "yeah, I'm a punkrocker actually, yeah for sure! I still live on those principles" (Kosta).

'*Boodschap*' was used most often in conjunction with the music rather than the subculture as a whole. *Boodschap* is most easily expressed lyrically and therefore is an important realm in which punk musicians may express their wider politics. For Bart having a '*boodschap*' defines punk music: "[punk is] primarily music with a *boodschap*" (Bart). Something could be similar musically, but without a message he wouldn't consider it punk. In lyrics we see one of the ways that punks' political ideas may be expressed. Gregor says that bands having a clear message is important for spreading political ideas: "you spread a *boodschap* as well of course and hopefully you can inspire people, at least you can vent your opinion" (Gregor). In Chap. 6 I discuss the political importance of such dissemination of political ideas. Many participants agree that lyrics are the most important (or for some, the only) way that *doing* punk can be political. However, others argue that underground and DIY approaches to punk can be political, thereby reinforcing Dale's (2012) arguments.

When discussing DIY we see, again, how important this is to participants in the strong links they make between punk and underground culture. "If you say the word punk I immediately have this reference to [the] underground" (Erik). "[Compared to metal,] punk is much more based on DIY ethics" (Ruben). The DIY aspect is also a reason that some participants particularly like punk: "for me the most fun was really the DIY culture of doing it yourself" (Suzanne).

The political importance of punk practices that are run along DIY principles ties into anti-commercial and anti-capitalist ideologies: "yeah about DIY I think it's also very important that you can remain [...] independent, creating your own culture within a bigger culture. Then it's important that you can remain autonomous and do your own thing and then you don't have to give into commercial demands" (Jasper). DIY allows Jasper and others such as Erik to position themselves as ideologically opposed to mainstream commerce. Moreover, this is a move in the creation of autonomous subcultural space *as* a political strategy (see Chap. 6).

Contested Areas of Ideology

The importance of DIY underpins the ever-raging debate in punk circles about whether or not punks can (or should) be engaged in any commercial activities and what constitutes 'selling out', thereby possibly taking away the 'right' to be considered punk (Dunn 2012). Again, this is seen by some as a marker by which punk can be defined:

Kirsty: Can punk ever be commercial?
Johan: By definition—actually not, really?

Those who debate the possibility of something being commercial *and* punk draw on discourses of DIY and independence (Dale 2008, 2012; O'Hara 1999): "I think some people may disagree with me but I think those bands like Green Day, are for me not punk, that's for me nearly pop music actually. No that's not on, it must remain independent, it must stay small" (Lotte). For Lotte, Green Day are not punk explicitly *because* they are no longer independent. Mark extends this debate beyond music and bands to critique those who would use commercial Internet services such as Myspace (at the time still a popular social networking site, owned by News Corp): "If you take any idea of punk and DIY seriously, what are you doing with Myspace? I mean, [...] 'don't trust a punk with a Myspace account!'" (Mark). Mark believes that punks should not interact with such products of global corporations.

Whilst nearly every participant in this research project would prefer punk and commercialism to remain separate worlds, many allowed for the possibility that punk bands can become 'successful' beyond the underground. Many also believe that these bands might remain punk. For most participants, therefore, the most pertinent issue is not whether the band makes money from selling records but rather that the music and the ideals remain the same as when the band was 'underground'. "Say a band like Rise Against. Yes, they are quite commercial but, if you look at the lyrics not so much has changed since when they started" (Bart). Some even express admiration for those who are able to make a living from punk as long as they can do so without losing their ideological 'roots':

> I am not a guy who is gonna yell "sell out" at a band because they sign with a major label. It has more to do with how you act after that, is your message changing? Because if you were in punk bands all your life and you still are, that's your thing, and if you are able to make money out of it, if you can live from your band, well kudos to you because deep in most of the punkers hearts it is like, "I want that too, I want to do my music and nothing else". (Larry)

Other respondents critique this debate by questioning the assumptions on which it is founded. "I don't really think that commercial punk is not punk, but what's not commercial anymore? It's very hard, nowadays it's very hard: is a band selling their own t-shirts being commercial?" (Theo). Sander adds that sometimes a band doesn't necessarily have control over their popularity, and dealing with larger commercial enterprises can come out of necessity. "If a punk band for instance just makes this awesome music, that a lot of people like, and it just sells and the gigs sell out, yes that is of course fine [...] I don't think that's a contradiction or anything" (Sander). Johan draws attention to the futility of the debate; if punk should change the world, it must communicate this widely, but instead there is an 'elitist' attitude in favour of staying underground.

> But that is then always an awkward dilemma really, because on the one hand you'd want everyone, [...] lots of people to start thinking about it, but when that happens it will again turn commercial, that is always the same, the same difficulty, because what's the point in wanting to change

the world but that it has to remain elitist, that's of course a bit of non-sense. (Johan)

This debate's existence and the rehearsal of various aspects of it by participants in the research project illustrates how punk practices can be based on political beliefs. This is connected to—but dinstinct from—the manner in that there are ideological foundations to individualised aspects of *being* punk that will be discussed later in this chapter.

In the Dutch punk scene, another key debate centres on the issue of 'protest' or 'resistance' (see Chap. 2). Whilst some claim that '*punk is het verzet*,' ('punk is the resistance'), others counter that '*punk is niet het verzet*,' ('punk is *not* the resistance'). As a 'catchphrase' this draws explicitly on (and is used as often as) 'punk is dead'/'punk is not dead' in English. Gregor, Menno and Tom all use this phrase in defining what punk means. For Gregor this aspect is important: "punk originated primarily as a kind of *verzet* movement" (Gregor). For Menno this marked out what made early punk *punk*, whilst later 'punk' lost the way. "We thought punk was in a way a kind of *verzet*, a sort of anti-culture. Whereas in the 1980s part [of the scene] got into heroin and part [of it] turned commercial" (Menno). Tom attempted to use the phrase in order to avoid coming up with his own definition (see introduction): "punk is *verzet*! Right? That's what they say! Don't they?!" He quickly followed up that he did, indeed, agree with the sentiment.

However, there are those, within the punk scene, who argue that punk is *not* '*verzet*'. For Daan, the phrase was used by punks as empty posturing and often not backed up by resistant action: "I said something like 'this is what you sing—but why don't you *do* something?' They said 'punk *is* the *verzet*,' but punk is not *verzet* if you ask me" (Daan). For Daan, the 'ideological' underpinning of punk served as '*aanzet*' rather than '*verzet*': initiation into resistance rather than resistance in itself.

Wouter, as we have seen, agrees that many punks engage in 'empty' posturing rather than actual political engagement; however, he argues that the subculture is 'useful' insofar as more politically engaged people (such as, in his opinion, in the squatters' movement) can raise money for their causes through allowing punks the use of their spaces: "if we just charge for admission, [and] with a lot of their money [spent on our] beer [...then] we can sponsor lots of things. [...] You can make a lot of money with these kinds of gigs" (Wouter). In this sense wider political organisations sometimes mobilise the punks rather than the other way around (as discussed in Worley 2012).

A further contested area is whether or not punk—or punks—can be right wing. This brought up strong feelings amongst some respondents, the vast majority of whom identified themselves as left wing.[5] Lotte became very angry with the question of whether Nazi punks existed in Groningen, arguing that they did not and *could not* exist: "I think [...] you can't be right wing if you're punk, that's not on, you have to be left [...]. No, Nazi punks, that's unthinkable. Yes, 'Nazi punks *fuck off*'. [...] To me that is not punk, absolutely not, they are just trouble makers ([spoken angrily]). I think that that, maybe that punk comes from the English, *maybe*? No I think that's very wrong, really wrong" (Lotte, emphasis in original).

Jeroen, whilst also being critical of righ-wing beliefs, does not negate the possibility of punks being right wing. He recognises this as a similarly extreme—but opposite—approach to his own politics. He argues that instead of attacking right wing punks or denying their existence, talking to them to try and convince them otherwise would be more productive: "they just think completely differently about certain things, maybe I am also very extreme about some things, like they are—you always have an opposite and that's a pity, that that is the case, and it absolutely shouldn't be. But, yes, they are there and I'd rather not have them, but shutting them out doesn't help either" (Jeroen).

Lotte and Jeroen hereby tap into a long tradition of debate within punk circles over the place of right-wing politics within punk. Worley (2012) discusses how the National Front attempted to co-opt disaffected UK punks to the far right and Ward (1996) claims that individuals with right-wing beliefs have only a spurious claim to be punk. However, Pilkington (2014b) shows how it is perfectly possible for right-wing beliefs to sit alongside punk practices, drawing on a Russian context.

A number of specific viewpoints were also brought up by participants in discussions of punk politics. Nico suggested links between environmentalism and punk, which for him culminates in a passion for recycling and bicycles (see Clark 2004; and Chap. 6). Marieke and Gregor both brought up 'nihilism' as part of punk; for Gregor this was what separated early punk (as more nihilist) from contemporary punk, whereas for Marieke nihilism still ran through punk. Menno and Theo both suggested that an 'anti-establishment' position was important for punk: "punk *is* very anti-establishment" (Theo, emphasis added, see also Dunn

2008). Maarten brought up the importance of anarchism and also discussed anti-authority, anti-consumerism and anti-(normative) approaches to society. Kosta and Erik both defined punk as a form of protest. "[Punk rock is] a natural human reaction to overcome oppression" (Kosta). Sem, Andre and Bram all talked about punk as "about being critical about society" (Bram).

Whilst we see that ideology is important to Dutch punks, the specific forms that this might take remains heavily contested, as suggested by O'Hara (1999) amongst others. The manner in which these debates have impacted individuals' lives in the Dutch punk scene will be further discussed in Chap. 6.

Punk as Individual Practice

This section elaborates on themes of punk as an individual practice, occasionally in contrast to ideas of punk as a social practice. Widdicombe and Wooffitt (1990) discuss the way in which punk can be an identity to be claimed rather than a set of social practices. Whilst I do not reject punk as a set of practices, the evidence in this section will suggest that for some participants punk *can* be an identity. First I will turn to discourses of *being* punk and what this entails. For many participants the role of being a punk was key to their individual identity, and I include examples of individuals' relationships to punk. Punk will be positioned as an expression of individuality, and there will follow a discussion of the personality traits that participants identify as necessary to *being* punk. The section ends with a selection of responses to the question 'are you a punk?'

Being Punk

A number of participants responded to the question, 'what is punk?' not (only) with discussions of the music, social practices, and/or ideologies associated with punk, but with ideas of punk as an identity or a social category. "[Punk is] who you are, it's your way of expressing how you feel" (Erik). Assertions of what it meant to *be* (a) punk and what was—or was not—involved in punk identity were common. For some, this included having a taste for the music and the politics; however, many brought up personal qualities or personality traits that they associate with *being* punk.

A great number of respondents suggested that having a punk 'attitude' was crucial to a punk identity. "Mostly, [punk] is an attitude" (Jasper). Andre, Maarten, Kosta, Jeroen and Luka also bring up punk 'attitude' as part of their definition. Whilst often the specifics of this attitude were left unelaborated, some respondents gave further clues as to what a 'punk attitude' meant for them. For Jeroen, a "fuck off attitude" were common to the hardcore and punk scenes around the Steenwijk area. Luka suggested that a punk attitude entails a proclivity for 'provocation', especially in his hometown of Belgrade. Mark even 'exemplified' this attitude during his interview, when discussing his straightforward approach to work as a sound technician (and in reference to a falling out with The Ex): "people don't want to work with me, that's fine. They can't fuck me around, no bullshitting me, don't do it!" (Mark).

Kosta suggests that attitude is the crucial element to defining punk. Whereas the outward elements such as style, music and political practices, may shift over time or from place to place, *attitude* will designate whether someone (or something) can be defined as punk. "The music has changed but the attitude is the same. Punkrocker is punkrock is the attitude. Yeah it's all about the attitude, how you approach [and] how you perceive and how you deal with it. That is punkrock!" (Kosta). Goshert (2000) also suggests that punk is an 'attitude', although his focus on attitude is in terms of being a site for radical politics.

Mark believes that a certain element of 'roughness' is required to be punk: "it's got a sort of low-life element". In addition, he also looks for a high degree of passion in order for him to consider something as 'interesting' punk. He looks for people to be "personally engaged, and they're trying to find out more [about] it and they're trying to really bring the message across and that they care and why they care" (Mark). "[I]f people really have an idea about something and they're passionately engaged it helps, it doesn't necessarily have to be something I really agree with" (Mark). Whilst Mark doesn't designate the ideological stance that a punk must take, he asks that they do so passionately in order to be taken seriously. In this sense attitude is seen as more important than content.

There is another personality trait that a number of participants link to being punk that also follows from the need for passion. The idea of being '*bewust*' (being 'conscious') was raised by Marieke, Gregor and Andre, amongst others. This is largely used to describe a person's approach to how they live their lives; being 'conscious' and 'understanding' the consequences of the choices they make, and being aware that they *can* make choices that go against social norms. Andre talked about this in terms of questioning one's surrounding, while Gregor described being '*bewust*' as inherently a part of being punk: "consciousness and also critically reflecting and that sort of thing, those are things I would associate strongly with punk". This form of consciousness is therefore linked to practices of resistance.

Such 'consciousness' results in a number of individualised practices of resistance that punks may take part in and that some participants included in their explanations of what 'punk' meant to them. Squatting was therefore often linked to definitions of punk, especially given the historical context of the Dutch punk scene (see Chap. 3). Daan joked that leaving home at a young age—implicitly associated with rebellion against parents or guardians—is a 'punk' cliché: "I left home on my fifteenth [birthday], very punk!" (Daan). This shows a recognition of one's own actions as a self-aware, ironic parody of punk norms (see Pilkington et al. 2014).

Marieke discusses how being '*bewust*' has been important in guiding her decisions; from her youth, when she sought to live ascetically, to more recent years where she has allowed a relaxation of her rules.

> I think, say, for me it's been a tendency [...] since I was seventeen or so, of first looking for the extremes of what do, [what] I stand for and how do I want to live, [doing] that in an extreme fashion like, [to] live without gas, water, or electricity, and also that year I also only ate from dumpsters and that sort of thing. And then really as I grew older, I found out [...] yes it isn't really all black and white. I also think that the people who all lived much more extreme[ly] than I, much more sex and drugs and rock 'n' roll, and far more political activities and—really also things that can put you inside [prison] for a year—[...] that for many people [...] in the end it's very much about your own freedom [...]—freedom is not really the right word, but [...] your own choices or something—and as long as you make these consciously, then it's really okay. (Marieke)

In this way, being '*bewust*' has underpinned Marieke's approach to living life in a way that she understands as 'punk'. Marieke used this definition of punk to say that she thinks of some squatters as far more *punk* than some of the 'punks' she knows. Punk, therefore, can be considered an individual approach and ideology.

This desire for consciousness in approaches to living choice has resulted in many participants bringing up particular 'lifestyles' as part of what it means to be punk. "And if I would define punk? A lifestyle, a lifestyle indeed" (Maarten). "[A] lot of punks [have] an alternative lifestyle, an outrageous outfit is already seen as an act of revolt, which of course it is. I mean, on a personal level you don't conform, you revolt against conventions" (Daan). Jacob expands on what these 'norms' are: "people who listen to this kind of music, [...] don't go for the '9–5 job and 2.4 children' but are a bit more bohemian" (Jacob). These Dutch punks therefore do indeed seek to *resist* normative culture (see Chap. 2).

We see in these participants' discussions that punk can be understood as an identity. The claiming of this identity is rooted in a variety of individualised practices, such as an attitude or an approach to life that is underpinned by punk ideologies. By committing to a punk identity, and expressing this through a number of practices, punks claim subcultural capital (Thornton 1995) and authenticity (see Chap. 2).

Being an 'Active' Punk

Many participants, when discussing their 'punk careers', made distinctions between becoming involved with punk, becoming an *active* punk, and sometimes then becoming less active. This designation was occasionally also applied to others. This suggests that for some, the assignation of 'punk' has various hierarchical levels. 'Activity' was linked to a number of practices with which the individual might get involved. These often involved musical activities, such as attending gigs, running gigs, playing in a band, or becoming more involved with political actions.

Daan's 'activity' started with him becoming more involved, socially, with other punks: hanging out and sharing music. "From then on I've really been active, nearly every day I went to the squat where the people in Lärm together with some [other] friends ran a sort of punk cafe and there we listened to music" (Daan). For Ruben, activity is ascribed by going regularly to underground gigs: "in Groningen we saw a complete scene going on here, we were amazed how many—all—people were actively busy here and how much people were going to the shows here" (Ruben).

Luka saw going to shows as part of what 'active' meant, along with the political, organisational and creative aspects of punk. "I started getting into more political aspects, you know and environmental aspects of music you know. Like getting more active, and [I] started doing [a] fanzine you know, going to every single show, and organising shows"

(Luka). Tom also discusses being busy with running shows and festivals as part of what comes with a more active position in punk.

Nico suggests that simply going to gigs, and even taking part in further 'lifestyle' elements of punk, did not make him feel like he was an active member of the punk scene compared to others who were more involved in active roles. "I mean it's not like I was involved, I went to shows and I knew people who played in bands and organised shows but I was not really active in the scene other than going and seeing shows and supporting a certain lifestyle" (Nico).

For some being 'active' *was* being punk. For others, being an 'active' punk was used to delineate a punk with more subcultural capital (Thornton 1995) from other punks. Some therefore identified with being an 'active' punk, whereas others didn't. We see here echoes of the discussion in Chap. 1 in regards to the complexity of participants' own understandings of their insider/outsider status (Kempson 2015).

Punk Individuality

The desire amongst punks to resist social norms, and to seek the freedom to make '*bewust*' choices, feeds into another prevalent discourse amongst participants. Many talked of the links between punk and individuality. Punk provides the social space for individuals to experiment with their identity; *being* punk is about *being* individual. This was discussed in a number of different ways: being punk is that "you don't just conform" (Lotte), that you can "think for yourself" (Bart), and that you are able to "develop what you think about your own identity" (Jasper). Marieke talked about the importance of finding her own path, and how this was an important quality in her friends.

> I [had] the feeling I had to find out more for myself—or wanted to—how consciously I could live my life. And I think that's always been somewhat attractive to me from when I was fifteen or so, I also always had—well not really *punk* punk—but always friends who very much made their own choices. So not the well-trodden, normal paths—whatever you can call normal, because I don't think you can call anything really normal—but anyway [people] who were always very much looking for a sort of *bewust* life (Marieke).

In seeking out individuality, Ruben likes always to maintain a sense of difference: "if I'm in a metal crowd I always call myself a punk, if I'm in a punk rock crowd I always call myself a metalhead. Yeah!" (Ruben). Ruben's identity is not fixed and is produced contextually on the basis of the crowd he is with. However, rather than being a process of *belonging* to the group, he finds in identity construction an opportunity to highlight his individuality; another example of 'genre evasion' (Steinholt 2012).

Conversely, 'difference' was not always a sought after choice. For instance, Luka describes himself as having always felt like a "black sheep in every school that I was [in]" (Luka). For him, punk therefore offered the opportunity of meeting others who similarly felt rejected by mainstream society: "I was looking for—probably unconsciously—a group" (Luka). Here we see the strong relationship between individuality, difference and belonging, which as Shank (1994) argued, is crucial to any scene. Individuals may seek to differentiate themselves from normative society, and from others within their own subculture, but will do so on the basis that enough ties them to punk to create a sense of belonging.

Individual Relationship to Punk

In discussions of what punk 'is', participants sometimes reflected on what punk meant specifically to them. Just as Luka valued group solidarity with other punks, others found similarly individualised reasons for their attachment to punk.

For Larry the attraction of punk could be found in the coalescing of musical qualities and the particular life-stage at which he discovered them. "What is punk? [...] Especially when you are a teenager it's really an outlet to use, that's why you start [as] a little teenager, you are fed up with everything and you have this music that is loud and aggressive and you can really let it go, go to a gig and go nuts really have a fun time" (Larry). Erik found a similar outlet in punk:

[Punk is] your way of expressing how you feel in a passive[ly] aggressive way. I don't go out drinking myself to the ground and punch a guy in the face or something. Punk is the outlet for things that are not really well, if you have a really hard week it's really relieving that you can go out to a punk show and just enjoy the moshing and the dancing and the singing along. And unity is a really important issue in that matter, that the unity feeling makes you forget the week before and the feeling, hardcore punk is the feeling for me, yeah (Erik).

Both Larry and Erik positioned the embodied social practices at gigs—the aggressive dancing and music—as a cathartic escape from the tribulations of daily life. This is similar to the energy boost that Andre received from the music, as discussed earlier.

Lotte also discussed having a particularly emotional connection to the music: "it's really, something that your whole life, [it's] what is in your heart, with which you are in love. It is a kind of love for the music for me, the attitude and the being-in-love and everything that comes with it" (Lotte).

Whilst these rationales for involvement with punk are rather more specific to individuals, they open up the possiblity to recognise the embodied, physical (Riches 2011; Tsitsos 1999), and emotional, affective responses that music and subculture can initiate.

Are You Now, or Have You Ever Been, a Punk?

Punks have an often contentious relationship with claims to individuality. Individuals' search for differentiation is usually aimed at a normative other (Shank 1994), meaning that aligning oneself broadly within a punk group is possible whilst still claiming individuality. However, as Steinholt (2012) notes, punk tendencies towards 'genre evasion' highlight the complex relationship between punk and self-categorisation. For bands, Steinholt argues, punk authenticity derives from maintaining an 'authentic voice' based on "consistently resist[ing] and undermin[ing] any outside attempt at defining what you do" (269); by extension resisting definition of who you are. This section contains a variety of answers given in response to my question "are you a punk?" No one answered in a straight-forward manner. Those who allowed the 'imposition' of such a definition did so only with elaboration:

Kirsty: Are you a punk?

Lotte: Yes

Kirsty: Yes?

Lotte: I am, no wait, I'm a punk-rocker!

Kirsty: You're a punk-rocker? What is the difference?

Lotte: The difference is maybe [the] interpretation you give it in Dutch language? [...] I think I associate the word "punk" a little bit more with also the clothes and a little bit more, you know, like Sex Pistols—boring—for me. I am a punk-rocker, thats more a way of life, more like, yeah, I see that, it's a better word, really, [... I'm] definitely a punk-rocker.

For Lotte, punk is not an identity, but punk *rock* is a lifestyle to which she adheres. 'Punk', for Lotte, retains the stigma of being attached to early UK punk, as understood by the first wave of punk theorists and led by the Sex Pistols and their stylistic practices. To differentiate herself from this ('boring') punk, the marker is altered to 'punk-rock'.

Some felt that punk, as a label, was something associated with their youth (such as Sem and Bram, further in this chapter). 'Old age' has tempered the *attitude*—notably one of 'rebellion'—that Sem would have once termed 'punk':

Kirsty: Are you punk?

Sem: No, I no longer am.

Kirsty: But were you before?

Sem: Yes, I did rebel against a couple of things in those days, so in that sense I was a punk but nowadays I am just a good boy as far as that is concerned.

Sem has dropped the 'label' as well as some of the practices, a modification of the behaviour described by Haenfler (2006), who discusses older straight edgers who drop the label yet remain committed through the lifestyle. However, Sem has not dropped punk entirely, remaining involved in the scene through his record label, photography and writing.

Bram similarly understood punk as an identity that was linked with his youth, drawing in particular on the social practices involved, thus positioning his understanding as closer to later conceptualisations of punk. However, after a brief spell rejecting the label in an attempt to better stake out his own individuality, he has now come back round to embrace being a punk:

Kirsty: Are you a punk?

Bram: Yeah!

Kirsty: Yeah?

Bram: [I] always have been, [I] always will be.

Kirsty: Why?

Bram: Umm, well that's a difficult one! Well yeah actually, at some point
I always [...] identified as a punk because I loved the music and I
was looking the part and it was the politics and stuff. And at some
point I was like "ah I'm not punk, I'm just me", you know? And
then I thought later on I was like, "no, fuck it, I'm just a punk".

Other participants rejected 'punk' as a label applicable to them. For
Larry this is due to a perceived lack in his own subcultural capital
(Thornton 1995); he is not 'insider' enough (Kempson 2015) to claim
punk as an identity. Similarly to Lotte and early punk theorists he views
punk in terms of its stylistic practice in which he doesn't partake:

Kirsty: Are you a punk?

Larry: Jesus! Umm, "am I punk?" [...] No, I never had a Mohawk, I
never dyed my hair, have no piercings, no tattoos, no, just regular
hair. [...] No I can't say I am like "the punk guy".

Jacob, like Bram above, preferred to assert his individuality, certainly in
the face of categorisation by a researcher:

Kirsty: Are you punk?

Jacob: No. I'm [Jacob].

Similarly, Gregor also rejects punk as a label. In doing so he both epit-
omises Steinholt's (2012) 'genre evasion' and recognises the irony
(Pilkington et al. 2014) in his own response:

Kirsty: Are you punk?

Gregor: No, I don't think so.

Kirsty: Why not?

Gregor: Yes, I don't know. I don't see myself like that, but in any
case I don't see the point in those labels. But saying that
is of course very punk [laughs]. That's a bit of a vicious
circle [laughs]!

We see in this section—and throughout the chapter—how multifarious 'punk' is and the many *different* meanings participants have attached to it. Mark, therefore, feels that the only conclusion to draw from all of this is that 'punk' has become meaningless:

Kirsty: Would you call yourself a punk?

Mark: I guess, yes.

Kirsty: Why?

Mark: Because it's really fun and it doesn't mean anything anymore.

CONCLUSION

Is punk meaningless, as Mark would have us believe? Penny Rimbaud (of Crass) certainly agrees: "I've got the answer to [the question] what is punk? And it's very simple. It isn't" (Rimbaud 2011). So why, then, attempt to define punk? There is a tension here between the desire to be able to clearly communicate what it is we are talking about and the demonstrated futility of imposing a concrete definition on punk(s).

There remain countless individuals around the Netherlands (indeed, the world) who continue to claim punk as *theirs*: as their subculture, as what they do, and/or as who they are. So, even as punk is "a notoriously amorphous concept" (Sabin 1999: 2), it is clear also that the label 'punk' retains a great deal of importance. In order to express why this is, this chapter has sought to understand what it is in punk that people feel drawn to.

As shown in this chapter the meanings that punk has for its participants are multifarious, and sometimes can even be contradictory. Punk can be a favourite style of music, a deeply held ideology or a set of practices. Some research participants conceptualise punk in terms of *social* practices, whereas for others the emphasis is on the *individuality* that punk offers (for some it is both, and yet for more it is neither). Research into punk has tended to focus on the former, in part due to its more observable nature, although some studies have examined punk as identity work. This chapter has drawn out four particular strands of individuality in punk: being punk, being an 'active' punk, punk individuality, and individual relationships to punk. The first strand encompasses a number of ways in which wider personality traits or approaches to life can be read as punk, often drawing upon themes of resistance. The notion of 'activity' suggests that participants understand a hierarchy in punk identities; that one can be a punk with minimal interaction with the scene, but greater involvement will bring with it the status of 'active' punk. The section on 'punk individuality' brings to the fore the tension between punk as an outsider status in which individuals seek to resist normative culture and punk as an insider group of other such 'outcasts'. The final section concludes with a discussion of individualised relationships to punk, and the question 'are you a punk?' Evidence presented shows that individual practices of punk are linked with group practices, thereby suggesting that in order to fully understand the meanings attached to 'punk', it is important to retain a lens on the individual as well as the social.

This chapter as a whole has shown the complexity and variety in Dutch participants' understandings of what punk is to them. In doing so it destabilises the narrow definitions of punk that have persisted in academia, directing the reader instead to a looser understanding. Punks may have agreed on the fact that music was central to punk, but they agreed on little else. Punk as an identity, punk and sociability, or punk as individuality: all were more or less contentious claims, advocated by some and opposed by others. Equally, there were a few that argued against the idea that punk is an ideology, or that it draws on a set of political beliefs.

Given the predominance of those who argued that politics *are* important to punk and the many detailed discussions held with participants about their 'extra-curricular' political activities, the next chapter will consider the different ways that politics have impacted on punk's lives.

NOTES

1. The complex relationship between punk and UK class positions has been further dissected (Laing 1985).
2. Squatters' 'surgery'; organisational meetings that take place usually weekly.
3. Dutch hardcore techno, a style that emerged in the early 1990s.
4. 'Cunt'. Its use here was more akin to 'like fucking shit', although that loses the gendered aspect of the expletive.
5. The overwhelming majority of those involved in the Dutch punk scene were firmly left wing (see Lohman 2013). They usually identified as *far* left, although at least one respondent understood themselves as more centre-left (see Chap. 6). This is broadly characteristic of the Dutch punk

scene as a whole but was also due to methods of snowballing for participants. A number of respondents claimed that I could have spoken to right-wing punks had I extended my research to Rotterdam.

REFERENCES

Clark, D. 2003. The Death and Life of Punk, the Last Subculture. In *The Post-subcultures Reader*, ed. D. Muggleton, and R. Weinzierl, 223–236. Berg: Oxford.
Clark, D. 2004. The Raw and the Rotten: Punk Cuisine. *Ethnology* 43 (1): 19–31.
Clarke, J., S. Hall, T. Jefferson, and B. Roberts. [1975] 2006. Subcultures, Cultures and Class. In *Resistance Through Rituals: Youth Subcultures in Post-war Britain*, 2nd ed., ed. S Hall and T Jefferson, 3–59. London: Routledge.
Dale, P. 2008. It was Easy, it was Cheap, So What?: Reconsidering the DIY Principle of Punk and Indie Music. *Popular Music History* 3 (2): 171–193.
Dale, P. 2012. *Anyone Can Do It: Empowerment, Tradition and the Punk Underground*. Burlington, VT: Ashgate.
Dunn, K.C. 2008. Never Mind the Bollocks: The Punk Rock Politics of Global Communication. *Review of International Studies* 34 (1): 193–210.
Dunn, K.C. 2012. If It Ain't Cheap, It Ain't Punk: Walter Benjamin's Progressive Cultural Production and DIY Punk Record Labels. *Journal of Popular Music Studies* 24 (2): 217–237.
Gololobov, I., H. Pilkington, and Y.B. Steinholt. 2014. *Punk in Russia: Cultural Mutation from the 'Useless' to the 'Moronic'*. London: Routledge.
Goshert, J.C. 2000. "Punk" After the Pistols: American Music, Economics, and Politics in the 1980s and 1990s. *Popular Music and Society* 24 (1): 85–106.
Gosling, T. 2004. Not for Sale: The Underground Network of Anarcho-Punk. In *Music Scenes: Local, Translocal, and Virtual*, ed. A. Bennett, and R.A. Peterson, 168–186. Nashville: Vanderbilt University Press.
Haenfler, R. 2006. *Straight Edge: Clean-Living Youth, Hardcore Punk, and Social Change*. New Brunswick, NH: Rutgers University Press.
Hebdige, D. 1979. *Subculture: The Meaning of Style*. London: Routledge.
Kempson, M. 2015. I Sometimes Wonder Whether I'm an Outsider: Negotiating Belonging in Zine Subculture. *Sociology* 49 (6): 1081–1095.
Laing, D. 1985. *One Chord Wonders: Power and Meaning in Punk Rock*. Milton Keynes: Open University Press.
Leblanc, L. 1999. *Pretty in Punk: Girls' Gender Resistance in a Boys' Subculture*. New Brunswick: Rutgers University Press.
Lohman, K. 2013. Dutch Punk with Eastern Connections: Mapping Cultural Flows Between East and West Europe. *Punk & Post Punk* 2 (2): 147–163.

Marcus, G. 1989. *Lipstick Traces: A Secret History of the 20th Century.* London: Faber and Faber.

Moore, R. 2004. Postmodernism and Punk Subculture: Cultures of Authenticity and Deconstruction. *The Communication Review* 7 (3): 305–327.

Moore, R. 2010. *Sells Like Teen Spirit: Music, Youth Culture, and Social Crisis.* London: New York University Press.

Nehring, N. 1993. *Flowers in the Dustbin: Culture, Anarchy, and Postwar England.* Ann Arbor: University of Michigan Press.

O'Connor, A. 2002. Local Scenes and Dangerous Crossroads: Punk and Theories of Cultural Hybridity. *Popular Music* 21 (2): 225–236.

O'Connor, A. 2003. Punk Subculture in Mexico and the Anti-globalization Movement: A Report from the Front. *New Political Science* 25 (1): 43–53.

O'Connor, A. 2004. Punk and Globalization: Spain and Mexico. *International Journal of Cultural Studies* 7 (2): 175–195.

O'Connor, A. 2008. *Punk Record Labels and the Struggle for Autonomy: The Emergence of DIY.* Lanham: Lexington Books.

O'Hara, C. 1999. *The Philosophy of Punk: More Than Noise!* Edinburgh: AK Press.

Perasović, B. 2012. Pogo on the Terraces: Perspectives from Croatia. *Punk & Post-Punk* 1 (3): 285–303.

Phillipov, M. 2006. Haunted by the Spirit of '77: Punk Studies and the Persistence of Politics. *Continuum: Journal of Media & Cultural Studies* 20 (3): 383–393.

Pilkington, H. 2014a. If You Want to Live, You Better Know How to Fight: Fighting Masculinity on the Russian Punk Scene. In *Fight Back: Punk, Politics and Resistance,* ed. The Subcultures Network, 13–33. Manchester: Manchester University Press.

Pilkington, H. 2014b. Vorkuta: A Live Scene in a "Rotting City". In *Punk in Russia: Cultural Mutation from the 'Useless' to the 'Moronic',* ed. I. Gololobov, H. Pilkington, and Y. B Steinholt, 143–195. London: Routledge.

Pilkington, H., I. Gololobov, and Y.B. Steinholt. 2014. Conclusion. In *Punk in Russia: Cultural Mutation from the 'Useless' to the 'Moronic',* ed. I. Gololobov, H. Pilkington, and Y.B. Steinholt, 196–211. London: Routledge.

Riches, G. 2011. Embracing the Chaos: Mosh Pits, Extreme Metal Music and Liminality. *Journal for Cultural Research* 15 (3): 315–332.

Rimbaud, P. 2011. *Rottenbeat: Academic and Musical Dialogue with New Russian Punk Workshop,* London, 4 May. Quoted in H Pilkington, 'Punk— But Not As We Know It: Punk in Post-Socialist Space'. *Punk & Post-Punk,* 1 (3): 253–266.

Sabin, R. 1999. Introduction. In *Punk Rock: So What?: The Cultural Legacy of Punk,* ed. R. Sabin, 1–13. London: Routledge.

Savage, J. 1991. *England's Dreaming: Sex Pistols, Punk Rock, and Beyond*. London: Faber and Faber.

Shank, B. 1994. *Dissonant Identities: The Rock'n'Roll Scene in Austin*. Middletown: Wesleyen University Press.

Steinholt, Y.B. 2012. Punk is Punk but By No Means Punk: Definition, Genre Evasion and the Quest for an Authentic Voice in Contemporary Russia. *Punk & Post-Punk* 1 (3): 267–284.

Steinholt, Y.B., I. Gololobov, and H. Pilkington. 2014. St. Petersburg: Big City—Small Scenes. In *Punk in Russia: Cultural Mutation from the 'Useless' to the 'Moronic'*, ed. I. Gololobov, H. Pilkington, and Y.B. Steinholt, 49–98. London: Routledge.

Thompson, S. 2004. *Punk Productions: Unfinished Business*. Albany: State University of New York Press.

Thornton, S. 1995. *Club Cultures: Music, Media and Subcultural Capital*. Cambridge: Polity Press.

Tsitsos, W. 1999. Rules of Rebellion: Slamdancing, Moshing, and the American Alternative Scene. *Popular Music* 18 (3): 397–414.

Uitermark, J. 2004. The Co-optation of Squatters in Amsterdam and the Emergence of a Movement Meritocracy: A Critical Reply to Pruijt. *International Journal of Urban and Regional Research* 28 (3): 687–698.

Wallach, J. 2008. Living the Punk Lifestyle in Jakarta. *Ethnomusicology* 52 (1): 98–116.

Ward, J.J. 1996. "This is Germany! It's 1933!" Appropriations and Constructions of Fascism in New York Punk/Hardcore in the 1980s. *Journal of Popular Culture* 30 (3): 155–185.

Widdicombe, S., and R. Wooffitt. 1990. "Being" Versus "Doing" Punk: On Achieving Authenticity as a Member. *Journal of Language and Social Psychology* 9 (4): 257–277.

Williams, J.P. 2011. *Subcultural Theory: Traditions and Concepts*. Cambridge: Polity Press.

Worley, M. 2012. Shot By Both Sides: Punk, Politics and the End of "Consensus". *Contemporary British History* 26 (3): 333–354.

CHAPTER 6

Punks' Wider Lives: Punks and Their Politics

There is a hotly contested battle over what counts as political engagement. From understandings of 'traditional *Politics*', to the 'New Social
Movements' of the 1960s–1980s, to the introduction of life politics
(Giddens 1994) or sub-politics (Beck 1994), and the subsequent rejec-
tion of these (Furedi 2005), the field of the 'political' is under constant
negotiation. This chapter draws on debates over definitions of politics in
the wake of theories of individualisation (see Chap. 2). It continues to
argue the importance of embedding the individual and their whole lives
into complex social structures.

This chapter will start with a discussion of differing conceptualisations
of politics before proposing that a wider definition is required in order
to encapsulate a variety of political engagements. It recommends that we
do not attempt to replace understandings of 'traditional political activity'
with 'new engagement'. Instead we should understand that individuals
may, and always have, enacted politics in multiple ways.

'Political activity' was a theme that was raised in every one of the
interviews for this project. It was a topic I was interested in and therefore asked about; however, participants often raised the subject of their
own political engagements before I did. They understood these political
engagements to be a part of their punk identity; if I was asking about
punk, many expected that I was also interested in politics. Whilst there is
an extensive discussion to be had regarding the ways in which *punk* and
politics are linked, and the potential for the music or subculture itself to
be political (Goshert 2000; O'Hara 1999; Phillipov 2006; Street 2012),

© The Author(s) 2017
K. Lohman, *The Connected Lives of Dutch Punks*,
Palgrave Studies in the History of Subcultures and Popular Music,
DOI 10.1007/978-3-319-51079-8_6

this chapter instead focuses on *punks'* engagements in politics: that is, the way in which individuals are involved with politics *beyond* the scope of the subculture. The chapter takes as given that the punk scene is populated by many politically active individuals (although of course not all punks are political, nor do they agree on the form that political engagement should take, see Chap. 5, Ward [1996] and Worley [2012]. It seeks to understand how punk can influence other engagements and how these engagements might in turn both shape the individuals concerned and be reabsorbed into the scene.

The variety of political engagements included in the discussion of this chapter reflects those brought up *as* political by participants. It is on the basis of this empirical evidence that I argue that previous theoretical frameworks for defining politics are too narrow. Participants in this project engage with a variety of 'traditional' political activities, including party membership and trade union activism, as well as other forms of politics, including grassroots awareness-raising projects and politically informed life choices such as squatting or veganism. Whilst individuals' particular reasons for their chosen form(s) of political engagement may vary, their understandings of these activities are *as* political involvement.

There will be five empirical sections to this chapter that include discussions of education, resistance and practices of consumption, demonstrations, as well as more 'traditional' political engagement. The first empirical section proposes that the act of *educating* oneself or another is inherently political. There is a long tradition of political discussion groups, anarchist bookshops and other peer educative initiatives that exist to spread and increase political engagement; however, the academic conceptualisation of these acts as political is underdeveloped. Furthermore, I propose that just as the act of educating another is political, the act of educating *oneself* is political. A number of my participants were engaged in grassroots activities in which they sought to educate one another on particular matters. There are also examples of participants' self-education and their eagerness to engage in political debate to demonstrate this. This section will discuss these various forms of engagement and why it is important to include 'education' as a category of political action. In doing so it brings together ideas of both individualised (Giddens 1994) and connected (Smart 2007) modes of education as political.

The following two sections will discuss politically informed life decisions that participants have made, for example, around work or consumption. I posit that these choices are symptomatic of the politically active subculture in which these individuals are embedded, and these choices are utilised as individual expressions of political conviction. Such choices are often made by those who are politically active in other ways, therefore countering arguments that 'individual' acts are stripped of political potential. I instead argue that these acts contribute to homologous political identities for the individuals concerned. Moreover, these individual choices are framed as expressions that participants are capable of making even where other avenues of action may be closed to them.

The final two empirical sections will introduce examples of participants' engagements with more traditional forms of protest and politics: demonstrations, democratic politics and trade union activism. I highlight how these forms of political engagement exist *alongside* other forms and thereby critique the model that suggests that these have been 'replaced' by 'newer' activisms. Moreover, these sections will present the ways in which 'traditional' politics are interconnected with participants' understandings of their other political engagements, suggesting that separating out trends of 'old' and 'new' politics draws us away from the 'connectedness' of social life (see Chap. 2).

WHAT IS POLITICS?

The 1990s saw a shift in the theorisation of what constitutes political activity. This was in the context of theories of late modernism and individualisation (see Chap. 2). With the proliferation of choice in individuals' lives (Giddens 1994, 2000) there comes a widening of the political implications of these choices and therefore also an accompanying encroachment of politics into many more spheres of individual life. Giddens (1994) posits this as 'life politics'; "[l]ife politics, and the disputes and struggles connected with it, are about how we should live in a world where everything that used to be natural (or traditional) now has in some sense to be chosen, or decided about" (90–91).

Giddens' (1994) 'life politics' encompasses "quite orthodox areas of political involvement—for example, work and economic activity" (91)—but is much broader than this, being a "politics of identity as well as of choice" (91). In this regard his work is a productive move towards recognising the necessity of widening theorisations around what constitutes politics, which this chapter will build upon.

Beck (1994) also addresses how individualisation has impacted political participation. He argues that "citizen-initiative groups have taken power politically" (18), forming a new mode of political participation. According to Beck, politics is no longer the preserve of the political elite but open to all citizens who choose to engage. He understands these modes of activity as 'sub-politics', distinguishing between "official, labelled politics (of the political system) and sub-politics (in the sense of autonomous subsystemic politics)" (35). 'Sub-politics' focuses on group mobilisation in order to effect societal change through alternative means to those offered by 'the system'. However, both Giddens' and Becks' understandings of these phenomena as twentieth-century developments are problematic in terms of their ahistoricism (Smart 2007; see also Chap. 2).

Other theorists' work has taken a more nuanced historical view. Norris (2002) recognises that the supposed 'modern' forms of political engagement are 'newer' rather than 'new'; having achieved a prominence in mainstream politics in the late twentieth century: "[p]rotest politics did not disappear with afghan bags, patchouli oil, and tie-dyed T-shirts in the sixties; instead it has moved from margin to mainstream. Now social movements, transnational policy networks, and internet activism offer alternative avenues of engagement" (4). She suggests that attempts to divide the 'social' from the 'political' are problematized by identity and lifestyle politics. Activities that are "commonly understood as broadly 'political'" (192–193) "include volunteer work at recycling cooperatives, helping at battered women's shelters, and fund raising for a local hospital, as well as demonstrating at sites for timber logging or airport runway expansions, and protesting [against] the use of animals in medical research" (192). Norris therefore allows for a wide range of activities to be understood as political.

However, the shift towards identity and/or lifestyles politics is not without its critics. Some critiques came from the left, with theorists such as Hobsbawm (1996) lamenting the fragmentation of oppositional politics into minority interest groups. Others, such as Crenshaw (1991) critique the movement from within. She argues that it carried with it problematic practices in which some voices were privileged over others. "The problem with identity politics is [...] that it frequently conflates or ignores intragroup differences. [...] [I]gnoring difference *within* groups contributes to tension *among* groups" (1242). She used the critique to recommend a more 'intersectional' approach to identity politics.

Furedi (2005), on the other hand, rejects any understanding of these new modes of engagement as political. He argues that unless new modes of engagement can constitute a practical alternative to representative democracy, they should not be understood as political challenges. Indeed, he states that they form an obstacle to political change by pacifying those who might alternatively challenge the political hegemony. "There is nothing objectionable about individuals participating in organizations in order to become members of an *emotional community*. However, when the pursuit of self-discovery becomes a principle objective of involvement it is likely to turn into merely another form of disengagement" (46, emphasis added).

A definition of politics as necessarily based on engagement with—or replacement of—representative democracy shows a misunderstanding of the contemporary political landscape. In a globalised world, it is not always the state that has utmost power in a situation. As Norris (2002) highlights, "privatization, marketization, and deregulation means that decision making has flowed away from public bodies and official government agencies that were directly accountable to elected representatives, devolving to a complex variety of nonprofit and private agencies operating at local, national, and international levels" (193). As such, 'protest politics' shows a necessary shift from democratic politics in order to target the relevant authoritative bodies in today's globalised world.

Moreover, Furedi's (2005) argument is characteristic of those who believe that *P*olitics might be open to anyone or everyone. As Collins ([1991] 2000) argues, in reference to black women in a North American context, this is not the case. Structural obstacles will always prevent marginalised groups from participating in *P*olitics, which invariably privileges the activisms of white men. Privileging *P*olitics over other forms of activity erases the political importance of the activities undertaken by large swathes of the population. Collins therefore argues for the inclusion of individualised instances of resistance in understandings of political activism; for many, their greatest political achievements will be centred on personal strategies for resistance and survival. These arguments are applicable beyond the realm of black women's activism for many who do not have the opportunity to engage in 'traditional' forms of politics. For social scientists to negate these activities as 'not political enough' erases centuries of activism.

Collins' proposal to recognise the struggle for survival can also be found in some CCCS work on the politics of subcultures (Corrigan and Frith [1975] 2006). The creation and maintenance of a cultural space in which working class young people may thrive *is* viewed as having political potential.

[A]ny political judgement of youth culture must be based on treating it first as a *working class* culture, secondly as a cultural response to a *combination* of institutions, and thirdly as a response which is as creative as it is determined. Our own, unsystematic, judgement is that even if youth culture is not political in the sense of being part of a class-conscious struggle for State power, it nevertheless, *does provide* a necessary pre-condition of such a struggle. Given the structural powerlessness of working class kids and given the amount of state pressure they have to absorb, we can only marvel at the fun and the strength of the culture that supports their survival as any sort of group at all. (Corrigan and Frith [1975] 2006: 201, emphasis in original)

Whilst this chapter does not delve into the realms of how far punk in itself may be a political act, it is important to recognise that the creation of alternative cultural spaces is one strategy for the survival of groups that do not necessarily have access to traditional forms of politics. Furthermore, these alternative cultural spaces enabled the development of new cultural norms that challenge wider societal expectations. "What [punk,] zines, and underground culture writ large offer is a safe place in which to test out new ideas and to imagine a different way of ordering things" (Duncombe [1997] 2008: 186). Subcultures provide autonomous spaces in which individuals meet, share political ideas and gain support from each other.

This chapter draws on broad theorisations of 'politics' in order to allow for an acknowledgement of individuals' agency where it is due. It takes on board Giddens' suggestion that politics includes those choices made about individuals' everyday lives. It utilises Beck's arguments for understanding grassroots activities that challenge 'the system' as political but does not propose that these activities are *sub*political, instead positioning them as an alternative form of political expression. It learns from Collins not to erase the political potential of those who cannot or do not engage in 'traditional' (privileged) forms of politics, and instead affords agency to those who oppose 'the system' in individualised forms of everyday resistance. Finally, it does this whilst highlighting Smart's model of individuals' connectedness: to others who share (or reject) their politics, to changing sensibilities and norms within both the punk scene and 'normal' society, to their own biographical histories, and to the societal structures that constrain them, in spite of their best attempts to resist.

EDUCATIVE POLITICS

Reading for a Revolution

Education, both formal and informal, has always carried with it political implications. Collins ([1991] 2000) discusses the crucial role that
education played in the post-slavery lives of Black Americans through
to the Civil Rights Movement and beyond. Many states had outlawed
the education of enslaved peoples in order to prevent their political
awakening. Following the abolition of slavery those who *were* able to
read and write felt it their moral obligation, as part of a process of 'race
uplift', to pass on their knowledge and educate one another. Education
took place formally at churches and (initially segregated, later unseg-
regated) schools; it also took place informally at homes. These Black
Americans' commitment to educate one another was a key part of their
political activism.

At English working men's reading clubs of the early 1800s, national
newspapers and radical political journals were purchased by the club
for all members in order to make knowledge affordable. Texts were
read aloud by those who could read in order to make it accessible for
the illiterate. Those with the skills to read and write taught their peers
in order to increase accessibility to knowledge, especially in regard to
class struggle and other reformist political traditions (Thompson [1963]
1980). Drawing on Gramsci, CCCS scholars argue that the revolutionary
potential of this 'grassroots' self-education was recognised as a problematic challenge to middle class hegemony, and formalised education was
brought in for the masses in the nineteenth century. The working class
were educated with middle-class values and culture in an attempt to pla-
cate radical class reform (Corrigan and Frith [1975] 2006). Therefore
there is a critical *political* need for alternative forms of education (Freire
[1970] 2000).

Cultural monopolies on formal education do not eradicate underground systems of education; educating oneself and each other remains a
key strategy in political struggles. Alternative political education, for the
most part, takes place outside the academy and often in forms that are
difficult to measure or record. They range from homeschooling in literacy skills and informal reading groups to unrecorded meetings, debates
and conversations between peers and individual reading choices. Formats
by which political ideas gain currency and provoke thought and debate

are multifarious. Today, high levels of literacy and the availability of the Internet heightens opportunities for individual self-education in political matters and provides platforms for debate.

This section investigates the multiple ways in which participants' political actions have taken the format of educative engagement with political ideas. These forms of engagement include educational organisations, the writing and distribution of political reading material, informal conversations and self-education. A key aspect through which participants 'performed' their political engagement during interviews was by engaging me in extensive political discussion.

A few of the participants in this research project had experience with setting up educative action groups or knew of others in the scene who had done so. These often took the form of consciousness-raising organisations created to tackle specific political problems. Lisa and Gregor both talked about their own experiences of self-organised grassroots political campaign groups, whilst Larry, Mark and Ruben discussed setting up political information distros or bookshops. Menno, meanwhile, found his interests lay with producing political historical texts.

Lisa set up an animal rights organisation that aimed to educate the meat-eating public. "We also put flyers out, for instance just before Christmas we put flyers out to make people consider buying organic meat or just eat[ing] vegetarian [meals] once in a while, that sort of thing" (Lisa). This activity was in keeping with broader trends within the punk scene, where vegetarianism is common and animal rights activists often have a presence. Larry discusses this in the context of gigs he played at: "[w]e always brought information with us, like leaflets from PETA,[1] other political leaflets, [and] we did a lot of benefit shows for animal rights activism" (Larry). A number of participants discussed seeing animal rights information at punk gigs, something that was present during events attended as part of my fieldwork. These were often part of 'distros' at which leaflets, zines and books as well as music and merchandise might be sold or made available at gigs.

Two participants had been involved in separate projects to make anarchist literature more available to the (punk and wider) public. Both had been in collectives that set up anarchist bookshops or distros: one in Amsterdam, and one in Groningen. Het Fort van Sjakoo has become an Amsterdam institution that no longer advertises its anarchist credentials or its squat history (it is instead labelled an 'International bookshop') but is still run to cater to anyone seeking radical political reading materials.

Gregor, along with his university peers, set up a non-governmental organisation in order to educate people about the genocide in Darfur. They organised a lecture series inviting a variety of guest speakers, including a UN official, to discuss the issue at Radboud University Nijmegen. This series had formal ties to the university; around 200 students were able to follow the lectures in return for degree credits. Both this series and practices of distributing literature represent methods by which participants seek to educate others on particular matters as a form of political activism.

If we accept that reading and discussing ideas is political, then, by extension, the writing of these ideas must also be political. A few participants were engaged in writing more formal political texts, such as pamphlets or websites for political groups. This practice will be discussed in more depth later in this chapter. The most common of these writing practices, however, is the writing of zines.

A great many participants in this research project had some history of involvement with the making of zines. Whilst a great deal of this writing was often focused around music—including reviews, interviews, and so forth—some was more directly political. These zines were copied and shared amongst punk networks. Nico, amongst others, discussed ways in which zines introduced him to new modes of thinking about issues and provided guidelines on how to live. Menno curated the Raket zine in line with his anti-censorship beliefs; he would publish anything—and everything—that anyone submitted.[2] For others, zines provided a space in which to express or explore their own opinions or political beliefs. In these ways Dutch zine culture resembles zine cultures in other countries (Dunscombe [1997] 2008; Kempson 2014; Worley 2015).

Similarly, many participants had been involved with writing lyrics for bands and discussed their tendency to write explicitly political lyrics. For example, "most of [...] [the lyrics are] about human rights and animal rights" (Theo). This is one way in which we can view punk music itself as a communicative process through which individuals are educated politically (Street 2012).

For Menno, however, punk's political potential was limited, and as such he sought more and different ways to express his views. His post-Rondos project was an exercise in documenting and spreading knowledge of Dutch workers' history. Menno and his ex-bandmates conducted oral history interviews in order to produce an account of Rotterdam's workers' movement in the 1930s.

We interviewed fifteen people who were all active in the unions. Yeah, that was very interesting and well, we typed it up and wrote it into a story, but these people really told their own story, often for the first time. One of them had fought in Spain, the Spanish civil war. And anarchists, freethinkers, communists, friends of Van der Lubbe.[3] [...] Those kinds of projects we really found a lot more interesting than spending every weekend in your leather jacket downing as many pints as [possible]. (Menno)

The previous examples all involve education of others and the communication of political ideas. These instances of communication form a political economy of ideas, developed intersubjectively within the punk community, as individuals influence one another. However, self-education is also important in terms of political potential. Participants were keen to give examples of their own political research and its role in the formation of their political ideas. Just as some were inspired by reading zines or lyrics, books and the Internet also formed key resources for self-education. Daan described his 'reading history' in the formation of his own political stance, name-checking Marx, Lenin, Stalin, Kerensky, Trotsky, Luxembourg, Tolstoy and Kropotkin. This can be linked to discourses that foreground the importance of reading for political education and political mobilisation (Collins [1991] 2000; Freire [1970] 2000; Thompson [1963] 1980).

Current Affairs

Participants were keen to discuss current affairs during interviews; one aspect of their political interest was following the news carefully and researching various aspects of contemporary politics. They were keen to share this 'education' with me in the research setting.

The fieldwork period for this project coincided with the first events of the ongoing Arab Spring in December 2010 in Tunisia. However, the international media did not start reporting on the events in question extensively until Al Jazeera begun their 24/7 coverage of events on 28 January 2011, three days into the protests that took place in Egypt's Tahrir Square (Alterman 2011). Seven of the interviews for this project took place in the 15 days between the start of this intensive coverage and the announcement on 11 February 2011 that President Mubarak was resigning. Nanabhay and Farmanfarmaian (2011) discuss this coverage as a media 'spectacular': "Al Jazeera audience patterns, for example, suddenly spiked after an unprecedented rise as people tuned in globally to watch the events in Egypt" (591). Certainly, a number of participants reported being glued to the Al Jazeera coverage in order to keep up-to-date with events. One participant, following an interview on 10 January 2011, sent me SMS messages with the latest news that Mubarak was due to give a speech and that he was expected to resign. Both Daan and Maxim talked of watching Al Jazeera multiple times a day during this period, Daan stressing the importance of watching "history [... as it] is happening" (Daan). He was also engaged in writing on the matter, sharing his education with others; he published a few articles for websites and newspapers he was involved with.

The Arab Spring therefore formed a particular point of reference for a number of participants. Maxim talked of his great admiration for those involved in the protests in Tahrir Square, and how this greatly eclipsed his own political actions in being straight edge and vegetarian:

> I've been vegetarian for as long as I've been straight edge so for fifteen years, but [... it] doesn't mean that you are revolutionising [...] people around you. I think, I mean, really to all the people who are on the streets of Egypt for the last week, I'm sure ninety-nine per cent of them are not vegetarians, but I think they're doing something which all the vegetarians in Holland combined have never ever achieved! I mean they're attacking a system so big, like enormous, and they're taking their lives into their own hands in a way that's unseen for western societies. So who am I to say that they're not the true revolutionaries because, well, "he ate meat before he came to the demonstration", "he drank some milk before he threw a rock at the cop", I don't care!. (Maxim)

Daan likened the emotion of watching the news unfolding as similar to listening to political hardcore punk bands: "look, what punk and hardcore provoke is of course a certain emotion which you have also in politics, for instance if you look what happens in Egypt then I'm filled with anger which is the same anger that I hear [...] when I listen to Discharge or Crucifix or MDC" (Daan). Thus we see how important music and politics are for Daan and how he is connected to both of these emotionally. His reaction to these events, and the likening of these to music, highlights how inextricably connected (Smart 2007) these various facets of his 'whole' life (Pilkington and Omel'chenko 2013) are.

Daan, Maxim and Kosta all talked about the events in Egypt in terms of their working-class revolutionary potential, echoing the terms by which Al Jazeera also discussed the events in question (Alterman 2011). It was hoped by some participants that this was a sign of wider global trends towards left-wing revolutionary change, with examples also given of the Greek national strike in May 2010 and subsequent protests in Greece, and the London student protests of November 2010.

Further current affairs interests discussed during interviews revolved around Dutch governmental politics; critiques of politicians are alive and kicking in the punk scene (and are a distinct part of punk's history, see Donaghey 2013; Laing 1985; O'Hara 1999; Street 2012). This was most notable in reference to the rise of Geert Wilders' '*Partij voor de Vrijheid*' (PVV).[4] This topic formed a nexus around which punks could discuss their own political (self-)education and could become a starting point for both anti-political (see Chap. 5) and anti-racist discourses.

The rise in far-right political extremism in the Netherlands mirrors that of many of the countries in Western Europe (Mudde 2007; Vossen 2010). Pim Fortuyn's party '*List Pim Fortuyn*' (LPF) first ran in the 2002 general election; political tensions soared, culminating in his assassination six days before the election. The LPF won enough seats to become the second largest party and had a place in the subsequent coalition government. Following the decline of the LPF, Wilders' PVV (est. 2005) filled the niche and gained some political power in the 2006 general election. The fieldwork for this project occurred after the 2010 Dutch general election in which the PVV came third. Whilst they did not take any cabinet seats, their formal support ('*gedoogakkoord*') was necessary in the formation and stability of the resultant coalition government (de Lange and Art 2011).[5]

During 2010–2011 Geert Wilders was on trial, accused of hate speech. The trial was televised on Dutch television and ran from October 2010 to June 2011; as such this was another prominent political event during the fieldwork period (van Spanje and de Vreese 2015). Geert Wilders and the PVV were regularly mentioned by participants in this research. Whilst Wilders was dismissed by participants as an idiot, '*rare vent*',[6] an anomaly, the potential dangers that his popularity signalled were discussed with concern: "this Wilders guy [is] a bad motherfucker" (Luka).

Some used the rise of the PVV as an example of why more people should be engaged with democratic politics. Anger was expressed at those who disagreed with the PVV but responded only with apathy rather than action.

I think a lot of people, a lot of younger people as well, think they'll just play it by ear or something. But it doesn't get them anywhere, many people have something like "it'll be all right on the night, it may not come to anything, it's anyway all ridiculous". So most people don't [think] this movement will come to much either, they don't really have [...] to really do something against it, to speak up against it [...] because they think it'll all blow over or something. And I ask myself will it just blow over? The last few years it has just become bigger. I think these are things, I won't say what you *should* go against them or something but it is important to notice it and to think about it, about what the consequences could be if it goes on [...] what are the consequences of your own behaviour? (Gregor)

Another participant reinforced this by discussing his daily interactions with those affected by the popularity of the PVV and the associated rise of Islamophobia in the Netherlands. "This school [(his workplace)] has about fifty per cent Muslim students. So you can't have a day without politics. [...] Here you are continuously confronted with racism, the effect of it and eh, it keeps you on your toes" (Daan).

Critiques of parliamentary politics were not just reserved for right-wing opponents. Maxim, at the time of the interview, was reeling after feeling betrayed by 'his own side'. He discussed the recent actions by the "unbelievable fucking backstabbers of *Groen-Links*"[7] (Maxim) who had recently voted to continue the Netherlands' involvement in the war in Afghanistan (despite widespread opposition) in the hope—as Maxim understood it—of being invited to form part of the next coalition government. Maxim's judgement was that politically, as well as morally, this was an incorrect political move. The strength of his feeling on the matter and his investment in parliamentary politics show that far from being disillusioned, Maxim was concretely angry at this betrayal:

Brilliant, brilliant move on their part really. I don't know how and where the fuck they came up with this idea and who was the brilliant strategist who did, but they're going to lose so many votes because of this. It's going to be they're going to be like—I mean we're going to have elections for city councils coming up in March—they're going to be so slaughtered, it's going to be ridiculous. I mean [...] this new leader of *Groen-Links* was on TV talking about it, I was really like "you piece of shit". Really, like, "you're the worst, the worst parasite that we've ever had on the left, really like, horrible, I will spit in your face if I ever see you!" (Maxim)

There are many means by which we engage in spreading political ideas. Here I have described a number of ways in which participants in the Dutch punk scene engage in self-education and education of others; I argue that this process forms a key method by which political ideas spread, and thus is, in itself, a political act. Some of these activities are collective communicative forms of education (the lecture series, distros, conversations, and writing for others) whilst others are more individualised (reading, watching the news). However, all are forms of critically engaging with political messages and working to inspire others. Whilst some, such as Furedi (2005), have dismissed these 'individualised' forms of politics, they form an important sphere of alternative political activity for those marginalised from—or unwilling to engage in—other, traditional, forms of involvement. In doing so these fit within a historical trajectory of political activism by various other groups such as working-class men (Thompson [1963] 1980), and Black American women (Collins [1991] 2000).

The spread of knowledge, critical political thought and alternate modes of resisting society allow for the creation and reinforcement of new political cultural norms. The next section will look at the ways in which political discourses, especially from within the punk scene, have impacted the ways in which participants choose to live their lives. Following Giddens (1994, 2000) and Collins ([1991] 2000), I argue that there are multiple everyday life choices that are imbued with political connotations. The choices that participants make (or don't make) form modes of resistance to societal norms. There follows an intersubjective process by which these choices create new subcultural norms for Dutch punks.

RESISTING NORMATIVE CHOICES

Given punk's stance as critical of authority, state and 'the system' (Cross 2010; O'Hara 1999), it follows that many individuals involved with punk have a difficult time negotiating institutions and social norms in their everyday lives. Punk does not exist in a vacuum nor do its' participants. Zines and texts such as O'Hara's *Philosophy of Punk* (1999), which is widely read by punks, contain debate on the (anarchist) 'rules' by which punks must live, grappling with the difficulties that punks face when interacting in communication interlocks (Fine and Kleinman 1979) with non-punk society. Chapter 2 discussed the importance of 'resistance' (J. Clarke et al. [1975] 2006; Haenfler 2006; Leblanc 1999; Williams 2011) to subcultural debates, particularly within punk. This section will unpick a number of the ways in which participants resist normative choices within the realm of everyday life. It posits these individuals' choices as political (Giddens 1994).

Whilst punk discourse positions punks as 'anti-system', many punks have a less clear understanding of which 'system' it is that they oppose. For many punks it is the government and other forms of authority—and the restrictions these place on individuals through rules or law—that constitute the reviled system. Others take a broader political stance against capitalism or neo-liberalism. For some, this broad approach is more a 'punk' figure of speech than any particularly considered political position. Bram describes his politics with impressionistic (punk) brush strokes: "oh very much like the anarchist politics and the anti-state anti-system fuck the system, those kind of politics" (Bram).

Participants exhibited various strategies in dealing with the very real challenges that their politics posed for everyday life choices. From the extremes of 'dropping out' of society to decisions regarding which aspects of society individuals *could* work with and to what extent, participants espoused politically informed choices in many aspects of their life. Their politics informed decisions regarding work, housing, and patterns of consumptions, all of which will be discussed in the remainder of this section. Each choice made by participants represents a strategy of resistance to 'normal' society, thus providing examples of politics enacted on an everyday level in a manner that is possible for these punks.

One (anonymous[8]) participant described themselves as living completely outside 'the system'. They were not registered in any traceable way with the authorities and wanted to maintain this. Another used similar language in discussing his past engagements with 'society' and how this continues to impact his adult life. "[I] never fucking had a job, never had to do any official shit [... I'm] so used to being outside the whole fucking system" (Bram).[9] However, Bram was claiming unemployment benefits during the time he lived 'outside of society', so there must have been some degree of engagement with 'the system'. As such, Bram drew differentially on available modes and levels of engagements, deciding what was acceptable to him. Moreover, we see that he still aimed to 'perform' (during interview at least) an ideal of being 'outside' society. Dropping out is a strategy that entails a great deal of effort and thus is not always open to all punks. Participants often, instead, drew differentially upon various strategies in order to live in a 'politically conscious' way.

Some acknowledge this tension in their political critiques, by discussing the ways in which they 'regretfully' engage in the system due to the difficulties of complete disengagement. For others, this becomes a key part of their life and their art: "[keeping art and money separate] doesn't make sense for me because [the] economic system is one of the systems which you have to include in your art thinking as well" (Marieke).

Work

All participants engaged in some form of acquiring money, whatever their opinions of the economic system that necessitated this. Even the anonymous participant mentioned above, who lived 'outside the system', engaged in some paid work.

Many participants live on—or had past experience of living on— the state's unemployment allowance. A difficult economic climate in the Netherlands during the 1980s (especially in the northern city of Groningen) meant that for the older punk generations: "most of us [...] were on the dole since we were like sixteen [or] seventeen" (Wim). Indeed, "it was [the] beginning of the eighties and I don't think anyone had a job really, I don't remember anybody having a job. [...] There was a big crisis at that time, so everybody was on the dole, so was I. I'd done my arts school and finished school and just directly into get[ting] money from the [government]. Yeah there were just no jobs available" (Henk).

However, Henk immediately followed this comment up with a statement showing another, 'less' political argument for living from unemployment allowances:

Henk: Not that I would've taken any job, I think, [even] if there was one available!

Kirsty: Why?

Henk: Because I was enjoying myself too much!

Conversations in the pub whilst on fieldwork suggested that participants felt justified in their choice to live from these allowances despite their anti-state politics. They understood this as their own means of exploiting the state; taking the government's money and using it to live a punk life *must* be resistance. Being on 'the dole',[10] therefore, became normalised in many punk circles.

These stories highlight the way in which punks are inextricably bound to a (global) economic system, however much they resist. The poor economy and often precarious social position of punks led to their widespread unemployment. Unemployment therefore became a social *norm* within the Dutch (especially Groningen) punk scene of the 1980s. Punk ideology was reformulated, both to allow for this and to ensure that even those who might otherwise be able to get a job might choose not to in order to fit normative *punk* standards. Being 'on the dole' became an important discourse within Dutch punk scenes, similar to the early UK punk scene (Fryer 1986; Simonelli 2002) and the later Oi! (Worley 2013, 2014) and L.A. punk scenes (Traber 2001). Money gained through 'the dole' allowed Dutch punks to spend their time on creative, cultural and political engagements.

A number of participants discussed how the dole enabled them to support their local scene through working as 'volunteers' for punk venues: behind the bar, as sound technicians, as stage hands or as promoters. This lowered the operating costs of running the venues that supported the punk scene. Jaap says: "so I became unemployed and started booking bands. [...] Unemployment was high then. It wasn't a [paid] job then. I did that for thirteen and a half years, [as a volunteer] on the dole and then we created a [paid] job for it" (Jaap). In this we see one way in which punks 'rerouted' state money in order to finance the punk scene.

There was, however, recognition amongst older punks that they had had it lucky and that times were changing. "In Holland we're pretty spoilt, with the dole you don't work [and] you've got €800 a month to live from and you don't have to do basically nothing for it. [... But] it's not [like that] anymore because it's getting stricter, it's hard to be on the dole. I'm talking about like ten years ago" (Ruben). Changes to regulations were having real impacts on younger people's ability to be involved in punk in the same way that they had been. See Chap. 3 for Bram's and Wim's discussions of how much harder it is for younger generations, who are encouraged to be more 'responsible'.

There were (at the time of research) still a few possibilities for punks not to work; one participant offered the example of a bandmate who was in the process of applying for an artist's stipend from the government. However, in line with changes to the law on squatting (see Chap. 3) and changes to the unemployment welfare system, the opportunities for Dutch punks to live without work were being eroded.

The acceptance of government money, in spite of anti-state political positions stems, in part, from discursively prioritising criticisms of *work*. Not only does work limit one's potential for engagement in cultural and political actions but respondents also report criticisms of work in a manner that is linked to an anti-capitalist position. Luka reported his confusion with the treatment he received for working on arrival in Amsterdam:

> I could[n't] really figure it out; what the fuck is going on? Nobody was working, nobody cared about [it …] like everybody [was] begging. And [...] who knows how [they were] getting money. And I was like, whatever, washing the cars' windows on the street, you know? Like I start bringing [in] food. They were all just like, "Ah! You have money, you're a capitalist!" (Luka)

For the most part, however, work was becoming a necessity for many punks at the time of my research. There was a regretful acceptance of some degree of interaction with the capitalist system. A number of punks were, or had been, engaged in multiple, low-earning, unstable jobs. Some, such as Andre, adopted this path deliberately. Whilst he had been university educated and therefore certainly had the option of following a mainstream career path, he chose a more unstable way of working. This was the only way, for him, that he was able to foreground his commitment to punk: "so I do all kinds of small [jobs]—I don't have a regular job or something—because you can't combine that with being on the road a lot. So I do odd jobs, from teaching guitar to care-work with the elderly to removal jobs and [being a] driver for a company of a friend of mine" (Andre).

Other participants did not necessarily have the privilege of choosing unstable work over something more secure: having multiple insecure jobs was especially prevalent for those who had migrated to the Netherlands (see Chap. 4). "[I] moved to Holland, and then here I did all kind of dishwashing, cleaning, I was putting posters in the street, I worked for like a mail company, like delivering mail [...] more cleaning, then [...] working in restaurants I mean a lot of—I wouldn't say shitty work—but I mean, you had to pay your bills so I was doing whatever [was] necessary" (Nico). By contrast, prior to this, Nico had studied in Portugal for a degree and then worked as an English teacher. However, whilst Nico was forced into working multiple insecure jobs, he also chose not to continue with the normative career path he had initially embarked on, as demonstrated later in this chapter. Necessity and opportunity therefore interact with individuals' political agency in complex ways; we see here how crucial it is to acknowledge the 'connectedness' of these individuals' whole lives to the economic and social structures that force them in, or out, of work.

A number of participants set up their own businesses and were self-employed. Others were in the process of getting a business off the ground. Participants set up companies in the fields of IT and Internet services, publishing, graphic design, merchandise, bicycles; one participant was also involved in setting up a pub. A number of these businesses drew directly on skills learnt first through punk; for example, the graphic designer made posters and zines as a teenager, and the pub owner had volunteered at punk venues behind the bar. In this way Dutch punks display similarities to punks and skins in Germany who have their own 'alternative' economy (Ventsel 2008). Whilst arguably at odds with anti-capitalist strands of anarchism, this process feeds into punk and political discourses of 'autonomy' from State and from employers, that is, from 'the man'. "[W]orking for somebody else? If I can *not* do it, yeah I will, I will try to avoid it" (Nico). Moreover this is an example of the influence that punk DIY practices have on participants' work lives.

For Nico, it was very important to work for himself and run his bike shop along DIY principles. Whilst he aimed to provide a good service at as low a cost as possible, his greatest pleasure was to enjoy his work.

> I would probably more define myself with DIY. [T]rying to be a little bit [...] independent. One of the reasons I really like having this bike shop is; well, I'm working more now than I ever did, but it's working for myself. I mean, I think I give a good service to [...] my neighbours let's just say, regarding prices and quality. [...] I'm actually happy that I'm doing something that is not like working for somebody else. [... If] you have good working conditions, if you are well paid, if you have a good working environment and it's all fine, but that doesn't really happen in a lot of cases. (Nico)

Nico's decision to set up his own business was informed by the politics surrounding working conditions and his own experience of having previously been poorly treated in a work environment. He felt disenfranchised in challenging his treatment and thus saw this option as a manner of *survival* (Collins [1991] 2000).

The majority of self-employed participants worked alone. However, in some cases the businesses were partnerships (the pub), or had grown to a point where extra staff were needed to keep up with demand (the bike shop). Whilst pleased at his business' success, the shift that Nico experienced from employment to self-employment to employer was one that sat uncomfortably with him. During the interview, conducted at his work, he expressed hope that his employee was satisfied with his working conditions but worried that if I were to question him privately, he might have his own reservations about working for Nico.

Participants who were engaged in more normative career paths emphasised the importance of fulfilment from their work. However, these participants were almost exclusively engaged in roles with cultural or political associations.[11] At least five worked in the arts: Henk is a graphic designer; Menno, Kosta and Johan all draw and work with cartoons; and Marieke is an artist and fashion designer. Others' work was more directly linked to the punk scene; Jeroen, Mark, Maarten, Lotte and Jaap all work at or owned punk venues (working behind the bar, as sound engineers, or as promoters) and Ruben designs and makes merchandise for bands. Such participants who were able to make money from their creative interests did not necessarily view this as work, as they would likely do it anyway.

Other participants were engaged in work within the public sector. These roles were in keeping with the broadly left-wing ideologies of the Dutch punk movement, if, again, at odds with more anti-statist discourses. However, in searching for the lesser of 'two evils', working for 'the *public sector* man' was more acceptable than for 'the *private sector* man'. Bram relates this choice directly to his punk experiences:

> Since about six months ago I started going back to school and I'm learning to be like a social worker, I'm working with the homeless and junkies at the moment. So I reckon that in five years I'm gonna end up working with [... the] disadvantaged and underprivileged. [...] I think I wanna work with problem kids you know, cos that's where all of us come from, so you've got most experience with that and I kind of enjoy that, I'm good at that as well. (Bram[12])

Daan's career choice—a secondary school history and politics teacher—stemmed from his passion for politics, which was first stoked by punk: "I have no other ambitions than teaching. There are people who want to climb the greasy pole, become a director or whatever, but I find actual teaching great fun" (Daan). He saw this role as particularly important given the contemporary political environment, especially with the rise of the Islamophobic PVV given his work in a school district with a relatively high proportion of Muslims (see earlier in this chapter). He discussed the daily challenges faced by his pupils as a particular source of continued inspiration for his political activism, one dimension of which was his band.

The majority of the younger participants in this research were either students or had recently completed their studies. In their choices of subject, we see similar patterns to those already in work in that they are all influenced by political and/or cultural interests. Many chose to study (traditionally left-wing) social science subjects such as sociology or politics, and three were studying various aspects of music, musicology or music business. For a few students, this choice was based on a clear career plan. Larry had studied political history before embarking on a career in politics, whilst Sander was studying politics and was as yet undecided as to whether he wanted to enter politics or academia. However, most often these choices were based on interests rather than plans.

The high numbers of students and graduates amongst Dutch punks is partly symptomatic of merit-based access to higher education (from 1977 onwards) with high levels of economic support for students and their families; however, a degree of inequality of access to those from poorer backgrounds persisted (Rijken et al. 2007). At the time of fieldwork there had recently been a number of changes to the way in which university study was financed. Participants argued that this would probably reduce access to higher education for those who could not afford to pay. Whilst this had not yet had an impact, there was a great deal of consternation over the future for young people.

To work, or indeed not to work, to study, or not to, is a political decision (Giddens 1994). However, as we have seen, these individuals are constrained in terms of choice and opportunity by the economic system in which they are embedded. Whilst many would prefer to opt out of the economic system entirely, all are forced to engage. A struggling economy will affect all, and migrants and those from less well-off backgrounds have fewer options open to them. However, participants, where they can, have chosen how they will interact with the world of work. Some choose not to work, to prioritise the ability to tour over stable work, or to be self-employed. Others choose to work in the cultural world or in public sector jobs based on their prioritisation of left-wing ideals. We see again, in the example of punk work choices, the connectedness between sub-cultural ideology and participants' whole lives. Moreover, the interaction between choice and opportunity is not stable. The punk scene is affected by the changing economy and by the rise of neo-liberal economic policies that have reduced access to unemployment support and to university education. Younger punks are less able to choose not to work and to focus on their punk activities than their forbearers were. The impact of this is likely to become more apparent over the next decade.

Squatting

In Chap. 3 there was an extensive discussion of the importance of squatting to Dutch punk, focusing in particular on the cultural and political opportunities that were historically afforded to punk. As discussed, squatting became a punk norm (particularly in the 1980s) that was set against mainstream societal expectations. However, again, the individual reasons for punks to choose to live in squats were varied. Some understood it as a political action (Ruben, Wouter), some did so out of necessity (Dikkie, Tom) and others focused on the sociability of doing so (Lotte, Sander).

As squatting became more difficult—through the 1990s and 2000s, up until it was outlawed on 1 October 2010—punk participation in squatting shifted. More and more respondents talk about squats as places to socialise (Herry Alex) or to volunteer (Suzanne, Luka) rather than as a viable choice for everyday accommodation. This process reinforces the politicisation of the choice to squat. Whilst necessity might still be a factor, the sociability of squatting has been eroded by the daily challenges and worries of fighting against evictions, both in the courts and in the streets (Marieke, Mark, Wouter; see also Chap. 3). Whereas at the height of the squatters movement (Owens 2009) squatting may have been an 'easy' option, it latterly became something in which one must be ideologically invested.

PRACTICES OF CONSUMPTION

Since the early 1980s, there has been a strong tradition of punk involvement with environmental activism (O'Hara 1999). Anarcho-punk called for conscious living and activist engagement amongst punks. Led by UK bands such as Crass, anarcho-punks were often engaged in anti-war activism, with a focus on revitalising the Campaign for Nuclear Disarmament (Worley 2011; Rimbaud 1998). Other punk bands, such as Flux of Pink Indians and Conflict focused instead on issues of animal rights, vivisection and vegetarianism (Cross 2010). There was a proliferation of punk zines at this time that discussed animal rights and ecologically conscious practices of consumption. A similar shift can be seen in the United States, with politicised old school hardcore bands in the early 1980s and the straight edge scene also developing strong animal rights politics. Bands such as Youth of Today and Earth Crisis later brought the message of vegetarianism and veganism to the straight edge punks of the 1990s and 2000s (Haenfler 2006).

This concern with animal rights fed into a wider politics of consciousness for the environment and opposition to wasteful practices of consumption. This can be understood as a form of continuity between (anarcho-)punk and earlier politicised countercultural trends such as hippie and avant-garde; "this connection is most clearly expressed as a shared sense of non-conformity, anti-consumerism, anti-materialism, and anti-capitalism" (Donaghey 2013: 151).

Vegetarianism

When posed the question of whether they were engaged in any forms of politics, some participants immediately brought up their vegetarianism, or in some cases, veganism. For many of those involved in the punk scene this is therefore is intertwined with notions of how one can live a *politically* conscious life.

Ruben: I got to into the politics stuff through a friend and through bands like Crass.

Kirsty: and what sort of politics are you talking about?

Ruben: anarchy—anarchist politics DIY, environmental stuff, vegetarianism, yeah.

In the Dutch punk scene vegetarianism has become an established norm: "within punk and hardcore there are lots of vegetarians and vegans" (Lisa). Like the Black Cat Cafe of Clark's (2004) research, many of the Dutch squats with 'VoKu's' that are frequented by punks serve vegetarian and/or vegan food only. Joe's Garage in Amsterdam, where I volunteered in the kitchen, served vegetarian food with vegan options, and Molli—the most renowned of Amsterdam's punk squats—serves vegan food twice per week.

A number of the participants in this research offered political reasons for their vegetarianism; "most of it's about human rights and animal rights" (Theo), and "that everyone in this world would have enough to eat if we all stop eating meat, and that it is enormously polluting, and that the animals all have to live in boxes of 1 × 1[m]" (Marieke). Their vegetarianism was one facet of a wider political engagement with animal rights issues. As previously noted, Lisa wrote and distributed leaflets about vegetarianism in her local community, and she also takes part in demonstrations on animal rights causes. For Daan it was part of the lifestyle politics with which he was engaged through the International Socialists. He understood vegetarianism and concern for the environment as a key element in revolutionary politics; he felt that no politically engaged person could *not* be vegetarian and that mass vegetarianism should be fought for in order to hasten revolution.

Whilst not everyone subscribed to the same evangelical 'lifestyle' politics that Daan displays, two participants took pride in having had an influence over others' decisions to eat less—or no—meat. "[M]y mum is now vegetarian but earlier she wasn't, I was brought up with the idea that it's normal to eat meat" (Lisa).

> [T]here are a lot of people who are aggressively vegan. But [...] my house mate for instance is a meat eater, if he's got meat in the fridge, [okay, so be it. ...] But he does join me three days a week [in] eating vegan [food]. Then I think, I actually stopped him three times [from] eating meat! [...] Well! Why would you always have to be extreme when you just [can] to do things more quietly? Maybe more logically, for me at least. (Jeroen)

Participants were often keen to establish that vegetarianism should always be a personal choice, for others as well as for themselves. "What I do find important is that people decide it for themselves" (Marieke). Individuals should follow punk norms of vegetarianism no less critically than societal norms of omnivorousness. It is in this process of conscious decision-making that the political importance of individual choice resides (Giddens 1994). Punks' 'think for yourself' mantra, and the emphasis amongst Dutch punks to be '*bewust*' (see Chap. 5) is inherently political.

Indeed, one vegetarian was highly critical of veganism's inflexibility, in terms of its negation of allowing individuals to 'think for themselves'. "There is no definition of 'this is how you must live'. That is I think also in a way what I have against veganism, it is so extreme that it nearly dictates to others 'this is how you should do it'" (Marieke). For Marieke, political agency was of the utmost importance in regards to individual decisions about vegetarianism.

In three interviews the participants emphasised that the decision to turn vegetarian was made on a 'landmark' birthday, as part of the process of becoming an adult, independent from their families' norms. "[It was on] [m]y twenty-first birthday exactly! [...] I was just saying like okay, now I have become of age, I have become twenty-one so less talk, more action" (Theo). Marieke turned vegetarian on her 13th birthday and Daan on his 18th. We see that these political choices can be part of the individuals' sense of identity creation (see Chap. 5).

For these participants both the choice to become vegetarian and the act of vegetarianism are politically loaded and form one method by which they can choose to lead socially and politically conscious lives. However, it is important to acknowledge that vegetarianism has become a punk norm, loaded with subcultural capital (Thornton 1995). Therefore, when individuals make this choice, they are able to choose differentially between different cultural and subcultural norms, placed as they are within various communication interlocks (Fine and Kleinman 1979).

Sustainable Consumption: Dumpster Diving and Recycling

Themes of ecological activism are present in other choices participants make in regards to consumption. A number of participants, whilst talking about their political engagements, discussed concerns with waste and their attempts to reduce this on a personal level. One participant had noticed a recent trend amongst his peers towards 'punk gardening': Theo had recently started growing his own vegetables and was surprised to find that he wasn't alone in this passion. However, this trend is certainly in keeping with wider punk discourses on ecological activism and

DIY. Other methods of sustainable punk consumption included 'dumpster diving', recycling as much as possible, and the purchase and production of ethical clothing. These practices were usually engaged in by those who were also linked to the squatters' movement and were vegetarian, as part of a wide set of personal practices influenced by political positions and political norms within punk.

'Dumpster diving' is the practice of reclaiming food from (often) supermarket bins where unspoiled food that cannot be sold (due to damaged packaging or being outside it's 'sell-by date') can be found. This practice spawned the 'freegan' movement (Stewart 2009), which has strong links to DIY anarcho- and crust-punk (Edwards and Mercer 2007, 2012); Clark (2004) discusses its role in the 'punk cuisine' of Seattle's punks based around the Black Cat Café; the dumpster 'cleanses' the waste products of the traces of capitalism, thereby making them acceptable to anti-capitalist punks.

During interviews for this research, this anti-capitalist trend was present in the discussions of dumpster diving by those who engaged in it. Whilst some discussed practices of only eating food "from dumpsters" (Marieke), others viewed it as 'recycling food'. 'Recycling food' was seen as broader than just taking it from bins: "In Amsterdam you can actually recycle a lot of food, you can go to several markets and, and get food at the end of the day, and [...] I don't have any problem going to big supermarket[s] and steal[ing] food from them. Kind of from the bins but actually in [the shop too.] In Amsterdam, for instance, there's this big supermarket [chain] called Albert Heijn" (Nico). This form of stealing was, for this participant, justified by their (punk-influenced) anti-capitalist stance:

> Well, the thing is they are all these companies I think they're making like so much money and, and of course their politics are probably not environmentally conscious, and they just want to try and get as much as possible. So there's, something I read in a zine a long time ago, it said; "stealing is not really stealing, stealing is making things more equal". So I sort of, yeah [...] that's something I support. (Nico)

Mark also explained that for him it was important to "not buy anything from big firms—only shoplift" (Mark).

This process of recycling, through dumpster diving or stealing, was applied beyond food recycling. Nico was proud that his bike shop was almost entirely furnished by these methods.

> In this shop [(his business)], you would be amazed with the things that actually were bought and the things that were found. Basically, I can tell you only these drawers, and maybe that I bought them [(points to his tools) too], but almost everything else, trust me, is ['found']; all those shelves, all that wood, these things on the floor, [...] really a lot of stuff was found on the on the street[13]. So, I think already for that I think I'm happy that I'm doing it, I really see it as a kind of must [do] thing. And you know, a lot of people do this kind of stuff, you still get a lot of scavengers and people take stuff from the trash, and I think it's really a very good thing to do. (Nico)

Ethical clothing was an issue of discussion amongst two participants. One, a fashion designer, had built her career around making artistic statements about "being conscious about the clothes you wear" (Marieke) and had made collections entirely out of recycled and repurposed materials. Lisa discusses her concern with wasteful purchasing of cheap and unethically produced clothing ('fast fashion'), made using underpaid child labour, and her (not fully achieved) desire to only buy clothes that have been ethically produced and/or from second hand shops.

> I also buy more second hand clothing. [...] It might still be made by children or something but anyway you stop that process [...] [or] you don't stop it really, [but] you disrupt the process of production, and [all] this consuming and buying new clothes all the time and that sort of thing. [But] I find it very difficult, on the other hand I also do just want to buy nice dresses and things. (Lisa)

Both Marieke and Lisa discuss the problems brought about by the cost of ethical clothes, limiting their availability to many. "I do for instance have one pair of jeans that were quite expensive and they were Fairtrade, biological cotton say, and that is nice but it's so expensive, you can't do that for all your clothes or things. Yes and also these jeans just fitted perfectly, it's not that I would have bought them if they hadn't looked good" (Lisa).

Both the role of consumption in 'creating space' (Collins [1991] 2000) in which subcultural participants can live by alternative norms, and the practice of consumption as 'resistance' have a long history in subcultural theory (Clarke et al. [1975] 2006; Hebdige 1979; Williams 2011; see also Chap. 2). However, I argue that practices of consumption go beyond this in being a clear site in which individuals make politically informed choices in their everyday lives. Moreover, as opposed to areas such as work and housing, in choices of consumption these individuals are less constrained by structural factors.

DEMONSTRATIONS AND DIRECT ACTION

Nearly every single participant talked of having been on a political demonstration at some point in their lives. The issues addressed by these demonstrations varied widely with themes including squatters' rights and housing shortages, anti-monarchy, anti-government, student politics, anti-nuclear weapons, anti-nuclear energy, anti-war, anti-religion, anti-globalisation, anti-racism, anti-homophobia, anti-islamophobia, workers' rights, women's rights and animal rights.

The importance of the squatters' demonstrations to the punk scene was outlined in Chap. 3. They were both historically important at the height of the squatters' movement in the 1970s–1980s, as well as contemporaneously at the time of the squatting ban (Fig. 6.1). Other causes were also rooted to particular times. Only older punks talked about women's rights, or workers' rights, or anti-nuclear weapons demonstrations. Many of the younger punks were more involved in student politics or anti-war protests in relation to the wars in Iraq and Afghanistan in the 2000s.

Maxim values demonstrations as a means to radicalise people: "It was nice to see that there were people demonstrating because it was good to see the outrage, I mean, I'm a socialist, and I think that people really change, I mean nothing changes you as much as going to a demonstration and getting pepper sprayed, I mean that teaches you so many things at once about how the world works" (Maxim). In this sense, Maxim echoes those who saw the squatters' and punk movements become radicalised in the 1970s and 1980s through eviction and coronation protests (see Chap. 3).

This was certainly true of Bram who took great pride in the reputation of the Groningen punks in the 1990s as particularly radical and fearless at protests: "we were kind of known throughout Holland that we didn't give a fuck so, you know, so they always put us up at the front of the demonstration so even if there's like fights with cops or with skinheads or something we'll just fucking kick the shit out of them you

Fig. 6.1 The Bucket Boys, an Amsterdam punk-squat band, serenade the pro-testers at a Squatters' demo. Photo taken by author, 8 November 2010

know!" (Bram). For Bram, protest is particularly valued as a site for affective social ties to develop between him and his fellow punks (see Chap. 2).

However, others favour more 'direct' forms of protest over demon-strations: "I find it hard to motivate myself to go every week and hold a placard, I'm more someone who *does*" (Jeroen). These other forms of direct action often cause much debate and consternation within activist scenes.

A group of punks smashed the windows of the Rabobank. They claimed [(publically)] that they were from the squat scene. But the squat scene is made up of so many dfferent types of people. It was all because the squat evictions didn't happen, they were delayed. So they had some bricks left over and they thought, haha! "Well, we've got to do something, and yeah bankers are wankers, fuck the economic system, we'll throw bricks at it" haha! [But] then there were massive debates, online, within the squat scene [about the use of this as a tactic on 'behalf' of so many poeple with various opinions]. (Marieke)

With forms of direct action and demonstration, we see that punks maintain connections with other political activists. In participating in demonstrations we see a variety of political causes in which punks are often engaged. They do so alongside their other forms of political activism rather than in place of them. Most importantly, as with all of punks' choices, Gregor stresses that the choice to support a particular cause must be made consciously: "you mustn't go and demonstrate just to demonstrate, of course" (Gregor). As in other realms of politics, participants placed an emphasis on the deicision to be involved as inherently political (Giddens 1994).

'Traditional' Politics

Punk is often traditionally understood as standing in opposition to all Political structures. This anti-government feeling stems from a suspicion of those in authority and often encompasses a dislike for (all) politicians (Gololobov 2014a; Lahusen 1993). However, as we have seen throughout this chapter, this does not translate into punks being apathetic. Indeed, we saw earlier how closely some punks follow the manoeuvrings of politicians. For many punks, political engagement is expressed in a variety of manners entailing either grassroots organising or individual action; however there are also punks who do become involved in governmental or democratic politics. For them this involvement is not at odds with their punk identities; on the contrary, their punk background shapes their entry into and their engagement with politics throughout their careers.

One participant in particular was heavily involved in democratic politics and had two roles in the 'Socialistische Partij' (SP)[14]: one within the provincial parliament, and a second as chairman of the local branch. Punk, he says, was directly responsible for his involvement in party politics. Not only did lyrics introduce him to new political themes that ensnared his interest but also the DIY ethic prepared him for the way in which he preferred to approach politics, thereby echoing Dunn's (2008) proposal of the revolutionary potential of DIY. Larry's band's lyrics touched on themes of:

"Capitalism sucks" and our "government sucks" and we have to fight the government—really not that great poetic stuff. [(laughs)] Of course that's how you start and I think that really is also punk for me, it's not only music, but it's also a way of working, of organizing yourself and from thereon I wanted to get more involved in politics and then [...] I joined a party but that started really with listening to punk music. (Larry)

For Larry, it was both the left-wing politics and the party's approach that attracted him. He saw similarities between politics and his punk interests. His local SP branch's emphasis on grassroots activism on a local rather than national level was in keeping with Larry's punk, DIY ethic:

Well it's cool to be in politics but when you are in the real city council, like a small parliament it's all people are like "blablabla" [...] and just a small part that you can do. I think it's good that I did that but now, when I look back and think what I've learned that it's not everything. That's the cool thing about what we do [now], that we also do a lot of work outside the city hall a lot of [...] grassroots politics with people. [...] We fight for, well it could be just like a basic thing like a bus stop that's gone and they don't have any public transport anymore, or it could be the forest that they are going to sell, that's the last thing we did; the town wanted to sell the forests and the neighborhood surrounding it, we went to them every night knocking at every door, [asking] "do you want to help us? Come on we are going to fight it". That kind of stuff that makes it really interesting. [...] Our way of working [...] is also a bit of the DIY mentality, [...] it's also that thing that you do when you're in punk, it's also, you can sit and wait until some politician does it for you or you can do something yourself and I think that's why there is a good connection. (Larry)

Punk furnished Larry with the methods by which he could best engage with the politics that interested him. He has built a career out of politics and sees no contradiction between his punk involvement and his professional role.

Some participants, when attempting to convey their own political position, would engage in the language of parliamentary politics by listing parties that they particularly did or did not identify with. Bart says: "I see myself as roughly in the D66[15] corner", and Sander suggests that opposition to liberal parties such as the 'Volkspartij voor Vrijheid en Democratie' (VVD)[16] is particularly punk. For others, a broad 'political spectrum' was used in order to position themselves:

I do tend towards a left wing spectrum [...] extreme left maybe, but yes
I can never find that really in a party or a person [...] It's very difficult to
have to categorise myself. I'm not an anarchist, I'm not a communist, I
am strongly socia[b]l[e] so maybe I'm a socialist! It's more about how I
see myself, I see lots of good things everywhere, anarchism can work very
well, but not on a large scale, but in 'compartments', so that just means in
commune-like living structures but then it quickly becomes like 'Animal
Farm' or like communism nearly [...] and that doesn't mean that communism is something bad, absolutely not. It just has to be applied in the right
way. That's where it most often fails. Maybe [I'm] a domestic anarchist
with communist tendencies in a social-democratic world, maybe that's it.
(Jeroen)

This unwillingness to align firmly with any particular political position is
characteristic of punks' suspicion of politics; moreover it fits with punks'
tendency to 'evade' genres (Steinholt, 2012).

A number of participants in this research project were members of
the International Socialists (IS). This was part of the wider tradition of
left-wing affiliations within the Dutch punk scene (as discussed in Chaps.
3 and 5, and in Lohman 2013). A number of early Dutch punk bands
had professed affiliations to communist or socialist groups and/or think-
ers. These included the bands that made up the Red Rock Collective—
Rondos, Rode Wig, Sovjets and Tandstickörshocks—as well as later acts
such as Lärm and Man Lifting Banner (Lohman 2013). Members of
these bands were actively engaged in politics outside of their music, and
as such normalised punks' engagement with left-wing political activism
on an individual basis.

For Daan, his involvement in politics directly impacted on the band's
direction. Having already changed their name from 'Profound' to 'Man
Lifting Banner', he said that his membership of IS marked the start of a
new chapter in the band's history: "in 1991 I joined the International
Socialists. That's when Man Lifting Banner became a revolutionary
socialist band". We therefore see that individuals' place in different inter-
locking spheres of influence and communication (Fine and Kleinman
1979) spreads influence in sometimes surprising ways.

Daan displayed a great deal of interest in left-wing ideas (as previously discussed), and during his interview spoke at length about political theory; he was keen to emphasise the need for political ideas to be
grounded in and to be sympathetic with people's struggles. A key part of

his engagement with this is in writing for the IS paper and website. This was another means by which he participated in educational practices as a political act not only in terms of communicating his ideas but also as a means to further educate himself.

Both Daan and Maxim discuss how their activities with the IS have been curtailed in recent years due to various personal circumstances that mean they have less time and ability to engage with it. Their contemporaneous activities seemed largely focused around communicating the ideas of IS to a broader audience in order to gain a larger membership. They both took part in selling the IS newspaper and distributing leaflets to the public but regret that this is all they are able to do. Maxim used to be involved weekly but now dedicates most of his time to his PhD study; Daan used to work in the leadership of the organisation until a nervous breakdown forced him to reduce the time he spent working with IS. "On the weekend we usually have a little action going on at the market like giving out leaflets and talking to people and trying to get some people to come to meetings and stuff so I help out when I can. I used to be involved on a weekly basis and I don't have the energy to do it anymore" (Maxim).

As well as his membership of the IS, Daan was also heavily involved in his workplace trade union. He was a union representative for his (large) school at a time when there were large-scale union demonstrations against the Dutch governments' cuts to the public sector.

This form of political engagement—with an established organization—requires a certain level of dedication. Individuals' ability to consistently dedicate time, often weekly if not more often, varies as other aspects of their lives demand more attention (similarly to the drop off in subcultural engagement as participants age, see Chap. 3 and Haenfler 2006). As such this engagement with traditional politics is not open to all. Political punks engage in other forms of resistance instead of, or alongside, these traditional forms; both Maxim and Daan remain committed vegetarians and abstain from alcohol even whilst their involvement with IS fluctuates. We see here evidence for Collins' ([1991] 2000) arguments for widening the scope of what constitutes political engagement beyond narrow definitions such as Furedi's (2005). Even those who *do* have access to 'traditional' politics might alter their engagement over time. This does not mean they are no longer politically active; they are still creating their own space for resistance by all means open to them.

Despite punks' professed anti-system politics, some do choose to engage in traditional forms of politics alongside the other political expressions that have been discussed during this chapter. Engagements are multifarious and encompass personal, educative and collective forms of traditional or grassroots activism.

CONCLUSION

This chapter has foregrounded the need to centre the discussion of subculture on participants' *whole* lives. It has taken 'political engagement' as a focus, due to the particularly political nature of the Dutch punk scene. Rather than drawing a boundary around subcultural political activity, or trying to understand whether punk or politics came first, it has uncovered the variety of ways in which politically aware participants are engaged in activisms.

The chapter has argued for a widening of the definition of 'politics'. Whilst there are problems with individualisation theories, especially in regards to their ahistoricism, the value that they place on individual actions and the political implications of choices that individuals make is important. However, this is not to say that participants are entirely free to make everyday decisions. This chapter has therefore drawn attention to a number of facets (in particular regarding work and housing) in which individuals' opportunities are shaped or stymied by structural factors.

By broadening the scope of politics beyond traditional Politics, I have highlighted the political potential inherent in educative practices, both in terms of self-education and educating others, as part of a trend that has a long history in punk distros and zine writing. I have also argued for an acknowledgement of the importance of political choices within everyday life regarding arenas such as work, housing, and patterns of consumption. Finally I noted that punks do not engage solely in these alternate forms of politics, as some are also active in more traditional forms of protest politics such as demonstrations, as well as trade unions and democratic politics.

NOTES

1. People for the Ethical Treatment of Animals.
2. The project ended in 1982 as it became unmanageably large.

3. A Dutch communist famous for setting fire to the Reichstag in 1933 to protest Nazism.
4. The PVV is the 'Party for Freedom', a far-right political party. Whereas Wilders is often positioned as an anti-politics populist (de Lange and Art 2011; Vossen 2010), he was viewed by these punks as part of the political establishment.
5. Further evidence of the extent of their power could be seen in 2012 when the withdrawal of their support for the cabinet led to its collapse and the 2012 general election.
6. Crazy guy.
7. Green-Left, a left-wing party with a focus on ecology.
8. This participant explicitly requested that the section of their interview in which they discussed these matters was not to be attributed to them. I have not drawn any quotes or given any information that could trace their location, and I used gender-neutral pronouns in order to mask their identity as far as possible.
9. See full quote in Chap. 5.
10. It is a sign of Groningen's connections with UK punks that they use UK slang there. See Chap. 4 for more discussion of these connections.
11. Of those who did not: one participant worked in the banking sector, another as a truck driver, a third as a mechanic. All of these participants saw their work life as entirely separate from their cultural affiliations.
12. Unfortunately, cuts to funding for the training of social workers prevented Bram from completing his studies.
13. In Amsterdam this practice is formalised and was noted during my field-work. On regular and pre-arranged evenings, households were allowed to put any unwanted large items onto the street. Anything that had not been claimed by midday the following day is collected by the local authority.
14. Dutch Socialist Party.
15. D66 is a centrist liberal party.
16. 'The People's Party for Freedom and Democracy', a liberal-conservative party.

REFERENCES

Alterman, J.B. 2011. The Revolution Will Not Be Tweeted. *The Washington Quarterly* 34 (4): 103–116.
Beck, U. 1994. The Reinvention of Politics: Towards a Theory of Reflexive Modernization. In *Reflexive Modernization: Politics, Tradition and Aesthetics in the Modern Social Order*, ed. U. Beck, A. Giddens, and S. Lash, 1–55. Cambridge: Polity Press.

Clark, D. 2004. The Raw and the Rotten: Punk Cuisine. *Ethnology* 43 (1): 19–31.

Clarke, J., S. Hall, T. Jefferson, and B. Roberts. [1975] 2006. Subcultures, Cultures and Class. In *Resistance through Rituals: Youth Subcultures in Post-war Britain*, 2nd ed., ed. S. Hall and T. Jefferson, 3–59. London: Routledge.

Collins, P. H. [1991] 2000. *Black Feminist Thought: Knowledge, Consciousness, and the Politics of Empowerment*, 2nd ed. New York: Routledge.

Corrigan, P., and S. Frith. [1975] 2006. The Politics of Youth Culture. In *Resistance through Rituals: Youth Subcultures in Post-war Britain*, 2nd ed., ed. S. Hall and T. Jefferson, 231–242. London: Routledge.

Crenshaw, K. 1991. Mapping the Margins: Intersectionality, Identity Politics, and Violence against Women of Color. *Stanford Law Review* 43 (6): 1241–1299.

Cross, R. 2010. There is No Authority but Yourself: The Individual and the Collective in British Anarcho-Punk. *Music and Politics* 4 (2): 1–20.

de Lange, S.L., and D. Art. 2011. Fortuyn versus Wilders: An Agency-Based Approach to Radical Right Party Building. *West European Politics* 34 (6): 1229–1249.

Donaghey, J. 2013. Bakhunin Brand Vodka: An Exploration into Anarchist-Punk and Punk-Anarchism. *Anarchist Developments in Cultural Studies* 1: 138–170.

Duncombe, S. [1997] 2008. *Notes from Underground: Zines and the Politics of Alternative Culture*. Bloomington, IN: Microcosm.

Dunn, K.C. 2008. Never Mind the Bollocks: The Punk Rock Politics of Global Communication. *Review of International Studies* 34 (1): 193–210.

Edwards, F., and D. Mercer. 2007. Gleaning from Gluttony: An Australian Youth Subculture Confronts the Ethics of Waste. *Australian Geographer* 38 (3): 279–296.

Edwards, F., and D. Mercer. 2012. Food Waste in Australia: The Freegan Response. *The Sociological Review* 60 (2): 174–191.

Fine, G.A., and S. Kleinman. 1979. Rethinking Subculture: An Interactionist Analysis. *American Journal of Sociology* 85 (1): 1–20.

Freire, P. [1970] 2000. *Pedagogy of the Oppressed*. New York: Continuum.

Fryer, P. 1986. Punk and the New Wave of British Rock: Working Class Heroes and Art School Attitudes. *Popular Music and Society* 10 (4): 1–15.

Furedi, F. 2005. *Politics of Fear*. London: Continuum.

Giddens, A. 1994. *Beyond Left and Right: The Future of Radical Politics*. Cambridge: Polity Press.

Giddens, A. 2000. *The Third Way and its Critics*. Cambridge: Polity Press.

Gololobov, I. 2014. Krasnodar: Perpendicular Culture in the Biggest Village on Earth. In *Punk in Russia: Cultural Mutation from the 'Useless' to the 'Moronic'*, ed. I. Gololobov, H. Pilkington, and Y.B. Steinholt, 99–142. London: Routledge.

Goshert, J.C. 2000. "Punk" After the Pistols: American Music, Economics, and Politics in the 1980s and 1990s. *Popular Music and Society* 24 (1): 85–106.

Haenfler, R. 2006. *Straight Edge: Clean-Living Youth, Hardcore Punk, and Social Change.* New Brunswick, NH: Rutgers University Press.

Hebdige, D. 1979. *Subculture: The Meaning of Style.* London: Routledge.

Hobsbawm, E. 1996. Identity Politics and the Left. *New Left Review* 217: 38–47.

Kempson, M. 2014, May 23. My Version of Feminism: Subjectivity, DIY and the Feminist Zine. *Social Movement Studies: Journal of Social, Cultural and Political Protest.* Available from 10.1080/14742837.2014.945157.

Lahusen, C. 1993. The Aesthetic of Radicalism: The Relationship Between Punk and the Patriotic Nationalist Movement of the Basque Country. *Popular Music* 12 (3): 263–280.

Laing, D. 1985. *One Chord Wonders: Power and Meaning in Punk Rock.* Milton Keynes: Open University Press.

Leblanc, L. 1999. *Pretty in Punk: Girls' Gender Resistance in a Boys' Subculture.* New Brunswick: Rutgers University Press.

Lohman, K. 2013. Dutch Punk with Eastern Connections: Mapping cultural flows between East and West Europe. *Punk & Post Punk* 2 (2): 147–163.

Mudde, C. 2007. *Populist Radical Right Parties in Europe.* Cambridge: Cambridge University Press.

Nanabhay, M., and R. Farmanfarmaian. 2011. From Spectacle to Spectacular: How Physical Space, Social Media and Mainstream Broadcast Amplified the Public Sphere in Egypt's Revolution. *The Journal of North African Studies* 16 (4): 573–603.

Norris, P. 2002. *Democratic Phoenix: Reinventing Political Activism.* Cambridge: Cambridge University Press.

O'Hara, C. 1999. *The Philosophy of Punk: More Than Noise!.* Edinburgh: AK Press.

Owens, L. 2009. *Cracking Under Pressure: Narrating the Decline of the Amsterdam Squatters' Movement.* Amsterdam: Amsterdam University Press.

Phillipov, M. 2006. Haunted by the Spirit of '77: Punk Studies and the Persistence of Politics. *Continuum: Journal of Media & Cultural Studies* 20 (3): 383–393.

Pilkington, H., and E. Omel'chenko. 2013. Regrounding Youth Cultural Theory (in Post Socialist Youth Cultural Practice). *Sociology Compass* 7 (3): 208–224.

Rijken, S., I. Maas, and H.B.G. Ganzeboom. 2007. The Netherlands: Access to Higher Education—Institutional Arrangements and Inequality of Opportunity. In *Stratification in Higher Education: A Comparison*, ed. Y. Shavit, R. Arum, and A. Gamoran, 266–293. Stanford, CA: Stanford University Press.

Rimbaud, P. 1998. *Shibboleth: My Revolting Life*. Edinburgh: AK Press.

Simonelli, D. 2002. Anarchy, Pop and Violence: Punk Rock Subculture and the Rhetoric of Class, 1976–1978. *Contemporary British History* 16 (2): 121–144.

Smart, C. 2007. *Personal Life: New Directions in Sociological Thinking*. Cambridge: Polity Press.

Steinholt, Y.B. 2012. Punk is Punk but By No Means Punk: Definition, Genre Evasion and the Quest for an Authentic Voice in Contemporary Russia. *Punk & Post-Punk* 1 (3): 267–284.

Stewart, T. 2009. *Waste: Uncovering the Global Food Scandal*. London: Penguin.

Street, J. 2012. *Music & Politics*. Cambridge: Polity Press.

Thompson, E.P. [1963] 1980. *The Making of the English Working Class*. London: Gollancz.

Thornton, S. 1995. *Club Cultures: Music, Media and Subcultural Capital*. Cambridge: Polity Press.

Traber, D. 2001. L.A'.s "White Minority": Punk and the Contradictions of Self-Marginalization. *Cultural Critique* 48 (1): 30–64.

van Spanje, J., and C. de Vreese. 2015. The Good, The Bad and The Voter: The Impact of Hate Speech Prosecution of a Politician on Electoral Support for his Party. *Party Politics* 2 (1): 115–130.

Ventsel, A. 2008. Punx and Skins United: One Law for Us One Law for Them. *The Journal of Legal Pluralism and Unofficial Law* 40 (57): 45–100.

Vossen, K. 2010. Populism in the Netherlands after Fortuyn: Rita Verdonk and Geert Wilders Compared. *Perspectives on European Politics and Society* 11 (1): 22–38.

Ward, J.J. 1996. "This is Germany! It's 1933!" Appropriations and Constructions of Fascism in New York Punk/Hardcore in the 1980s. *Journal of Popular Culture* 30 (3): 155–185.

Williams, J.P. 2011. *Subcultural Theory: Traditions and Concepts*. Cambridge: Polity Press.

Worley, M. 2011. One Nation under the Bomb: The Cold War and British Punk to 1984. *Journal for the Study of Radicalism* 5 (2): 65–83.

Worley, M. 2012. Shot By Both Sides: Punk, Politics and the End of "Consensus". *Contemporary British History* 26 (3): 333–354.

Worley, M. 2013. Oi! Oi! Oi!: Class, Locality and British Punk. *Twentieth Century British History* 24 (4): 606–636.

Worley, M. 2014. Hey Little Rich Boy, Take a Good Look at Me: Punk, Class and British Oi! *Punk & Post-Punk* 3 (1): 5–20.

Worley, M. 2015. Punk, Politics and British (Fan)zines, 1976–1984: While the World Was Dying, Did You Wonder Why? *History Workshop Journal* 79 (1): 76–106.

CHAPTER 7

Dutch Punk Lives: Contesting Subcultural Boundaries

This research has charted the development of the Dutch punk scene through the eyes and lives of its participants. At its core this book challenges those who attempt to draw clearly delineated boundaries around objects of study, arguing instead that we need to understand the messiness and connectedness of the social world. It dismantles the boundaries of subculture and its practices, destabilises geographic and spatial boundaries, and disrupts narrow definitions in understanding political engagement.

The choice of punk as the subculture with which to illustrate these arguments has facilitated this development. Punk is a highly contested term for those who identify with it and/or are involved in punk subculture. This has not always been reflected in academic literature that has often focused on particular elements of the subculture at the expense of others, thus making it appear 'neater'. With this book I have focused particularly on punk as a set of practices rather than, for example, punk as a musical genre, artistic form, cinema, comic strip style, fashion, a lifestyle or alternative economy (to name just a few spheres that punk has infiltrated). However, in doing so I have opened up possibilities for individuals to claim punk. Punk is, I argue, multifaceted. Punk influences many aspects of individuals' lives; just as those lives shape punk. Punk may have been the 'common denominator' in research participants' lives, but the experiences of these people and the meanings that they attach to them are by no means uniform.

© The Author(s) 2017
K. Lohman, *The Connected Lives of Dutch Punks*,
Palgrave Studies in the History of Subcultures and Popular Music,
DOI 10.1007/978-3-319-51079-8_7

This book places its punk participants' lives at the foreground of destabilising the boundaries of subculture, geography and politics. In focusing on participants' narratives and their practices it centres their punk subjectivity, embedding their lives and their punk subculture as part of wider culture. It argues that punks do not live their lives in a cultural—or a spatial—bubble. They interact with and learn from punks and non-punks from all over the world. Punk—and non-punk—local, national, and global cultural forms are therefore all available to them as they construct their own meaningful paths through life.

By approaching Dutch punk and (sub)cultural practices from participants' perspectives, this book regrounds theories of subculture (Bennett 2011; Pilkington and Omel'chenko 2013). It balances individualised choices in participating in various aspects of subculture and wider cultural practices whilst interrogating the social and cultural context that limits and guides their agency. It places punks as active agents in the intersubjective creation of meaning in their lives, whilst recognising the complexity of their position as not only objects but subjects of their complex structural locations.

In contrast to claims both that 'punk is dead', or that it "isn't" (Rimbaud 2011), this book contends that punk *is* and is most definitely alive. Punk has spread, mutated and fragmented, it has experienced highs and lows. Subgenres and subscenes of punk have taken to heart different styles, different ideologies, different practices and different identity markers over the last 40 years. However, 'punk' remains a powerful element of many peoples' lives.

By focusing on punk in the Netherlands, this book has illuminated a scene that has had little written about it. This book does not claim to have told *the* history of Dutch punk; however, it certainly has told *a* history of Dutch punk. By focusing on the stories of participants' lives, it is a jumping off point for further work on this under-researched scene. This book has further drawn attention to the multiple interacting hierarchies present in a global punk scene. Punk in the Netherlands is peripheral to that of the UK, the United States and Germany. However, it maintains a privileged position in relation to much of the rest of the world by dint of it being situated in well-connected, affluent Western Europe. Moreover, this book has complicated the idea of studying a locally (or nationally) bounded subculture, especially in the context of hyper-mobility. Dutch punk is too connected to its global context to be one specific object of study; nonetheless residence in the Netherlands, in multiple locations *within* the country, has shaped this global form.

The particularly politicised form of punk in the Netherlands, moreover, has allowed us to see how politics operates on multiple levels in participants' lives. Politics should not be understood just as governmental or democratic involvement, nor should it be extended only to include protest activisms, instead, any choices that participants make with a consciousness of their political weight can be understood as enacting politics. The lifting of these boundaries of what constitutes political activism allows us to include the resistive practices of subcultures in which participants make space in order to survive. The multitude of ways in which individuals seek to educate and engage with others on political matters can be understood as political actions. By recasting 'politics' we give agency to those who enact ideology and activism in the ways in which they are able to.

Firstly, this research project set out to uncover what punk *means* for Dutch participants and how this has changed over time. The seeds of punk in the Netherlands were germinated with a few initial points of contact with New York and London and the mass media coverage of the Sex Pistols' Dutch tour in January 1977. Initially a largely mimetic scene, with pub rock bands choosing this new style for their next musical direction, the Dutch scene soon came into its own. With new punk bands forming, close punk ties were forged between the Dutch art world and the burgeoning squat scene. As has been demonstrated, the connections with and overlaps between the squatters' movement and punks have had a significant impact on the trajectory of Dutch punk, fostering a particularly politically engaged, well-connected, and mobile scene.

Participants who were part of these formative years found in punk an artistic expression of otherness and difference. In this sense it is similar to the discourses of its contemporaneous UK scene (Hebdige 1979). However, there are signs that even in these early days the potential of punk to be political was more keenly felt with bands such as the Rondos proclaiming their communist stance. Definitions of punk that include 'political' begin to emerge around this time.

The 1980s saw a series of highs and lows as punk became better connected, to a global scene, and new genres were founded. A poor economy in the Netherlands pushed the punk scene and a large scale, well-organised squatters' movement even closer together. However, the 1980s also saw the fragmentation of the punk scene. The new subgenres all brought new styles and new ideologies, with fractures appearing between those who prioritised political forms of punk and those who enjoyed the parties and the drugs. However, whereas in other countries the 'drunk punks' (Phillipov 2006; Tsitsos 1999) tended towards apoliti-cism, in the Netherlands these punks got involved in demonstrating, in benefit gigs and even had political lyrics.

The 1980s brought with it a period in which punk started to be viewed more as a lifestyle, linking together social and individual practices. The dominance of squatting and the spread of vegetarianism meant that a number of politicised life choices came to be tied up with punk norms. The rise in numbers of individuals who remained involved beyond 'youth' meant that punk as an identity gained currency (Widdicombe and Wooffitt 1990). Meanwhile social practices focused around protest, partying or touring came to be more codified in the 1980s.

Throughout the 1990s and 2000s punk experienced ever greater frag-mentation. There was a series of highs and lows, and tensions emerged especially between different generations. Debates over pop punk's claim on the label 'punk' were particularly contentious and arguments over commercialisation in punk raged. Definitions that regarded punk as a set of ideological positions therefore gained currency, in spite of, or perhaps because of these quarrels. Punk today has as many meanings attached to it as there are subgenres of punk; moreover it has as many meanings as there are individuals involved.

By focusing on the development of the Dutch punk scene, I have argued against narratives that punk—ever—died. By conceptualising punk as open to change rather than by narrow definitions, it was pos-sible to view all the ways in which punk has mutated and, therefore, per-sisted. However, by charting the highs and lows that the scene has been through, I have placed this subculture within its wider cultural, social and economic climate. The proliferation of the punk scene in the 1980s was fuelled by unemployment as much as the well-organised squatting movement. The general shrinking of the scene throughout the 1990s and 2000s was in part the result of a more stable economy and politi-cal climate, which affected the diminishing squatting scene. Participants themselves recognised the wider economic and political context to punk and therefore hoped that the contemporaneous economic recession and the dominance of neo-liberal agendas alongside state repression of squat-ting might reinvigorate the punk scene.

By centring this book's discussion of punk on the meanings articu-lated by self-reflexive participants, I have shown that for these members there are many more definitions than have been recognised by prior aca-demic work on punk or subculture. This approach worked in particular to redress the errors made by Hebdige (1979) in reading meanings from style without taking into account how punks themselves understand its meaning. However, it also highlighted the tension between sociologists' predilection to study the social practices of subcultures, and the way in which subcultures concurrently operate as a set of social and individual practices, and group and individual identities. It argues that as theorists we must understand both the social and the individual in order to better conceptualise punk, or indeed any other facet of society or culture.

A second theme of this book is that it presents not only what punk might *be* but how it operates within a globalised world. By embedding punk in participants' embodied mobility and connectivity, I have shown how punk culture 'flows' rhizomatically (Deleuze and Guattari [1987] 2003) within and beyond the Netherlands. The intersubjective sharing of punk between those within the same locale, or those from various places, contributes to the continual reshaping of punk. In highlighting inequalities and differences in access to mobility and connectivity I have shown how punks' *sense of place* (Shields 1991) is affected. Centre-periphery relationships (Hannerz 1992) can produce a sense of locality in some scenes, whilst undermining locality in connected 'centres'.

The focus on the under-researched Dutch punk scene has not only illuminated the specifics of punk in the context of the Netherlands but has also allowed wider conclusions to be drawn on punk in other non-original locations. It has shown that whilst such scenes may be peripheral to 'central' scenes, they operate within a multi-layered system of centre-periphery in which there are multiple centres and multiple peripheries, and culture can flow in more than one direction. Further work on other 'peripheral' scenes will contribute to this model, allowing better knowledge of how locality and other spatial conceptualisations operate within subculture.

A third contribution made by this book is in further unpicking how punk operates by examining its link with politics. In doing so I interrogated the relationship between individual and social practices in participants' wider political lives. I argued that a wide definition of 'politics' is necessary to understand the range of activities in which participants engaged. I therefore included activities that ranged from the individual (including reading, writing, vegetarianism and work choice) to the social (debating, teaching or squatting); from the 'traditional' politics of party membership or trade union activism to wider definitions that include demonstrations and practices of education. I argued that these various practices *all* need to be understood in terms of their political potential, in terms of their potential not solely to challenge the establishment but also to challenge social norms and to create space in which alternatives may exist.

Educative practices in which the punks engage are particularly of note. Punk (rather than punks') activities of writing zines, writing politicised lyrics, talking on stage about their latest cause, and running and playing at benefit gigs clearly fit into a mould of spreading knowledge about political issues. In punk individuals' other practices they continue this work by debating and educating their (punk and non-punk) peers, by running distros and writing their own literature, or even organising lecture series. These forms of engagement fit into a long trajectory in which marginalised and disenfranchised groups work towards alternative forms of education (Collins [1991] 2000; Corrigan and Frith [1975] 2006; Thompson [1963] 1980).

The political potential of participants' actions is posited as linked with the choices they make (Giddens 1994); however, the accessibility of this 'choice' is always structured by the wider social, cultural and economic context. As such, in discussing participants' political involvement, I also examined the structuring factors that made certain choices more, or less, available in different periods. For example, Dutch punks were subject to a poor economy in the 1980s and thus many were unemployed. This fed into subcultural norms, reifying unemployment as a preferable status.

We therefore see in the realm of politics how 'punkness' has often affected punks' whole lives. Through involvement in a politically engaged subculture, ideological aspects of punk came to affect the way in which punks understood wider choices in life. For some this led to engagements with *P*olitics or with a concern for self/peer education. For others it affected more mundane aspects of life, for example, in the realm of consumption and employment. Beyond politics, engagement with punk has also shaped individuals' wider lives in other ways. For example, punk's close relationship with squatting helped foster international connections and personal relationships that aided punks' mobility; providing them with experiences of travel, and in some cases, the opportunity or impetus to uproot and resettle in new areas. Whilst this book cannot possibly begin to answer all of the ways in which involvement with punk might affect multiple aspects of individuals' lives, in discussing these few facets in which it has, it opens up the possibility of further research into other areas of life in which punk might have an impact.

With this book I have argued that to understand these complexities in the social world it is crucial to focus not solely on group or social practices but also on individuals' practices and their conceptualisations, for it is through the meaning that individuals attach to their world that social practices have importance. By understanding the political value of individualised choices such as vegetarianism or practices including reading and self-education, by recognising that punk can be an identity as well as a friendship group, and by noting how personal, individual transnational relationships can facilitate the spread of cultural forms and the sharing of punk ideas, not least through touring practices, we gain a far more nuanced picture of the shape of the punk subculture.

Moreover, this book reminds us that we must not focus on punk or punks as entities separate from their wider cultural context. They make choices not solely based on subcultural capital within punk circles but also through interactions with other non-punks in their lives; other friendship groups, families, co-workers, and so on, and, crucially, their opportunities to make choices are shaped by what is available to them in their social world. Ability to be an 'active' punk or to be a political activist requires time and/or money. Having either of these depends on the economic climate and the availability of work or state support. Those with a more privileged background have greater access to study. Women and people of colour remain less visible, active or involved in a subculture that remains dominated by White men. Whilst punks create their own social structures, they do not do so in a vacuum from wider societal structures.

The foregrounding of 'connectedness' as a theoretical approach has facilitated the embedding of participants and their subcultural as well as their whole lives in wider social, cultural and economic contexts. This book has argued that we cannot understand punk and punks in isolation and has demonstrated this with a series of empirical chapters in which punks' *punk* lives are interrogated as part of, and intertwined with, their *whole* lives. Further research must consider both individual and social practices and meanings of subculture, as well as individual and group connectedness.

As a whole, this book has addressed and destabilised a number of artificial boundaries: in punk, in politics and in geography. It has done so because the everyday lives of participants suggest that these boundaries are porous, although generally not to the point of meaninglessness. Whilst spatial boundaries are easily—and regularly—traversed and whilst punk scenes and punk individuals are well-connected with others globally, the Dutch scene's position within a small country in Western Europe gives it access to particular structures and facilities that are not available to others. The embeddedness of punks and their connectedness to others does not, therefore, render their national borders insignificant. This book has instead challenged those boundaries that constrain our ability to understand the meaningful practices of punk individuals; were we to focus solely on what takes place in one locality, or that which is connected to a specific understanding of punk or of political engagement, we would be left with a far less rich picture of what constitutes the cultural world of Dutch punks.

REFERENCES

Bennett, A. 2011. The Post-subcultural Turn: Some Reflections 10 years on. *Journal of Youth Studies* 14 (5): 493–506.

Collins, P.H. [1991] 2000. *Black Feminist Thought: Knowledge, Consciousness, and the Politics of Empowerment*, 2nd ed. New York: Routledge.

Corrigan, P., and S. Frith. [1975] 2006. The Politics of Youth Culture. In *Resistance Through Rituals: Youth Subcultures in Post-war Britain*, 2nd ed, ed. S. Hall and T. Jefferson, 231–242. London: Routledge.

Deleuze, G., and F. Guattari. [1987] 2003. *A Thousand Plateaus: Capitalism and Schizophrenia*. London: Continuum.

Giddens, A. 1994. *Beyond Left and Right: The Future of Radical Politics*. Cambridge: Polity Press.

Hannerz, U. 1992. *Cultural Complexity: Studies in the Social Organization of Meaning*. New York: Columbia University Press.

Hebdige, D. 1979. *Subculture: The Meaning of Style*. London: Routledge.

Phillipov, M. 2006. Haunted by the Spirit of '77: Punk Studies and the Persistence of Politics. *Continuum: Journal of Media & Cultural Studies* 20 (3): 383–393.

Pilkington, H., and E. Omel'chenko. 2013. Regrounding Youth Cultural Theory (In Post Socialist Youth Cultural Practice). *Sociology Compass* 7 (3): 208–224.

Rimbaud, P. 2011. Rottenbeat: Academic and Musical Dialogue With New Russian Punk Workshop, London, 4 May. Quoted in H Pilkington, Punk—But Not As We Know It: Punk in Post-Socialist Space. *Punk & Post-Punk*, 1 (3): 253–266.

Shields, R. 1991. *Places on the Margin: Alternative Geographies of Modernity*. London: Routledge.

Thompson, E.P. [1963] 1980. *The Making of the English Working Class*. London: Gollancz.

Tsitsos, W. 1999. Rules of Rebellion: Slamdancing, Moshing, and the American Alternative Scene. *Popular Music* 18 (3): 397–414.

Widdicombe, S., and R. Wooffitt. 1990. "Being" Versus "Doing" Punk: On Achieving Authenticity as a Member. *Journal of Language and Social Psychology* 9 (4): 257–277.

APPENDIX: PARTICIPANTS

For this project I conducted interviews with a broadly representative segment of the 'Dutch punk population'. I interviewed 33 individuals, including 5 women, and 28 men. All participants could be read as white and all but four were born in the Netherlands. These other four participants were born in Portugal (1), Russia (1) and Serbia (2). Ages of interviewees ranged from 21 to c. 61.[1]

In Tables A.1 and A.2 I show the historical and generational spread of the participants. Chapter 3 discusses the way in which an ageing punk population affects the scene, especially contemporaneously. Whilst most participants reported first getting involved in punk as a teenager, there were not many teenagers active on the scene at the time of my fieldwork. This was due both to changing fashions—punk was out of favour at the time—and a 'lull' in punk, with forms of dance music more popular amongst alternative young people.

The largest group of participants were in their late 20s and were still active punks at the time of fieldwork. Most of these individuals had become involved during the late 1990s and early 2000s. However, there is representation in this research from individuals involved in all eras of Dutch punk, and some of these older punks considered themselves to be actively involved in the contemporaneous scene.

As discussed in Chap. 5, the British notion of class structure is not directly translatable to the Dutch context. However, a recognition of socio/economic privilege, opportunity and the potential of disposable

© The Editor(s) (if applicable) and The Author(s) 2017   213
K. Lohman, *The Connected Lives of Dutch Punks*,
Palgrave Studies in the History of Subcultures and Popular Music,
DOI 10.1007/978-3-319-51079-8

Table A.1 Age of participants

Age	No. participants
Under 25	4
26–35	11
36–45	9
46–55	7
Over 55	2

Table A.2 Numbers of participants who were subculturally active in different 'eras' of Dutch punk[a]

Dates	No. participants
Pre-1976 (Pre-history of punk)	2
1977–1980 (Early Dutch punk)	6
Early-mid 1980s	10
Mid-late 1980s	14
1990s	23
2000s	28
2010–2011 (Active at the time of fieldwork)	22

[a]Data was based on when participants reported first being involved in punk and in which periods they still considered themselves involved. Some participants 'took a break', others 'left' and yet more have continued activity in some form. As such, individuals may be recorded as involved in multiple eras

Table A.3 The forms of employment of participants[a]

Forms of work	No. participants
Student	7
Creative arts	13
Public sector	4
Private sector	2
Unstable, causal or multiple jobs	6
Manual labour	7
Self-employed	11
Unemployed	2

[a]I provide details on both the forms of participants' employment, and the types of roles in which they work. As such, a self-employed artist who also has a casual job to support themselves will appear on the table three times

Table A.4 The 'punk' activities that various participants take part in, or have participated in[a]

'Punk' activity	No. participants
Plays in a band	23
Organises gigs	16
Volunteers in squats	12
Tour manager or tour assistant	7
Writes zines or reviews	9
Photographer	3
Artist	6
Works in a punk-related shop	3
Sound technician	2
Runs a record label	4
Helps in or runs a punk venue	6

[a]This is based only on activities that came up during interview and thus may not be exhaustive

income remains a useful signifier in sociological analysis. Table A.3 therefore shows the forms of employment of participants. It is worth nothing that an overwhelming majority of participants had studied (or were studying) at a higher education level. As discussed in Chap. 6, access to university level study was supported by grants and was common amongst participants of all backgrounds, especially in the 1980s when unemployment was high. However the link between access to education and (class) privilege means that higher education remains behind a barrier for individuals from low-income backgrounds (Rijken et al. 2007), and with recent changes to the funding of higher education, it was becoming even more problematic. The high level of participants who were studying at the time of the research, therefore, represents a group with a certain degree of privilege. At least ten participants[2] have experienced periods of unemployment throughout their lives. This was most common amongst those in their thirties and forties.

In Table A.4 we see the sorts of punk activities in which participants engaged. There are a high number of participants who have or were playing in bands at the time of my research. This, coupled with the prevalence of participants who have organised gigs, show how such 'activity' (see Chap. 5) is common within a subculture that puts such emphasis on DIY practices. The 'ease' of playing punk (again discussed in Chap. 5) or writing zines, and the sharing of knowledge of how to go about setting up gigs allows a large number of punks to get involved in such a way. However, it is also worth bearing in mind how the method

Table A.5 Where
participants live[a]

Location	No. participants living there
Alkmaar	1
Amsterdam	13
Arnhem	1
Drachten	1
Groningen	10
Leeuwarden	2
Nijmegen	4
Utrecht	1

[a]Again, data is based on at the time of fieldwork. In some cases the participant lives in a small village or town close to the city named

of 'snowballing' in locating interview participants affects this. Those who are 'more' involved become known by more people. They also hold a degree of 'subcultural capital' and are therefore held up as good examples of Dutch punk, and as founts of knowledge. Therefore such 'active' punks are more likely to be recommended to me as worth interviewing, to the neglect of punks whose involvement is less overt.

Table A.5 shows the geographical spread of research participants. There is a dominance of participants from Amsterdam, where I was based and had easiest access to participants, and Groningen, an example of peripheral scene in which participants were more invested in 'showing off' their local scene and recommending friends to interview (see Chap. 4). The majority of participants had not lived in their current location for their entire lives, and thus I also heard about their punk experiences when living in Rotterdam, Enschede, Amersfoort, Hoogeveen, Vlaardingen, Wageningen, Wormer, New York, Nottingham, Belgrade and Moscow, amongst others.

List of Participants

Andre: (28, male) plays in a band, and is based in Nijmegen.
Bart: (28, male) is a truck driver based in Nijmegen. He plays in a band and has driven bands on tour around Europe.
Bram: (44, male) is a student who lives in Groningen and has played with many bands.
Daan: (42, male) is a teacher in Amsterdam. He is straight edge and played in the Amersfoort scene for years with a number of bands.

Erik: (29, male) lives in Leeuwarden. He runs a record label and acts as a promoter and plays in two bands.

Gregor: (23, male) is a student in Utrecht who plays with one main band and has toured with other bands.

Henk: (50, male) is a graphic designer. He has lived in Enschede, Arnhem, and Groningen, made a zine and plays with a band.

Jaap: (55, male) is a promoter in Groningen, has played music and been a tour manager for a number of bands.

Jacob: (c. 41, male) is unemployed and lives in Groningen. He previously worked in IT and in venues in Groningen. He has played with a number of bands.

Jan: (c. 61, male) is an artist and publisher who in the 1970s ran a record shop and label and was a manager for a few punk bands.

Jasper: (23, male) is a student in Groningen who plays in a band.

Jeroen: (29, male) is from Drachten and now runs a youth club in Steenwijk. He organises punk gigs and is a tour bus driver for many bands.

Johan: (60, male) is a comic strip artist who has drawn artwork for gig posters and album arts for Dutch punk bands.

Jolanda: (28, female) is a social worker in Groningen. She has played with a number of bands.

Kosta: (44, male) is an art and music curator, who has played in bands and written zines. He grew up in Serbia and is now based in Amsterdam. He has also lived in Groningen (where he worked at gig venues) and Berlin, Germany.

Larry: (28, male) is a political activist in Nijmegen. He is straight edge and used to play in a band.

Lisa: (28, female) is a student in Nijmegen, originally from Drachten, she has also lived in Groningen. She plays with a band and regularly contributes to an alternative music publication.

Lotte: (42, female) lives in Groningen. She is a journalist, writer and runs a punk in hangout. She has organised gigs and run a radio show.

Luka: (37, male) is a student. Originally from Belgrade, Serbia he now lives in Amsterdam. He is straight edge and plays in a band.

Maarten: (50, male) works at a venue in Groningen. He has played and toured with a number of bands.

Marieke: (28, female) is an artist who works in fashion and who has lived and squatted in Arnhem and Amsterdam.

218 APPENDIX: PARTICIPANTS

Mark: (38, male) is from Wormer and has squatted all over the Netherlands. He is a sound technician and DJ who has worked with many Dutch punk bands and runs a record label.

Maxim: (30, male) is a student in Amsterdam, originally from Moscow, Russia. He is straight edge and plays in a band.

Menno: (c. 52, male) is a publisher and artist who was involved with early Dutch punk in Rotterdam. He played with a band and helped create a fanzine. Later he moved to Amsterdam and played briefly with later punk bands.

Nico: (38, male) runs a 'punk' bike shop in Amsterdam. He is originally from Portugal.

Ruben: (34, male) runs a silk screen company in Groningen, runs gigs and plays in various metal and punk bands.

Sander: (21, male) is a student from Amsterdam, he has squatted and plays in a punk band.

Sem: (52, male) is a computer technician and scene photographer based in Arnhem. He runs a record label and regularly contributes to an alternative music publication.

Suzanne: (40, female) lives in Groningen and works in the car industry. She has played with many bands.

Theo: (47, male) lives in Amsterdam and works in IT. He has played in bands since 1979.

Tom: (31, male) is a squatter and punk from Leeuwaarden.

Wim: (c. 40s, male) is from Alkmaar though is connected to the Groningen scene. He has played in a number of bands.

Wouter: (25, male) is a rock climber, a nurse, a punk, and a squatting activist based in Amsterdam and originally from Vlaardingen.

NOTES

1. Age is at time of interview. In some cases years of birth were given and thus actual age may be +/−1 year.
2. This is again based on what came up during interview.

POSTSCRIPT:
A PERSONAL NOTE FROM THE AUTHOR

The majority of this book was drafted in 2013–2015; the data on which it relies was collected in 2010–2011. I am now finalising the manuscript for publication in February 2017. As I do so, I cannot help but think of the radical social and cultural shifts that we have experienced in the global West over these last years, most acutely through 2016 and 2017 to date. While this book is a product of the years that immediately followed the global financial crisis of the late 2000s, it poses important questions and proposes new ways to conceptualise how we might move forward in response to the challenges of the contemporary world.

In the last year alone we have witnessed a rise in racism and in particular Islamophobia in the Netherlands, in the United Kingdom (where I live and work), as well as in the United States and beyond. There has been a political and cultural shift to the right. Politicians have sought to increase border controls, to build walls both literal and figurative between our nations.

This project started at a more optimistic time. That is not to say that it was an easy time; certainly the impact of the 2007–2008 global financial crisis was keenly felt by my participants. However, the idea that the crisis signalled the inevitable death of capitalism led to a feeling of hope on the left. The Arab Spring buoyed this anticipation as it highlighted the power that people could still wield over their political systems. Geert Wilders, a potent symbol of the Islamophobic right in the Netherlands, was on trial for hate speech during the majority of my fieldwork period,

© The Editor(s) (if applicable) and The Author(s) 2017
K. Lohman, *The Connected Lives of Dutch Punks*,
Palgrave Studies in the History of Subcultures and Popular Music,
DOI 10.1007/978-3-319-51079-8

his populist political threat seemingly tempered by an institutional recognition that his words and actions were/might be too extreme to be tolerated. He was acquitted in June 2011.

Fast forward to February 2017: we are just a few weeks from a general election in which it is expected that Wilders' *Partij voor de Vrijheid* will do well, perhaps even winning more seats than any other political party. Wilders is campaigning on an anti-Islam platform, along with a promise to seek 'Nexit', a break from Europe to follow Britain's 'example' of Brexit in 2016. France will go to the polls later in 2017, with far-right *Front National* candidate Marine Le Pen expected to perform well in the presidential elections. United States President Trump was inaugurated in January 2017. Across the West, rights for women, for workers, for ethnic minorities and for LGBTQ people are under threat.

In North Africa and the Middle East, the Arab Spring has given way to an 'Arab Winter', with ongoing and disastrous civil wars being fought in the regions that in 2011 were a focus for hope. Unknown numbers have died. Millions of refugees have fled these war zones seeking safety, but they face a proliferation of immigration regulations across the West and systemic violence instead of security.

Whilst this book's focus on punk may seem trivial in light of these huge and pressing problems, I hope that the chapters contained within can serve as an argument against putting up borders. It is a book that fundamentally questions boundaries, be they theoretical (in terms of how we define subculture, punk(s) and/or politics); or geographical. I instead argue for an understanding of connectedness, of recognising and centring our commonalities, our connections and our relationships across all divides. It is these commonalities, connections and relationships that provide a fundamental richness to our academic work, to our cultural worlds, and most importantly to our lives.

INDEX

© The Editor(s) (if applicable) and The Author(s) 2017   221
K. Lohman, *The Connected Lives of Dutch Punks*,
Palgrave Studies in the History of Subcultures and Popular Music,
DOI 10.1007/978-3-319-51079-8

Printed by Printforce, the Netherlands